A Drop from the Marvelous Ocean of History

The Lineage of Lelung Pema Zhepai Dorje,
One of the Three
Principal Reincarnations of Tibet

A Drop from the Marvelous Ocean of History

The Lineage of Lelung Pema Zhepai Dorje,
One of the Three
Principal Reincarnations of Tibet

By Lelung Tulku Rinpoche XI

Published by Tibet House US
New York
2013

Published by:

Tibet House US
22 West 15th Street
New York, NY 10011

http://www.tibethouse.us

Distributed by:

Hay House, Inc.
www.hayhouse.com

Printed in the United States of America on acid-free paper.

22 21 20 19 18 17 16 15 14 13   5 4 3 2 1

ISBN 978-0-9670115-9-2 (paper)

Library of Congress Control Number: 2013932592

Contents

Appendixes

MESSAGE

I would like to express my appreciation to the 11th Lelung Rinpoche, Tenzin Phuntsok Loden, for compiling the biographies of his predecessors, who performed numerous altruistic deeds for the benefit of the Dharma and the happiness of all sentient beings.

The real purpose of compiling the biographies of the previous Lelung manifestations is for us to learn from their great deeds and follow in their footsteps.

August 14, 2012

Author's Preface and Acknowledgements

The nonsectarian monastery of Thegchog Namdrol Ling was founded in the eastern region of Tibet near Lhunpo Dza, facing the great O-de-gung-gyal mountain, a gathering place of dakinis. This has long been the seat of the Lelung Rinpoches, who are human manifestations of Vajrapani, the Lord of Secrets. In 1984, when I was fourteen, I was recognized by His Holiness the Dalai Lama as one of their reincarnations.

I do not claim to possess any particular wisdom to penetrate the ocean of scriptures or to have any special inborn qualities. However, for over thirteen years I studied and took part in debates and prayer gatherings at that great seat of learning, Drepung Monastic University, like every other scholar monk. While I was engaged in my monastic education, I also read the collected works of the previous Lelung masters and thereby developed genuine faith in them. I thought that if I could find time to write their life stories, it would be a seed for developing my own devotion and that of followers karmically connected to them, especially as my ears were constantly ringing in those days with questions about their lives from people from other countries.

I have mainly relied on the biographies of four Lelung reincarnations, including that of Jedrung Gendun Choegyal Wangchuk, the fourth Lelung reincarnation, written by Omniscient Panchen Lama Losang Choegyen. I also consulted the following sources: *Scriptures of the Kadampa Father and Son Teachings* (*bka' gdams glegs bam*), the collected works of Lhodrak Khenchen Laykyi Dorje (*lho brag mkhan chen las kyi dor rje'i bkah 'bum*), the collected works of Jey Tsong Khapa (*rje tsong kha pa'i gsung 'bum*), the biography of Gyalchog Gendun Gyatso (*rgyal mchog dge 'dun rgya mtsho' rnam thar*), the collected works of the Third Dalai Lama (*rgyal mchog gsum pa'i gsung 'bum*), *A Chariot of Faith* by Panchen Lama Losang Choegyen (*pan chen blo bzang chos rgyan gyi dad pa'i shing rta*), *A Jewel Rosary: A Biography of Gyalwa Yonten Gyatso* (*rgyal mchog yon tan rgya mtsho'i rnam thar nor bu'i 'phreng wa*), the collected works of the Fifth Dalai Lama (*rgyal mchog lnga pa'i gsung 'bum*), *Yellow Lapis Lazuli: A Religious History of Ganden* by Desi (*sde srid kyi dga' ldan chos 'byung bee dhur ya ser po*), *Festive Joy for the Fortunate Ones: A Life Story of*

Jedrung Losang Trinley (rje drung blo bzang 'phrin las kyi rtogs rjod skal bzang dga' ston), Parts One and Two of the Seventh Dalai Lama's Biography by Chang Kya *(lchang skya'i gsung rgyal mchog bdun pa'i rnam thar stod smed), The Life Story of Mewang Pholha (me dbang pho lha'i rtogs brjod), Biographies of the Lamrim Lineage Masters* by Kachen Yeshe Gyatso *(dka' chen ye shes rgya mtsho'i lam rim bla ma rgyud pa'i rnam thar),* the *Collected Works of Longdol Lama (klong rdol bla ma'i gsung 'bum), The Wish-Fulfilling Tree: A Religious History* by Sumpa Khenchen *(sum pa mkhen chen gyi chos 'byung dpag bsam ljon bzang), A Melody of Sincere Utterances: The Life Story of Doring Pandita (rdo ring pan dri ta'i byung ba brjod pa zol med gtam gyi rol mo),* a *Biography of Trichen Jangchub Choephel (khri chen byang chub chos 'phel gyi rnam thar), A Stunning Jewel Rosary: A Biography of Gyalchog Tsultrim Gyatso (rgyal mchog tshul khrims rgya mtso'i rnam thar ngo mtshar nor bu'i 'phreng ba), The Magnificient Divine Melody of Saraswati's Lute: A Biography of Gyalchog Khedrup Gyatso (rgyal mchog mkhas grub rgya mtso'i rnam thar ngo mtshar lha'i rol mo dbyang can rgyud snyen pa'i tam bu ra), A Religious History of Nyingma* by Taggang Kheschog Guru Tashi *(stag sgang mkhas mchog gu ru bkra shis kyi rnying ma'i chos 'byung),* Parts One and Two of *A Magnificient Precious Gem: A Biography of the Thirteenth Dalai Lama* by Phurchok Jamgon Rinpoche *(rgyal mchog bcu gsum pa'i rnam thar ngo mtshar rin po che'i 'phreng ba bstod smed), An Ocean of Literature: A Religious History of Amdo (mdo smed chos 'byung deb ther rgya mtsho), A Biography of Khaywang Gendun Choephel* by Ragra *(mkhas dbang dge 'dun chos 'phel gyi rnam thar rag ras bris pa),* and *A Political History of Tibet* by Tsepon Shakabpa *(rtsis dpon shav sgab pa'i bod kyi srid don rgyal rabs).* As well as these principal sources, I also consulted the life stories of other lamas and reincarnations in Tibet, India and Mongolia.

Though lacking skills and experience in writing and composition, I have tried to assemble very short life stories of the previous Lelung reincarnations, and would very much appreciate any comments and suggestions.

*　　*　　*

I would like to express my heartfelt thanks to the great translator Lotsawa Tenzin Dorjee, Assistant Professor, Department of Human Communication Studies, California State University, Fullerton, U.S.A. for translating this book from Tibetan. He agreed to do this while in the middle of his PhD studies, and worked on the translation early in the morning and late at night, on weekdays and at weekends, while simultaneously working and studying. It was a mark of his wonderful friendship. I am deeply touched by his hard work, and will always appreciate it.

I would also like to offer a big thank you to Jania Napier-Burrows, who has given so much time to editing this book. When we first began, it must have seemed a hopeless task because of my lack of English, but she did not give up. She was very patient with me and devoted one day a week to it. I enjoyed working with her very much and appreciate all she has done for the book.

Finally, I ought to share the good merit with Connie Dusek and her family, without whom it would not have been possible to complete this work. She has helped me like a wonderful mother, put me up, given me lifts whenever I needed them, and much more. She jokes that she is the best landlady in the UK, and I really do think she is one of the best.

I am also very happy that my old friend Professor Bob Thurman is going to publish this book. He knows about the teacher-student relationship of the first Lelung and Lama Tsong Khapa. Through this publication he will increase awareness of this important history and make known the first Lelung's great deeds for all sentient beings and also the Lelung lineage.

Lelung Tulku Tenzin Phuntsok Loden

Editor's Introduction

Whenever the name of Lhodrak Namkha Gyaltsen was mentioned, His Eminence Kyabje Lingtsang Rinpoche, the late senior tutor of H. H. the Fourteenth Dalai Lama, would put his hands together in the gesture of deep reverence, and express his infinite gratitude to the 14th century lama. "He was so kind to Tibet. Thank Buddha he stopped Jey Rinpoche [Tsong Khapa] from going on pilgrimage to India after his enlightenment, and persuaded him to spend his years teaching the Dharma in Tibet."

When I visited Tibet during the 90s, I saw Lhodrak Namkha Gyaltsen's special vajra and skull bowl in a display case in one of the few reconstructed buildings in Ganden monastery (completely destroyed during the Cultural Revolution in the late 60s), and received their blessings. Way back during the 70s, when I was editing a volume of translations by others and myself from Tsong Khapa's *Collected Works* (published by the Library of Tibetan Works and Archives, as *Life and Teachings of Tsong Khapa*, in 1980), I translated a short work called *Garland of Supremely Healing Nectar*, which is in the *Collected Works*, a recording by Tsong Khapa of a dialogue between Lhodrak Namkha Gyaltsen and the divine bodhisattva Vajrapani himself, done as a teaching for Tsong Khapa and his companions. Though the text does not say so, it must have been a remarkable event, since the tradition says that when Namkha Gyaltsen taught Tsong Khapa, the former was perceived openly as Vajrapani himself, not as an ordinary human being (when Tsong Khapa on other occasions taught Namkha Gyaltsen, Tsong Khapa was perceived openly as Manjushri himself).

Among the invocations of Vajrapani that Namkha Gyaltsen expresses at the beginning is this: "Since You are all beauty of form, please teach the personal instruction that fills the eyes with tears born of the vision of the precept that generates the undissipating bliss!"

When Vajrapani is asked about the actuality of the clear light of emptiness, he gives a statement that is still so important for practitioners today:

> First the pattern of mistaking the actuality; in general.
> What we call "actuality" is the introspectively known reality that exists just like this, free from the adulteration of

present artificial consciousness, originally clear emptiness wherein nothing is intrinsically established. When a person meditates on emptiness without focusing just on that, he falls into the error of cutting off enlightenment at emptiness, by not freeing his mind from the holding on to emptiness. The sign of error is that thoughts arise such as "above there is no Buddha, below there is no hell, the utter lack of establishment of anything is emptiness." The fault of the error is that the mind that thinks everything is empty, on the positive side, abandons all religious practices such as devotion, purification of perception, refuge-taking, the spiritual conception of love and compassion, and engages in the enterprises of this life, and, on the negative side, all his practice is contaminated by the activities of sin....

Among the other very interesting teachings given by Vajrapani, he states that Tsong Khapa was the famous Kashmiri pandit (scholar/practitioner) Sumatikīrti in a previous life. He also predicts that there will come a time when war will come and the deities and demons of Tibet will be driven out by foreign invasion, but that if the lamas and masters teach and practice well, the Dharma can be restored in Tibet.

In the light of the relevance and greatness of the Great Abbot of Lhodrak, Namkha Gyaltsen, how wonderful it is to meet the present incarnation of that lama, known today as the Lelung Tulku (conscious incarnation), and have his energetic activities to help us today. Now with his first book beginning to track the history and search out the works of his predecessors, we can appreciate the impact of the Lelung line over the last half millennium.

The first Lelung, Namkha Gyaltsen (1326–1401), was instrumental in empowering Tsong Khapa's huge renaissance in Tibet. His biography shows that he was already a highly developed bodhisattva, an actual manifestation of the bodhisattva Vajrapani, considered the emanation of Vajradhara Buddha, born to collect and guard all Tantric teachings. In the Tibetan tradition, he may be considered the reincarnation of the enlightened soul-continuum of the famous Kadampa Geshe Potowa, a direct disciple of Dromtonpa. The biographies make no suggestions about intervening lifetimes.

The second Lelung Jedrung incarnation, Gedun Tashi, appeared after 85 years in 1486. He also had a very distinguished life, becoming a heart disciple of His Holiness, the Second Dalai Lama, Gendun Gyatso (1475–1542). Once matured and realized, he was entrusted with prodigious tasks in developing monasteries in the Flower Valley where Gendun Gyatso had constructed the Choekhorgyal monastery, near the "Soullake" (gLatso) of the powerful protector goddess, Palden Lhamo. He subsequently became an important teacher of His Holiness Sonam Gyatso (1543–1588), the Third Dalai Lama, transmitting key teachings of all the Unexcelled Yoga Tantras as well as super-secret teachings of various powerful protectors, such as Mahakala. Gendun Tashi, though a member of the "New Kadampa," Gandenpa, or Gelukpa order, was very much involved in the nonsectarian study and teachings of the Nyingma order. He shared these interests and practices with both the Second and Third Dalai Lamas. He passed away from his body into the clear light in 1559.

The Third Lelung Jedrung Rinpoche was Tenpa Gyatso, born in 1560. Recognized at the age of three by the Third Dalai Lama, Sonam Gyatso, he was installed as a youth in Choekhorgyal and also at Jamba Ling in Chamdo. He received all the heart teachings of his own previous incarnation from the Third Dalai Lama Sonam Gyatso. In his twenties, he accompanied Sonam Gyatso to Mongolia to the momentous meeting with Altan Khan, the ruler of Genghis Khan's Central Asian empire. Sonam Gyatso converted Altan Khan to Buddhism, and was in turn given the Mongolian name, "Dalai Lama" ("Dalai" being Mongolian for Tibetan "Gyatso," "ocean"). The emperor felt the "Presence" (Kundun) of Sonam Gyatso as being just like an ocean of compassionate bliss. The Third Lelung Jedrung, Tenpa Gyatso, was then sent by Sonam Gyatso to the Wanli Emperor (1563–1620) of China's Ming dynasty (Altan Khan refused to let Sonam Gyatso himself accept the Chinese invitation). There the Third Lelung Jedrung became the emperor's root guru, and in return was laden with offering gifts he brought back to Tibet to further the Third Dalai Lama's works. Around the same time, the Lelung Rinpoche became the root guru of Panchen Losang Choekyi Gyaltsen (1570–1662), the very important Fourth Panchen Lama, the key figure in teaching and supporting the Great Fifth Dalai Lama (1617–1682). The Fourth Panchen Lama wrote of him as follows:

> You do not merely masquerade as a learned master,
> You are free of the artifice of a phony realized master,
> Your holy conduct is worthy of praise from the holy—
> Therefore your qualities are reflected in the clear pool of
> my mind!

Finally, Tenpa Gyatso served as an important teacher of the young Mongolian Fourth Dalai Lama, Yonten Gyatso (1589–1617), before he "manifested the appearance of dissolving his body and mind into the sphere of ultimate reality"—as the traditional expression goes—in 1625. This Lelung Jedrung Rinpoche served two Dalai Lamas, a Panchen Lama, thousands of disciples, as well as a Chinese emperor.

The Fourth Lelung Jedrung lama, Gendun Choegyal Wangchuk (1646–1696), was recognized, ordained, and initiated by His Holiness the Great Fifth Dalai Lama Losang Gyatso. He became one of the root gurus of the Fifth Panchen Rinpoche, Losang Yeshe (1663–1737), who wrote his biography and praised him very highly. Like the Fifth Dalai Lama, he was born in an illustrious Nyingma order family, was educated in all the vast teachings of the Ganden order, and had many visionary experiences of the great precious Guru Padmasambhava and many Nyingma deities.

The Fifth Lelung Jedrung, Losang Trinley (1697–1740) was recognized as a small child by the Nyingmapa master, Tertoen Choeje Lingpa, and was much admired by the mystical adept and poet, the Sixth Dalai Lama, Tsangyang Gyatso (1683–1706?). Growing up, he received major teachings form both the great Nyingma masters of Mindroling and the mainstream Gelukpa masters such as the Fifth Panchen Rinpoche, Losang Yeshe. He suffered through the dislocations that happened due to the Mongolian warlords' interventions in Tibet, beginning with the deposing and apparent death of the Sixth Dalai Lama in 1706, the war between two factions of the Mongols in the next decade, and finally the installation of the Seventh Dalai lama, Kelsang Gyatso (1708–1757) with the overwhelming intervention of the Manchurian empire in 1720. He had very close relations with the Seventh Dalai Lama during the latter's youth.

The Sixth Lelung Rinpoche, Jedrung Losang Lhundrup Trinley Gyaltsen (1641–1811), was recognized at the age of three by the Seventh Dalai Lama, and considered His Holiness to be his root guru for his whole life. He was educated at Drepung and afterward at the Gyuto Tantric University in Lhasa, where he served as abbot for some time.

The Seventh Lelung, Oelkha Jedrung Rinpoche Losang Ngawang Tenzin Gyatso (1812–186?), participated in the brief lives of the Ninth (1805–1815), Tenth (1816–1837), Eleventh (1838–1856), and Twelfth (1857–1875) Dalai Lamas, which is probably why little is known about him in comparison with most of the other Lelung incarnations. Nobody really knows why all these Dalai Lamas were so short-lived. But during this period, the Manchurian emperors had representatives (Ambans) and garrisons in Lhasa. They could easily interfere with the Tibetan government and society by not having a Dalai Lama come into a spiritually and socially fully developed majority with the ability and experience to oversee personally the development of the country.

The situation of the Eighth Lelung Jedrung, Kelsang Tenzin, was even less clear. His birth and death dates are not clearly known; a report circulated that he passed away before finishing his education. The Ninth Lelung Jedrung (1905–1909) passed away as a child.

The Great Thirteenth Dalai Lama (1876–1933) recognized the Tenth Lelung Jedrung, Thubten Lungtok Choekyi Wangchuk (1909–1962). The Thirteenth Dalai Lama very effectively stabilized Tibet, defeated an assassination plot, coped with the British invasion along with the last bit of Manchurian interference in Tibet, discovered the world of international politics during the terminal phase of European imperialism, and proclaimed and maintained Tibetan independence as a recognized nation from 1913 until 1951. The Tenth Lelung Rinpoche worked with and helped the Thirteenth Dalai Lama during all these difficult times. In 1959, he did not escape the Communist Chinese invasion and occupation of Tibet, and passed away in 1962.

This book presents in much richer detail the lives of these incarnations by the author's careful showing the positive entanglement they have all experienced with the Dalai Lamas and the Panchen Lamas, in the center of the powerful Ganden Renaissance movement dating from around 1400 CE.

Finally, after a gap of nine years, the Eleventh Lelung Jedrung Rinpoche, Tenzin Phuntsok Loden, was born in 1970, and recognized by the Great Fourteenth Dalai Lama (b. 1935) in 1984. He was educated in Drepung Monastic University for another thirteen years. After graduating, he offered back his monastic vows, considering that, due to the nature of the times, he could be more of help to His Holiness and to Tibet by working in the lay world. He has done years of research in the effort to revive the

Lelung Jedrung lineage, finding and publishing in Tibetan many of the rare works of his predecessors. Here he has presented us with this lovely little book, which we are very pleased to publish. We are particularly happy, in these hard days of great division and contention, to hold up to view the example of an ancient lineage within the true "New Kadam"— or Ganden or Geluk order—that clearly demonstrates the beauty and power of the normal nonsectarian approach to the Buddha's Dharma as inherited, preserved, studied, practiced, realized, and performed in Tibet down the centuries until today.

> Robert A. F. "Tenzin" Thurman
> Editor-in-Chief, Tibet House US Books
> Jey Tsong Khapa Professor of Indo-Tibetan Buddhist
>   Studies, Columbia University
> President, Tibet House US
> President, American Institute of Buddhist Studies
>
> Ganden Dekyiling, Woodstock, New York
> Saga Dawa, June 4, 2012

A Drop from the Marvelous Ocean of History

*The Lineage of Lelung Pema Zhepai Dorje,
One of the Three
Principal Reincarnations of Tibet*

དཔལ་གསང་བའི་བདག་པོ་ལ་ན་མོ།

I. Salutation and Inspiration

With unshakable faith and respect throughout all my lives
I bow down to Your Holiness the Dalai Lama,
White Lotus Holder—embodiment of the compassion of
      all enlightened beings,
You brilliantly manifested in the Land of Snows in order
      to bring benefit and happiness!

I bow down to Buddha Shakyamuni—unsurpassable guide
      of the three worlds.
With the paths of the three vehicles,
You liberate mother sentient beings, kind to us in the three
      times,
From the ocean of the three poisons, and establish them in
      the state of enlightenment!

Respectfully I bow down to Vajrapani,
Powerful deity and lord of the secrets
Of the Vajrayana—the essence of Buddha's teachings,
And the heart treasure of the thousand Buddhas!

Respectfully I offer countless prostrations
To the three renowned brothers,
Supreme lights of Dharma in the Land of Snows,
Human emanations of the lords of the three families!

Respectfully I bow down to the Three Principal
      Reincarnations,[1]
Who nurtured the abundant crop of the three vehicles,
And irrigated the fields of the fortunate disciples with the
      water
Drawn from the womb-like clouds of the buddhas'
      wisdom and compassion!

---

[1] A title given to three seventeenth-century lamas, Lo Sempa, On Gyalse and Lelung Jedrung, who were manifestations of the three buddha families.

As if finding a precious jewel, I feel boundless joy,
At being able to give visible form to some part
Of my predecessors' life stories,
Through the slight merit of my positive karma and prayers.

II. A Liberating Story of Vajrapani, Source of the Lelung Reincarnations, with the Names of some of his Manifestations

> In the holy land of Changlojen
> Resides the great Lord of all secret Tantras
> He who destroys hosts of negative and obstructive
> forces—
> Salutation to Vajrapani, holder of the vajra!

With that positive note and salutation, I will present a brief account of the source of the Lelung Jedrung emanations and the line of Lelung reincarnations.

The source of the reincarnations of Olkha Jedrung, known as Lelung Zhepai Dorje, is Vajrapani, the powerful Lord of Secrets. He is the compiler and protector of all the profound Tantras, the ultimate vehicle of the Buddha's teachings.

In the far distant past during the Zinpa Chenpo Kalpa[2], there was a universal king named Tsibkyi Mukyud, who had 1,000 sons. The two eldest were Migmi Zum and Rabtu Tenpa, also known as Thuchen Thob. The chief minister, Brahmin Gyatso'i Dul, had eighty sons; the youngest, Gyatso'i Nyingpo, had the enlightened name of Sangye Rinpoche Nyingpo. He prophesied that King Tsibkyi Mukhyud would be enlightened as Buddha Amitayus in the Pure Land of Sukhavati, and that later his eldest son, Migmi Zum, and then his second son, Rabtu Tenpa, would become enlightened in their turn. He also foretold that Rabtu Tenpa would become Vajrapani. Some sutras speak of a prophecy stating that when Vajrapani became enlightened in the Pure Land of Sukhavati, its qualities and those of its inhabitants would increase threefold.

According to the *Sutra of Inconceivable Secrets*[3], during the far distant Zespar Nangwa Kalpa, Buddha Yonten Thaye Rinchen Natsog Koepai Gyalpo[4] manifested in the World of Magnificent Adornment. Here

---

[2] One of the very early aeons.

[3] *Gsang wa bsam gyi mi khyab pa'i mdo.*

[4] Enlightened King Bejewelled With Endless Qualities.

he was served for ten million years by the universal ruler Yulkor Sung and his 700,000 queens and 1,000 womb-born sons. Two of the queens, Mamed Ma and Pemed Ma, miraculously gave birth on their laps to Prince Choe Sem and Prince Choekyi Lodoe respectively. The ruler learned that all his sons had taken part in enlightened activity and wanted to discover which of them would first become an enlightened being. He put their names into a vase and performed a divination, which indicated the following: first his son Nampar Dagpai Lodoe would become Buddha Khorwa Jig,[5] the first of the 1,000 Buddhas of this fortunate aeon; then Nampar Gyalwai De would become Buddha Ser Thub;[6] later Wanpo Shiwa would become Buddha Od Srung;[7] subsequently Don Thamche Druppa would become our teacher Buddha Shakyamuni; and finally the other sons would become the remainder of the 1,000 Buddhas. When the 1,000 womb-born sons asked the two miraculously born sons what they prayed for, Choe Sem said he prayed he would be their protector Vajrapani, that his actions would not transgress the bounds of the buddhas' secrets, and that he would hear all of the outer and inner teachings, and revere and understand them.

Choe Sem did indeed become Vajrapani, and it was prophesied that he would become Buddha Dorje Nampar Nonpa in the World Completely Filled With Resources during the Nampar Jongwa Kalpa. It was also fore-told that there would be a counterpart of glorious Vajrapani behind every one of the millions of emanations sent forth by the 1,000 bodhisattvas of the fortunate aeon, including Maitreya, and that the number of his emana-tions would equal that of Buddha Shakyamuni's.

During this present era of Buddha Shakyamuni's teachings, Vajrapani emanated in sixteen forms while residing as lord of the Yakshas on the topmost floor of Great Changlojen Palace to the north of Mount Meru before he manifested as Laykyi Dorje, the great master scholar of Lho-drak,[8] for the benefit of sentient beings. The emanations were as follows: King Drowa Zangpo, the elder son of the Indian king Shri Ratnabodhi, an emanation of Arya Avalokiteshvara; the Nepali king Dharmapala; a

---

[5] Buddha Krakucchanda.

[6] Buddha Kanakamuni.

[7] Buddha Kashyapa.

[8] The first Lelung incarnation.

member of Naga Zhulang's family under Kongpo Shula; a son of Bonpo Raja in Yarlung; Prince Jangtsa Lhawon, a son of King Me Ag Tsom; a non-Buddhist teacher in western India who led many non-Buddhists into Buddhism; a Kashmiri; a divine son in the Thirty-three celestial realm; Yogi Choekyi Senge from Paro; a parrot; an antelope; a householder; a directional guardian; Abbot Drubpa of Ding Ma; the great leader Senge of Shud Phu; and a cannibal in Ngayab Ling. He emanated these various forms to benefit sentient beings in accordance with their mental aptitudes and capacities.

> You are an object of prostration,
> A deity who embodies all the powers of enlightened
>   beings,
> Supreme leader who protects and spreads
> The teachings of the thousand buddhas of this fortunate
>   aeon,
> To eliminate the darkness of the ignorance of beings.

ཡོངས་འཛིན་ཆེན་གསལ་བ།

III. The Three Kadampa Brothers

I supplicate the three Bodhisattva brothers;
Potowa who effortlessly generated bodhicitta in his mind,
Chen-ngawa who cultivated cherishing of others over self,
And Phuchungwa who devoted himself intensively to
    practice.
(lines from the supplication to the lineage masters of
    Lamrim)

Who would not respect those with the seven divine
    dharmas,
Moon and sun emanations of the lords of the three
    families,
Vishnu-like Dromtönpa, minister of Indra-like Atisha,
His radiant eyes of wisdom shining like a thousand beams,
Who rides majestically on the elephant of the five
    sciences.[9]
(lines from a text describing how the three renowned
    Kadampa brothers served their lamas and preserved
    and spread their teaching)

The incomparable Kadampa tradition stands out like Mount Meru from the many Buddhist traditions of Tibet. It teaches seven divine Dharmas: the three pitakas and the four deities—Arya Avalokiteshvara, Arya Tara, Krodhachala and Buddha Shakyamuni, lord of the three-fold pith instructions of view, conduct, and blessing. These are taken as stages of the path and branches for the three classes of practitioners. They constitute primary and secondary methods for a practitioner to progress from the level of beginner to the fully awakened state of enlightenment exactly as taught by the authentic Indian realized master scholars, including the two pioneer philosophers, Arya Nagarjuna and Arya Asanga, and Bodhisattva Shantideva. This tradition includes all the practices from the *Collected Precepts* ethical guide to the glorious Guhyasamaja.

---

[9] Language, logic, philosophy, medicine, and arts.

9

The word "Kadam" or "instructional guide" was used to refer to glorious Atisha's *Lamp for the Path to Enlightenment* and its autocommentary with the four greatnesses. It gave rise to the name "Kadampa" (*bka' gdams pa*),[10] one who realizes that all Buddha's teachings in the Greater and Lesser Vehicles are a personal instructional guide for an individual practitioner to become a fully enlightened person. Other derivations of the word have been suggested. One is that Kadampas practice their lamas' instructions and moral ethics purely, not adulterating them like milk sold in the marketplace, and thus are called *bka' bsdams pa*.[11] Another suggestion is that they are called *bka' 'dam pa*,[12] a reference to the final words of Dromtönpa, the Kadampa forefather, who strictly followed Atisha's teaching on the four deities and three pitakas and practiced mind training. However, the first of these is the definitive etymology. Kadampa is usually divided into two categories, textual Kadampa and instructional Kadampa, with pith instructional Kadampa sometimes added as a third category.

While the Kadampa tradition was upheld by every one of great Atisha's devotees, the master Dromtönpa was the main source of his teachings like the root of the wish-fulfilling tree. He was entrusted with all the precious master's teachings and empowered as his spiritual regent, and it was thanks to his remarkable work that the Kadampa tradition flourished like an ocean swelling in all directions. His appearance in Tibet under the name Genyen Choephel was predicted in sutras such as *Karunapundarika* and *Gandhavyusutra*, and Arya Tara prophesied to Atisha that he would be an emanation of Arya Avalokiteshvara.

Dromtönpa was born in 1004 AD, an Earth Dragon year, twenty-three years before the beginning of the [first] Rabjung,[13] in the upper reaches of Todlung Gatsa Kyemo in the foothills of Lhachen Thanglha. His father, who belonged to the Drom lineage, was called Tagsum Kushen Yagzher Phen, and his mother Khu Od Za. He studied with Yung, Choe, Gon, and Lo, from whom he learned to read, write, and so on, and received

---

[10] *bka'* — a teacher's words; *gdams* — personal instruction.

[11] "Carefully protecting the teachings and purely keeping discipline."

[12] *'dam* refers to a dying person's final words.

[13] A sixty-year cycle.

the complete *upasaka*[14] celibacy vows from Zhang Nanam Dorwang. This master, who was one of the four pillars of Lume, named him Gyalwai Jungne.

At the age of nineteen, he went to Denma in Kham and for twenty years received Tantra and Sutra teachings, including the Heart Sutra, from Lama Jowo Setsun Wangchuk Zhonnu, the Abbot of Drum. (Dromtönpa had previously met him on the road to Nepal when the lama defeated a Nepali pandita in debate.) At the same time he also studied Sanskrit grammar such as Vivykarta with Pandita Drai Tsanma Miti. Some said that he further studied the Abhidharma with Dru Namkha, but *Lamrim* states that he served only five spiritual guides. Subsequently he traveled through the northern region and visited Ngari in western Tibet, where at the age of forty-one he met precious Atisha in Pureng. He at once became the great master's spiritual son, and from then until the latter's death eleven years later, lived with him and manifested the appearance of receiving teachings on both Sutra and Tantra. Atisha poured every positive quality from his vase of knowledge into Dromtönpa, who became an erudite scholar and practiced and observed the view and conduct in accordance with the traditions of the two great pioneer commentators. He became known as Genyen Choephel.

On the first anniversary of Atisha's passing away, Dromtönpa performed the memorial rites. After handing a certain Kawa Shakwang the keys to the treasure house, he was presented with a portion of the precious master's relics and Acharya Suvarnadvipa's silver parasol among other objects. He took these to Reting and stayed at Lion Cliff Face, where at the age of fifty-four he founded the Garuda-Headed Temple. This had been revealed in Kadam scriptures as an auspicious location and described in the *Manjushri Root Tantra* as "the center of the northerly Land of Snows." Here he placed Atisha's silver reliquary stupa, which was constructed by the Indian sculptor Acharya Manu. Its interior was filled by a mandala with a host of deities such as Shakyamuni with the arrangement of the three samayas, Maitreya and the Medicine Buddha with their retinues facing in the four cardinal directions; on the outside of the stupa's vase were carved the host of Guhyasamaja deities. All this

---

[14] Lay person.

was completed in the Female Fire Bird year. Dromtönpa taught and bene-fited the Dharma and sentient beings for eight years at Reting Monastery, producing great, realized scholars shining like Mount Meru's golden slopes and filling the monastery with a galaxy of fortunate disciples.

In reality Dromtönpa was Arya Avalokiteshavara, who performed blessings and exhibited positive qualities for the benefit of ordinary percep-tions, and particularly delighted his spiritual guides with guru devotion. He was altruistic, erudite, skilful and patient in abandonment and cultiva-tion practices, firm in his commitments and endowed with wisdom, discipline and nobility. The very sound of his name is captivating. A great friend to everyone, he was a highly realized being, who concealed his realizations and showed humility to all. This great upholder of Dharma passed away at the age of fifty-nine in 1064 AD, a Wood Dragon year of the first Rabjung. His numerous disciples included the three Kadampa brothers, Shakya Yonten and others who upheld his tradition with erudite scholarship and realizations.

The most senior by ordination of the three Kadampa brothers was Geshe Phuchungwa, renowned as an emanation of Arya Avalokiteshvara and the principal upholder of the textual pith instructional tradition. Born in the Iron Sheep year, 1031 AD, to the Kyira Zingkhar family in Phenyul, he received ordination from Zher Chenpo and Len Tsuljang, who named him Shyönnu Gyaltsen. He considered Atisha and Khuton among others as his spiritual guides, and in particular served and studied with Dromtönpa for eleven years, becoming an erudite scholar. He did not cultivate many disciples but instead dedicated himself to solitude and practice, focusing mainly on the twelve dependent links of the liberated side of phenomena, making offerings to the Three Jewels, and the pith instructions contained in Kadampa treatises. In 1106 AD, a Fire Dog year of the second Rabjung, he passed away at Riwo Monastery at the age of seventy-six.

Phuchungwa Shyönnu Gyaltsen gave teachings to most of Chen-ngawa and Potowa's devotees. However, his main disciples were as follows: Gyalgyi Shapo Gangpa Pema Jangchub, who founded Shawo Gang Monastery, authored the mind-training text *Colorful Scriptures*,[15] taught four dharmas for abandoning roots of delusion such as alcohol, women, attachment and aimless activity, and passed away at the age of sixty-five;

---

[15] *be'u bum khra bo.*

Bendingpa Sherab Gyaltsen; Zhogkyi Karma Dragpa, who mainly focused on the practice of Samantabhadra; and Ben Gurgyal.

Geshe Potowa, the middle of the three brothers, was an emanation of Manjushri and widely known as a reincarnation of Arhat Yanlag Jung.[16] An heir to Atisha's tradition and the principal upholder of the textual Kadampa lineage, he was born at Drao Thang in Phenpo in 1027 AD, a Fire Hare year of the first Rabjung. His father was called Sidpo, from the family name Shensid, and his mother Lemo. From childhood onwards he showed strong and spontaneous altruism, love and compassion for others in pain. He had a deep heartfelt dislike of seeing people suffering, and constantly turned his thoughts to how they could become free of it, while he loved to see them enjoying happiness, and wished it would increase forever without diminishing.

At an early age, Potowa received upasaka vows from Bagom and later took ordination at Yerpa from Ngog Jangjung and Len Tsuljang, who named him Rinchen Sal. He received teachings from Atisha and Khuton among others, and in particular served Dromtönpa for seven years, becoming an erudite scholar. Potowa Rinchen Sal lived at Drolag, Kharthog, Zhungkhan Drag, Taglung and Phenyul Tras, where he subsequently founded Poto Monastery. It had been predicted that he would be an erudite scholar and known as Potowa from Taglung, as shown in the passage from the Kadam Scriptures beginning: "Then Rinchen Sal will [...]." In the places mentioned above he taught the Six Kadampa Treatises[17] and Atisha's *Lamp for the Path to Enlightenment*. Potowa Rinchen Sal actualized many qualities such as bodhicitta and clairvoyance, and had visions of numerous deities. His works included *Blue Scripture*[18]—a miscellaneous collection of Lamrim teachings—and *A Mound of Jewels of Examples and Meanings*.[19] In 1105

---

[16] One of Buddha Shakyamuni's sixteen disciples, who vowed to preserve the Dharma until the coming of Maitreya.

[17] *The Bodhisattva Bhumis (Bodhisattvabhumi)* by Asanga; *The Ornament of the Mahayana Sutras (Mahayanasutralankara)* by Maitreya/Asanga; *The Compendium of Trainings (Shikshasamucchaya)* by Shantideva; *A Guide to the Bodhisattva Way of Life (Bodhicharyavatara)* by Shantideva; *A Garland of Birth Stories (Jatakamala)* by Aryasura; *The Collected Sayings of Buddha (Udanavarga)*.

[18] *be'u bum sngon po.*

[19] *dpe chos rin chen spungs pa.*

AD, a Wood Bird year of the second Rabjung, when he was seventy-nine and had no more direct disciples to benefit, he manifested the appearance of passing away.

Geshe Potowa had as many as 2,000 fortunate disciples. One of the most important was Langri Thangpa Dorje Senge, called Gloomy Face, who was known as an emanation of Amitabha. He was born at Serma Shung in Phenyul Nyagong, received ordination from Drogkhar Wa, and founded Langthang Rinchen Gang Monastery. Subsequently he benefited sentient beings mainly through his sublime text *Eight Verses for Training the Mind*. His disciples included Shawo Gangpa; Khawa Jangchub Pal of Gya Chagri Gong, who was a spiritual guide of Khyungpo Ranyen Gampo; and Langthang Zhangwa, who was a spiritual guru of Phagdru Wa. For eighteen years Sharawa Yonten Drag served Potowa, who became an incomparable master and was known as an emanation of Manjushri. He was born in Patsab Rompo, where at birth he left an imprint of his foot in solid rock and hence was also called Shang Rompowa. He had great intelligence and famously memorized all the sutras. Potowa Rinchen Sal thus had many authentic upholders of his lineage.

Chen-ngawa Rinpoche, the youngest of the three brothers, was known as an emanation of glorious Vajrapani, and was the principal upholder of instructional Kadampa. He was born into the lineage of Nangra in Nyangyi Langra Gang in 1033 AD, a Water Bird year of the first Rabjung. His father was called Shakya Dorje and his mother Limo Yeshe Dron. When he was eighteen, he received ordination at Tsathog Monastery in Todlung from Mel Sherab Sempa, who named him Tsultrim Bar. At Nyenmo he met Atisha, to whom he offered auspicious verses, and the precious master gave him Acharya Suvarnadvidpa's vase in return. Tsultrim Bar attended upon Dromtönpa for eight years at Reting Monastery, regularly serving him and preparing his bed, and thus came to be kown as Chen-ngawa.[20] He internalized all Dromtönpa's instructions and had clairvoyance and visions of many deities. At the age of sixty-three, in the female Boar year, he founded Lo Monastery. In 1103 AD, a Water Sheep year of the second Rabjung, he passed away at Myugrum at seventy-one years of age. He had 800 disciples.

---

[20] "close one."

Of all Chenga Tsultrim Bar's disciples, these were his three incomparable spiritual sons:

> Chenpo Rinchen Nyingpo of Todlung, who also served spiritual guides such as Great Yogi Gonpawa, popularly known as Senge Drazin Pandita Bumtrag Sumpa. Founder of Tsandro Monastery, his disciples included: Dingpowa Choebar, Nyangro Thangpa of Tsang, Khyung Khampa—who founded Dingphu Monastery in Tsal—Lha Od, Nyaga Mopa, Zarpa, Jadul Zin and Log Kyawa;

> the elder Dargom Tsombar Myugrumpa, a spiritual guide to Gampopa, who resided at Myugrum Monastery in Lungsho and later built a newer temple called the New Rooftop of Thangkya;

> Tulku Jayulwa.

His other main disciples included the following: Zarwa Phaggom Yeshe Dorje, who founded Zer Temple in Upper Meldro; Rug Gyagom, who founded the chapel of Lungsho Rug; an earlier Dargom; the four great meditators of Ralwa Sanggom, who built the chapel of Lungsho Rug; four upholders of Vinaya—Lagur Tonpa, Tser Ton, Thang Dul, and Drom Dul; Kharuwa, Rompo Dorje, Ae Gewa Chenpo, who founded Ae Chung Monastery Zhangton Paltseg; Gyatse Dro, Drolagpa Chenpo from Phenyul; Pagya Wa, Lhodrak Pawa Ton, Tsangpa Jopad from Tsang; Tsangpa Gyiton, Oyugpa Ami, Kusung Tonpa, Zhang Kamawa, Zarwa Jotsun, and Kumer Shakya. After Geshe Chen-ngawa left for Myugrum, other disciples such as Nastan Zhonnu Monlam succeeded him in taking care of Lo Monastery.

True Kadampa practitioners never do the following: use their bodies to indulge in irreligious activities, practice dishonest livelihoods, entertain deluded thoughts, employ the three doors[21] in meaningless activities, sell the Dharma for money, or do retreats on demonic beings. They have strong faith and patience, talk and travel about less frequently, and cherish their vows and commitments. They have fewer expectations, doubts, and

---

[21] Of body, speech, and mind.

attachment, are diligent in developing renunciation, and reduce jealousy, competitiveness, and dissension. Consequently other traditions may have many enemies, but the Kadampas, like a golden elixir, have excellent relations with all.

With regard to the three brothers, the Kadam scriptures state that King Dadpa Tenpo was reborn as the spiritual guide Dromtönpa, his eldest son Sangye Zin became Geshe Potowa, and his other sons Dharma Zin and Gendun Zin became Phuchungwa and Chen-ngawa respectively. Furthermore, according to the king's biography, within a few years Prince Sangye Zin would become Rinchen Sal[22], Gyalwai Jungne's[23] chief disciple. In addition Prince Dharma Zin would become a sublime master and holder of Vinaya texts and Prince Gendun Zin would be Chen-ngawa, a holy master benefiting Dharma and practising many of Gyalwai Jungne's instructions.

The Kadam scriptures also state that the three brothers are emanations of the lords of the three families, as in the following quotation from the Prophecy Chapter:

> Henceforth an emanation of the deity Avalokiteshvara,
> Also one of Manjushri and one of Vajrapani,
> And another of Manjushri,
> And a spectacular emanation
> Will come here from Five Peak Mountain.
> The first three will be my sons
> Named Potowa, Phuchungwa, and Chen-ngawa:
> The three Kadampa brothers.

Furthermore it is stated that when Drom Rinpoche made extensive offerings to Atisha, the latter told him, "I can see that this white-colored boy has sixty-five emanations in Tibet." There was also a yellow-colored boy, who said, "I have ninety emanations," and a blue-colored boy, who said, "'I have 165 emanations in the north, but here I have six for my karmically linked disciples." The boys should be understood as Phuchungwa, Potowa, and Chenga Tsultrim Bar, respectively. These sources indicate

---

[22] Geshe Potowa.

[23] Dromtönpa.

definitively that the three Kadampa brothers are manifestations of the lords of the three families.

The tulkus known as the Three Principal Reincarnations of Tibet are renowned as emanations of the three brothers. The Kyabgon Gyalse Rinpoches are known as reincarnations of Phuchungwa Shyönnu Gyaltsen, the human emanation of Arya Avalokiteshvara, and the Kyabgon Lo Sempa Rinpoches as reincarnations of Chenga Tsultrim Bar, the human emanation of glorious Vajrapani. None of the texts that I have seen show clearly from which Kadampa brother the Kyabgon Zhepai Dorje[24] line descends. However, since the reincarnations of the other two lines of Rinpoches have been clearly identified in several biographies as illusory manifestations of Geshe Phuchungwa and Geshe Chen-ngawa, it is felt that Zhepai Dorje's line were intended to be understood as reincarnations of the remaining brother, Geshe Potowa. Some might question this on the grounds that the latter was known as an emanation of Manjushri while Lelung Zhepai Dorje was known as emanating from Vajrapani. However, this need not be felt as a contradiction because the following prophecy by Acharya Padmasambhava shows that Lelung Zhepai Dorje was also a manifestation of Manjushri:

> One with the name Tenpa—an emanation of Manjushri—
> Will in future appear at Dawa Thang in Domey.[25]

The lords of the three families constitute the complete resource body,[26] which embodies the enlightened body, speech and mind of the Buddhas of the three times. While they manifest in multiple forms, they all have identical nature and thus there is no manifestation of theirs that does not share the same mental continuum. Consequently there is no need for such narrow thinking. If any authentic scriptures should be found relating to this subject, they can be added later as an appendix.

The Three Principal Reincarnations were shown enormous appreciation by the Great Fifth and the Great Seventh Dalai Lamas, who bestowed on them titles and praises and for valid reasons. They did this without

---

[24] The fifth Lelung Jedrung.

[25] Cf. Chapter VIII.

[26] Sambhogakāya.

even a sesame seed's worth of influence from well-connected people, external powers or foreign nationals, but solely in accordance with their power and status as kings of Tibet. Historians have honored them for governing in this way.

> I humbly bow down to the three brothers—supreme guides
>   of the Land of Snows—
> Manifestations of the lords of the three families for the
>   people of the Land of Snows.
> Their tradition of instructions unprecendented in the Land
>   of Snows,
> Flourished widely for the benefit of the people of the Land
>   of Snows.

ཀྱེ་བྲག་སྒྲུབ་ཆེན་ནམ་མཁའ་རྒྱལ་མཚན།

IV. Lhodrak Namkha Gyaltsen, the First Lelung Jedrung Reincarnation

The great master Lhodrak Namkha Gyaltsen, commonly known as Dorje, was born in the Fire Tiger year, 1326. His father was the master Namkha Zangpo of Shudphu Palgyi Senge's[27] lineage, and his mother was Rinchen Gyen. When he was born, he recited the buddhas' names in Sanskrit and revealed signs indicating that he had deliberately chosen his birth there. At the age of two, he performed the gestures of offering tormas,[28] remembering these from his previous life. At three, he received the Vajrakilaya empowerment, when he saw in a vision the lineage dakinis performing dances. He also had visions of many other special deities. When he was five, he received the Dzogchen empowerment and through the power of previous positive imprints had visions of his kind spiritual guides, from whom he felt he was receiving teachings. He said that when a rooster crowed and a conch shell sounded on hot days, they sounded like the music of dakinis in Oddiyana summoning demons into the Dharma and the conversations of many celestial beings.

At the age of seven, Lhodrak Namkha Gyaltsen received upasaka vows from his uncle, the great abbot Gyalse Pa. With no feeling of attachment to family life and a strong thought of renunciation, he also received novice monk ordination from the great abbot Gyalse Zangpo,[29] as well as the teachings of the compassionate Arya Avalokiteshvara. Subsequently he did many retreats on this deity.

When he was ten, he received from his uncle Lamrim teachings according to the lineages from both Neuzurpa and Jayulwa; teachings on Arya Avalokiteshvara, Akshobhya, Hayagriva with four deities, and the twenty-one Taras, among others. Many special auspicious signs occurred. At the age of thirteen, an obstacle year, Lhodrak Namkha Gyaltsen engaged in virtuous actions every single day. While he was circumambulating the

---

[27] One of Guru Rinpoche's twenty-five disciples.

[28] Ritual cakes.

[29] Gyalse Pa.

stupa at Drowa Monastery one night, light could be seen from afar radiating from his body, and hence it was reported that the stupa was being encircled by fire. At fifteen, he studied the Vinaya extensively, and at seventeen, he said that although he was teaching and listening to the Dharma day and night, his one thought was to practice meditation in a remote area.

At the age of nineteen, Lhodrak Namkha Gyaltsen made a pilgrimage to Lhasa to meet Atisha; every day he did many circumambulations of Jokhang Temple. When he was in the courtyard of Ramoche Monastery one night, an iron gate opened and a ferocious black-colored man in a black robe appeared. The man told him that he was the one called Laykyi Dorje Dedan and that he should now go to Rinchen Gang, where he would meet an emanation of Manjushri. He said that this man must have been Gonpo Drigug. He went there accordingly and received full ordination from Rinpoche Tashi Gyalwa, who gave him many teachings on lamrim, lojong, bodhicitta, and numerous Tantric practices. Afterwards, he received many teachings from Rizang Dogpa, such as the Great Commentary on Ethics. At the age of twenty-two, he engaged in the practice of the Thirty-Five Confessional Buddhas, committing himself to doing 700 prostrations in every session. He said his practice had developed so well that his mind was completely settled and he had uninterrupted, genuine experiences of compassion and bodhicitta every single day.

When he was twenty-three, he did a six-month retreat on Manjushri and Don Zhag at Drowa Monastery; and at twenty-five, he received many teachings from Lama Dewai Jungne, who was visiting Kharchur. In the same year, the great abbot Gyalse Pa invited Mondra Wa to Drowa. They held a great teaching event, where Lhodrak Namkha Gyaltsen received numerous teachings, such as the empowerment of Vajrapani With Five Garudas, and Eight Verses for Training the Mind. When he was thirty-one, he built a huge golden statue at the passing away anniversary of Gyalse Pa, and at the request of the local monks and lay people, he sat on the Dharma throne of Drowa Monastery, becoming its abbot.

At that time, Vajrapani gave him teachings on the twenty-two [similes of] bodhichitta altruism, saying:

> O Laykyi Dorje!
> No one becomes a buddha by paying lip service to the
>   Dharma.

Birds with no wings cannot fly.
Water in a mirage cannot quench thirst.
But no one dies of thirst at the ocean.
Uncle Mitri spoke thus:
Just like earth, gold, moon and fire [...]

At the age of forty, he requested and received from Vajrapani profound instructions on the seriousness of transgressing the three sets of vows, and also an inconceivably secret method of purifying trangressed commitments. These were later recorded in his writings. When he was forty-two, Vajrapani spoke to him as follows:

It is a lie when individuals claim to have had visions of deities and to have actualized noble experiences and realizations, without first developing faith in and respect for spiritual guides. They are lying when, without a deep heart-felt remembrance of death, they claim to have renounced worldly activities; when, without conviction in the karmic law of action and results, they tell others not to commit negative actions; when, without having even atom-sized beneficial thoughts, they say they have generated love and compassion; when, without realizing conventional phenomena as empty of true existence, they say they have realized emptiness. To practice the Dharma genuinely, faith is of crucial importance.

When Laykyi Dorje asked what causes faith to arise, Vajrapani gave him many instructions, such as the following:

If you see your lama as the Buddha, you will have faith. If you remember death and impermanence, you will have faith. If you socialize with friends who have faith, you will have faith. If you reflect on the faults of samsara, you will have faith.

Once he met a master who said he was the great Brahmin Saraha, and extensively instructed Laykyi Dorje on the vital points of the vajra body. Furthermore, Lhodrak Namkha Gyaltsen said that at the age of sixty-one he had seen a great palace in the upper part of the central valley in Liyul, where three valleys join. On asking who lived there, he was told it was Dipamkara Shrijnana Atisha. As he wished to meet the great master, Lhodrak Namkha Gyaltsen went to the palace and earnestly requested a meeting with him. Consequently he saw great Atisha, huge in size, with a white face and wearing the red hat of a learned scholar. At his request to be taken care of as a disciple, the great master gave him many instructions.

When he was seventy, at dawn the day after he had given the empowerment of Dorje Namjom at Jamkar, a deity prophesied that four men would visit him with a letter from an emanation of Buddha Maitreya. The following day four men came with a letter from the spiritual guide Losang Drakpa.[30] He felt uplifted when he heard about the great master, remembering their teacher-disciple relationship from a previous life. Subsequently, one night in a dream he heard Losang Drakpa faintly telling him that he had invited seven Buddhas to come. As Lhodrak Namkha Gyaltsen wished for the happiness of meeting them, he immediately saw them coming to him in the form of twelve-year-old boys, with their ushnishas[31] prominently erect, seated on the five colors of a rainbow. Even after he woke up and looked at them, they remained there for a long time. He said that at that time Losang Drakpa had been consecrating the temple of Zingchi. On another occasion, a white-colored girl told him that he would be visited by a person who had been blessed by Maitreya, was inseparable from Manjushri, had received wisdom from Saraswati, and with whom he had made a connection fifteen lifetimes previously. The girl said that they would have a mutual teacher-disciple relationship, and that he should give this person Dharma instruction unstintingly and also receive teachings from him. At another time, he heard a faint voice announcing that Maitreya was visiting, and he understood this to mean that at that time Choeje Kazhipa was visiting Gyamo Ritreng.

In 1395, a Wood Boar year of the seventh Rabjung, Jey Tsong Khapa visited Drowa Monastery on the fourth day of the sixth month, the day of Buddha's first turning of the wheel of the Dharma. Laykyi Dorje stated that when he went to welcome him, he saw Jey Tsong Khapa as Manjushri, while he heard that Jey Tsong Khapa for his part saw him as Vajrapani. As he said:

---

[30] Jetsun Tsong Khapa, commonly known as Jey Tsong Khapa.

[31] The crown protuberance on top of the head of the Buddhas, a symbol of their wisdom and openness as enlightened beings.

That night Jey Tsong Khapa asked me for a Guru Yoga [teaching], and when I gave it to him, Vajrapani came and dissolved into Jey Rinpoche. Then, at dawn on the fifteenth day, a voice said that I should request Maitreya himself to teach me the *Compendium of Bodhisattvas' Trainings*. I asked Jey Tsong Khapa for this teaching and he gave it to me, having first enquired whether a deity had asked me to request it. At that time, I saw Maitreya sitting on the crown of Jey Tsong Khapa's head, with White Manjushri to his right, Saraswati to his left, and Jey Rinpoche himself encircled by hosts of Dharma protectors and dakinis. Many divine beings and demons were also listening to his teachings. I experienced unique faith in Jey Tsong Khapa and great respect for him. I also received from him the Sosor Drangma empowerment and altruistic mind generation. I gave Jey Tsong Khapa the following teachings among others: a commentary on the instructions on the two lineages[32] of Lamrim; an inconceivably secret commentary, oral transmission, and permission blessing given by Vajrapani; a permission blessing of Vajrapani with five deities; *A Vajra Garland of Questions and Answers*; an oral transmission and permission blessing of *A Cherished Garland of Questions and Answers*; an empowerment and permission blessing of Vajrapani With Five Garudas; an empowerment of the Subduer of All Aggressors; and a permission blessing of Three-Faced, Six-Armed Solitary Hayagriva. At that time, dakinis performed the activities of empowerment and permission blessing, and when Jey Tsong Khapa was offered a skull cup filled with nectar, he saw in the bubbles Manjushri, Jambhala and Vaishravana. Many other special indicative signs occurred. Furthermore I gave numerous teachings such as Lama Jamkarwa to Jey Tsong Khapa's wonderful circle of disciples, and by gaining faith in both the teacher and his disciples, I also

---

[32] *bka' babs gnyis kyi khrid.*

developed a few positive qualities myself. During my teachings, Jey Tsong Khapa for his part said that he saw Buddha Shakyamuni on my head, Vajrapani to my right and Sitatapatara[33] to my left.

As mentioned above, the highly renowned holy being Lhodrak Drupchen Namkha Gyaltsen received Lamrim according to both the lineages transmitted by Geshe Tonpa: the one to Gonpawa and subsequently Neuzurpa, and so on; and also the one to Chenngawa and then Jayulwa, etc. After receiving the quintessential instructions on these two lineages intermixed like two streams of water converging, he practiced them and attained supreme realizations. He also taught Lamrim widely to fortunate ones and thus nurtured many holy lineage holders. A prophecy by the deity Vajrapani, the Lord of Secrets, states:

> One hundred thousand will attain devotion,
> Fifty will definitely be liberated,
> Eight will be undisputed adepts,
> And the incomparable one will be Losang!

Many holy beings indeed appeared, but the one who was matchless and carried out the most tremendously beneficial activities in the Land of Snows was the Dharma King, Losang Drakpa the Great. On one occasion, he had decided to visit India to meet Acharya Nagabodhi and Mahasiddha Mitra in his search for the ultimate vital points of Sutra and Tantra, such as the ultimate profound Middle View and the illusory body of glorious Guhyasamaja. However, while he and his disciples, thirteen in all, were carrying out auspicious ceremonies for the journey, the great abbot Lhodrak Namkha Gyaltsen requested that he should stay in Tibet. In accordance with a prophecy from Vajrapani, the Lord of Secrets, he said that if Jey Tsong Khapa were to visit India, he would surely meet with Acharya Nagabodhi and Mahasiddha Mitra and attain special qualities. However, he would also become the abbot of Bodhgaya Temple and thus be unable to return to Tibet. Raising many other objections, for instance that his circle of altruistic disciples would die of heat in India, Lhodrak Namkha Gyaltsen earnestly entreated him not to go, and after serious

---

[33] The White Parasol Deity.

consideration Jey Rinpoche abandoned the plan. Consequently he stayed in Tibet, where he established and clearly elucidated systems of Sutra and Tantra, the precious teachings of the Buddha, and the sole source of benefit and happiness for all beings in the Land of Snows. He thus opened the door for prospective disciples to advance to the state of omniscient knowledge.

Je Tsong Khapa established monastic communities to uphold and spread the complete flawless precious teachings of the Yellow Hat tradition. This resulted in a pearl string of great realized master scholars, who have appeared ever since, due solely to Vajrapani, the Lord of Secrets, and the great master Lhodrak Namkha Gyaltsen, who was incomparably kind to the people of the northerly Land of Snows. He was under the constant care and guidance of Vajrapani and did everything according to his advice. Thus he was renowned as Lhodrak Vajrapani and also known as Lhodrak Drupchen Laykyi Dorje[34] in the cool Land of Snows.

This master founded monasteries in many places, such as Thigchi Monastery in the Lhodrak region, and 108 hermitages, as detailed in numerous great biographies. At the age of seventy-six, after greatly serving the Dharma and beings and having benefited every one of his direct disciples, he manifested the appearance of passing away. This was in 1401, an Iron Snake year of the seventh Rabjung. Inconceivable indicative signs occurred. At the cremation of his body, there appeared a self-arisen deity image and tens of thousands of relics, which became fields of merit for innumerable beings. In recent times these relics have also been known to be effective in treating sicknesses such as smallpox and leprosy.

His most important legacy was a large volume of his collected works, which included a liturgy for accomplishing the deities, and an ear-whispered Tantra from Vajrapani intended for his disciples. These teachings have been practiced by many practitioners from all the different traditions. Thus he made a huge contribution to the scriptural and realization aspects of Buddha's teachings.

> I supplicate at the feet of Namkha Gyaltsen!
> With an altruistic mind he saw all beings as his children,

---

[34] Laykyi Dorje, the great master of Lhodrak.

He was taken care of and blessed by a deity,
As a supreme spiritual guide leading beings of the
    degenerate era.

I supplicate Laykyi Dorje, the Lord of Secrets,
Who knows the three times without obscurations,
Who subdues hosts of demons with his power,
Who has actualized the four enlightened bodies and
    swiftly benefits all others.

འཇིགས་དྲུང་སྤྱགས་རམ་པ་དགེ་འདུན་བཀྲ་ཤིས།

V. *Ngagrampa Gendun Tashi, the Second Lelung Jedrung Reincarnation*

The noble translator Ngagrampa Jedrung Rinpoche Gendun Tashi was born in 1486, a Fire Horse year of the eighth Rabjung, in Upper Nyang. Nyang, which is part of Tsang[35], extends between Phu Habo'i Gang Zang in the north and Da Chugpa Yuwa Dong in the south, with Kuru Valley separating Upper and Lower Nyang. Gendun Tashi's father was head of the Keme Norbu Khyung Tse family.

At the age of eight, Gendun Tashi was admitted to Tashi Lhunpo Monastery, where he learned reading, writing, and all the chanting prayers, and completed his studies. One of his contemporaries was the Second Dalai Lama, Omniscient Gendun Gyatso, also studying there. At twenty, Gendun Tashi visited Ngamring Monastery and Palkhor Chode for debates, and there mastered the ten fields of knowledge—such as grammar and poetry—studying with Gyalchog Pa, the Abbot of Narthang Monastery. At about this period the King of Ney Nying stirred up discontent towards Gendun Gyatso among the followers of Panchen Yeshe Tsemo,[36] and it became awkward for the Omniscient Master to continue living at Tashi Lhunpo. He therefore had to move to Central Tibet, where Jedrung Gendun Tashi also went. The latter sat for Tantric debate at the Upper Tantric College, where he became known as Ngagrampa[37] Gendun Tashi.

After discussions between Panchen Choglha Ozer[38] and Depa Chong Gye,[39] Omniscient Gendun Gyatso and Ngagrampa Gendun Tashi went to Chong Gye and other nearby places to perform Dharma activities. Subsequently Jedrung Rinpoche was entrusted with the task of collecting funds in Kham to build the great statue of Maitreya at Chokhor Gyal. In

---

[35] A province south west of Lhasa.

[36] The regent of Tashi Lhunpo.

[37] Doctor of Tantra.

[38] A well-known lama who wrote about metaphysics and whose teachings are held at Ratoe Monastery.

[39] A ruler from Chong Gye, the area south of Lhasa.

Tsawa Gang, one of the monks in his entourage died from a naga's harmful attack and he performed a fire offering ritual to subdue it. Then the naga offered him 2,800 monks in compensation for the deceased one, entrusted its brother, Buteng, to them and also granted Ngagrampa Gendun Tashi the fortune of being a priest to the Chinese emperor in his next rebirth. Subsequently he was invited by Jampa Ling Monastery in Chamdo to become abbot. He received from organizations and individuals throughout Kham 3,000 ounces of gold, 80 copper coins, and mandalas of Guhyasamaja, Chakrasamvara, and Yamantaka set in roofed houses for the statue. He sent all these back to Chokhor Gyal with an emissary, while he himself stayed behind to build monuments at Chamdo. During this time the statue of Maitreya was almost completed.

Je Ngagrampa sat on the throne of Chamdo Jampa Ling Monastery in 1546, a Fire Horse year of the ninth Rabjung. At this time Omniscient Gendun Gyatso had already passed away into the sphere of emptiness, and his reincarnation, Omniscient Sonam Gyatso,[40] was very young. In 1547, on the fifth day of the sixth month of the Fire Sheep year, this noble erudite realized scholar, who was a truly great vajra master, sent a delegation with gifts for Omniscient Gendun Gyatso's supreme reincarnation. These consisted of a golden canopy with the image of a mandala and its doors, sixty-two deities of Heruka cast from finest silver, canopies with images of Nine-Deity Amitayus and Nine-Deity Hevajra, and a brocade canopy. Also included were numerous religious adornments such as banners, tea for a reception to welcome Omniscient Sonam Gyatso, hundreds of butter lamps and other offerings, and tea and gifts for the assembly of monks. The delegation consisted of Chief Treasurer Choedak, Lama Dakpa, Guru Yang and Ponpa Kunga, who presented the gifts on his behalf.

The Phagde Translator Jedrung Rinpoche Gendun Tashi served as abbot of Jampa Ling for seven years before relinquishing the throne in a Water Mouse year. The title Jedrung has been given to the line of the abbots of Chamdo Jampa Ling ever since.

After appointing Jedrung Miyowa Nyingpo as his regent, Ngagrampa Gendun Tashi went to Lhasa to meet the supreme reincarnation of his root guru Omniscient Gendun Gyatso, and also to do retreat at Chokhor

---

[40] The Third Dalai Lama.

Gyal hermitage. He first set up an encampment in Me Tog Thang valley,[41] and then opened a vase of unending wealth, making a great heart offering to the supreme reincarnation of the Omniscient Master. He also gave gifts to his attendants and followers, and generously made tea and gift offerings to the assembly of monks on twenty different occasions. He received numerous teachings such as a long-life empowerment and a Palden Lhamo permission blessing from the supreme reincarnation of his root guru. Afterwards he gave Gyalwa Sonam Gyatso a multiple-deity Amitayus empowerment and a peaceful and wrathful Guru Padmasambhava empowerment. The Omniscient Master did a retreat on the Small Red Wrathful Guru[42] and had a face-to-face vision of the host of deities, after which he wrote *Praises for Continued Blessings*.

Subsequently Ngagrampa Gendun Tashi left for Drepung, and on the journey fulfilled the spiritual requests of people of all backgrounds in places such as Oelkha and Dechen. He and his attendants returned to his residence, and he offered Dharma teachings and material gifts to the builders for constructing the retreat house called Island of the Wonderfully Blissful Garden. Shozangpa Choeje Jinpa Dhargye, who had arrived from Shosang in Amdo, was one of many who came to the feet of this master to receive numerous teachings on sutra and Tantra.

The following passage appears in the biography of the Third Dalai Lama, *The Ocean Chariot of Real Attainment*:

> The tenth month of the Water Bird year was the appropriate time for Gyalwa Sonam Gyatso to receive the ocean of secret teachings. The noble translator Ngagrampa Gendun Tashi was chosen to give them, being highly respected for all the following: ripening empowerments; liberating commentaries; supporting scriptural quotations; commentaries and explanations of Tantras; permission blessings, instructions and retreat fulfilments; the four virtuous activities; ritual dances, mandala plans and chanting; mandala drawings; making ritual cakes, and so on. In short, he had thoroughly mastered every skill from the

---

[41] "Flower Ground"—an area in Choekhor Gyal.

[42] Padmasambhava.

very smallest, such as how to hold the vajra and bell, and had accomplished many beneficial activities. He had also authentically accomplished the prescribed and supplementary retreat fulfilments, prerequisites for performing activities related to mandalas. He was a great vajra master who authentically actualized profound meditative stabilizations of the coarse and subtle levels of the generation stage and the highest levels of the completion stage. This master was Vajrapani in person, the Lord of Secrets and compiler of all Tantras, who intentionally manifested in the form of a fully ordained monk who had taken the three types of vows so that he could be a tutor to the supreme reincarnation of the Protector of the Land of Snows, a human manifestation of Arya Avalokiteshvara. He was worlds apart from those elderly intellectuals who pretend to be great meditators and pass themselves off as vajra masters despite having no expertise in Tantra, like donkeys masquerading in the skin of a leopard, deceiving many disciples. Thus this glorious master was invited from his upper residence in Chokhor Gyal called Island of the Greatly Blissful Garden to glorious Drepung Monastery.

At the Residence of Perpetual Sunshine, he first gave Gyalwa Sonam Gyatso a series of empowerments including Avalokiteshvara Donyoe Zhagpa, Eleven-Faced Avalokiteshvara and Nine-Deity Amitayus. The following day, the Omniscient Master said that at night he had dreamed of a white rainbow appearing from a clear blue sky, with a full moon above. In the center of the moon he had seen a large red-colored man holding a vase, surrounded by eight small men of the same color, all holding vases and wearing garments identical to the first man's. He said these must have been auspicious indicative signs of his receiving the Nine-Deity Amitayus empowerment the day before. He then received blessings from holy objects held by Ngagrampa Gendun Tashi, and the skull cup endowed with all the essential qualities was brought to his private residence. He placed this by his pillow with offerings and made prayers. The next day at dawn he dreamed of walking through the door of a huge building in whose courtyard he saw someone making tea or something similar in a huge brimming pot on a hearth. On asking what they were doing, he was

told that it was to give to sentient beings. He walked downstairs, and seeing a staircase leading to the loft area, went up and knocked at the door.
It was opened by a young girl who looked at him, and when he asked
who was inside, she replied that Vajravarahi lived there. Looking in, he
saw that Ngagrampa Gendun Tashi was also there and thought he could
see Sungrabpa too. He asked if he could enter but was told it was not the
right time yet, whereupon the door was closed. Tulku Trengkhawa[43] said
that the doorkeeper was someone who had great compassion for us, the
people of the Land of Snows.

In the past there used to be many lineages of the *Vajramala* empowerment, but the one received by the holy master Ngagrampa Gendun Tashi
and given by him to Gyalwa Sonam Gyatso was the four-mandala lineage
exclusive to the Choejey Vajradhara Evam spiritual father and sons. This
was unknown even to most of the other famous lineage holders. It originated
with Sazang Phagpa, when the *Vajramala* and *Kriyasammuchaya* mandalas
were mixed together like two streams of water converging. Ngagrampa
Gendun Tashi gave the entire lineage empowerment to Gyalwa Sonam
Gyatso and also many other empowerments, commentaries and oral
transmissions. These included the following: Zurka empowerments,
Guhyasamaja according to both Arya Nagarjuna's and Sangye Yeshe's
traditions, Heruka according to Mahasiddha Luyipa, the outer mandala
and body mandala according to Mahasiddha Ghantapa, the *Samputa Tantra*,
Hevajra according to the pith instruction and Ngog lineages, the Fifteen
Goddesses of Selflessness, the combined lineages of Mahakala mentioned
in the *Vajrapanjara*, Wrathful Danchan, Yamantaka according to Ra's
lineage, Dranag both with the Eight Zombies according to the Nyoe
lineage and with the Forty-Nine Deities according to the Zhang lineage,
the Thirteen Red Yamantakas according to Palzin's lineage, Five-Deity
Red Yamantaka according to Nejor Wangchug, Great Circle Vajrapani,
the Twenty-One Wrathful Garudas with the Four Wrathful Ones, Kunrig,
Mitrugpa, the White Parasol, Dranga, Avalokiteshvara according to
Mitri's lineage, the Kalachakra empowerment, permission blessing of
Vajrapani with the five Garudas, Acharya Drozang's lineage, Namjom,
Drubgyal Amitayus, Norgyunma, Oezer Chenma, Jambhala, the four

---

[43] A great lama who was an influential master of thangka painting.

empowerments of Three-Faced and Six-Armed Mahakala according to Saraha's lineage, the permission blessing of Thirteen-Deity Mahakala well-known to the Ganden Tradition, the permission blessing of the Four-Armed Goddess with Yakshas, the uncommon permission blessing of the Transfer of the Protector Mahakala into the Heart, the empowerment of Four-Armed Avalokiteshvara based on a cloth-drawn mandala and body mandala, permission blessings of the three brothers Gur, Zhal and Legdan, the accumulations of Heruka and Yamantaka mantras, the *Yedharma* consonants and vowels, the hundred syllables of Vajrasattva, empowerments of Gonpo Zhidrag and Duetsan Ma, the empowerment of the Lion-Faced Goddess according to the five Buddha lineages along with the liturgy for accomplishing her range of activities, the empowerment, permission blessing and oral transmission of the collected works on Manjushri, the empowerment of the White Parasol, Green Secret Vaishravana flanked by the eight great Nagas, permission blessings of White Serchen flanked by the four demonic females, accomplishing Yama as a deity, Kangthang Ma, the permission blessing of the six commentaries of Mitra, white and black miscellaneous pith instructions with regard to the Six-Armed Wisdom Protector,[44] and practices of the circle of great ritual propitiation among others, pith instructions and practices from the writings of the great translator Ra Lotsawa, the Yogic Circle of Yamantaka, Drugchuma[45] and so on. In short, the Omniscient Master received innumerable empowerments, commentaries, and oral transmissions like one vase filled from another. Before the teaching event was completed, Jedrung Rinpoche also gave teachings to many others who were interested, such as master scholars of Drepung, the reincarnation of Geden Tse Drakpa Dorje, the precious reincarnation of Jey Lhawang Paljor, Drungne Rinpoche and members of the inner circle.

He also gave Gyalwa Sonam Gyatso the empowerment of the Thirteen-Deity Secret Avalokiteshvara through a colored sand mandala. Shortly before its dissolution, it happened to be the torma-throwing ritual of the twenty-ninth day of the twelfth month, and that great Dharma

---

[44] Mahākāla.

[45] The sixty ritual cake offering.

protector, the Nechung oracle, appeared at the mandala in a trance. He made the following pronouncement:

> The quintessence of the heart of the thousand buddhas in general is Padmasambhava. I am his appointee and have not transgressed his words even to a thousand-way split of a horse's tail hair [...] When I see this perfectly pure practice, the order of details and the number of empowerments exactly as the Buddha taught in the discourses on Tantra, I say to all you dakinis and wisdom Dharma protectors on my level and above, wherever you are, in whichever of the twenty-four regions or thirty-two places, or in whatever cemetery, come here joyfully in fulfillment of your previous commitments. Worldly protectors below me and regional and local deities, you must also come, remembering your individual commitments. Today I too have happily come here to express my appreciation. Some pretend to know what they do not know; some pretend to understand; some pretend to have realizations. They falsely maintain that one thing can be replaced or substituted by another and do whatever is easiest for them, using deception to trick foolish devotees. Thus they claim to be adepts among the foolish and pretend to be highly realized. When I see such deception and waste of lives, I, Pehar Gyalpo, feel very sad. But I have been extremely happy to witness this water of empowerment exactly as found in the precious Tantric sources, untainted by the mud of errors, and also pure waves of authentic practices. Anyone who experiences these will be victorious over the demon of death and covered in the nectar of the great exalted wisdom. That was excellent work. Jedrung Rinpoche, you should carefully complete the remaining teachings. Now I shall leave for the ritual cake offering.

With these words he left. At another time, when Jedrung Rinpoche, the Lord of Secrets, was giving the remaining teachings, the great Dharma protector Nechung came and told him to build a huge and magnificent statue of Guru Padmasambhava, set it up at Nechung's monastery and perform a great consecration ceremony. Accordingly, on Jedrung Rinpoche's instructions, a larger-than-life-size statue of Guru Rinpoche was constructed by the sculptor Jamyang Gyatso.

On a later occasion, Vajradhara Ngagrampa Gendun Tashi enthroned Jey Thongwa Donden[46] on a lion throne with a canopy above his head, a parasol to his right, and a victory banner to his left. He also attired him in the robes of a universal king and put into his hands a vajra and bell, empowering him as his Vajra Regent. Jey Ngagrampa himself held a vajra and bell and presented the Omniscient Master with outer, inner and secret offerings as prescribed in the Highest Yoga Tantras. He also put into Gyalwa Sonam Gyatso's hands a volume entitled *Clear Lamp, a Chanting Text of a Vajra Garland*, which he himself had composed. After the elaborate mandala offering he requested the Omniscient Master to turn the wheel of secret Tantra far and wide, whereupon Gyalwa Sonam Gyatso began teaching from the *Clear Lamp*, thus creating magnificent auspiciousness.

In 1556, a Fire Dragon year, Gyalchog Sonam Gyatso visited Tsethang, which is south east of Lhasa. One night a Brahmin with garlands of human skulls encircling his torso came to him and said it would be tremendously beneficial for him to practice Yamantaka as the outer deity, Chakrasamvara as the inner deity, and the Four Vajra Seats as the secret deity. The Omniscient Master told Jedrung Rinpoche of this at Gyal and requested him to compose a liturgy for accomplishing the Four Vajra Seats. On being presented with this, he practiced it unfailingly. When Omniscient Sonam Gyatso established a workshop to build a silver reliquary stupa of his omniscient predecessor, Jedrung Rinpoche visited and perfomed rituals to get rid of obstacles, bless the workshop and the environment, empower the builders, and consecrate the materials and tools. Thus Jedrung Rinpoche, the all-encompassing lord of the mandalas of all lineages, was supreme among the spiritual teachers of Omniscient Sonam Gyatso.

The following passage appears in Gyalwa Yonten Gyatso's biography by the Great Fifth Dalai Lama:

---

[46] A respectful term for the Dalai Lama meaning "the mere sight of him is meaningful."

In 1588, Gyalwa Sonam Gyatso withdrew his bodily manifestation into *dharmadhatu*[47] on the twenty-sixth day of the third month of the Male Earth Rat year. He first went to the Pure Land of Vajrayogini, with his exalted wisdom body arisen from mere wind energy and mind because he kept his exclusive heart-bound kernel practices confidential. He continously practiced the Transfer of the Protector Mahakala into the Heart, a profound practice of the realized scholar Kyung Po and the incomparable Riwo Gandenpa school, which he received directly from Ngagrampa Gendun Tashi, the all-encompassing lord of an ocean of mandalas.

These words appear in the Omniscient Master's own testament:

I request blessings from the protector Mahakala,
Inseparable from the guru and the thirteen glorious
      dakinis.

as does the following passage, which indicates his realization of the special core path of the profound vajra yoga grounded in the central psychic channel:

I have experienced the vast ocean of bliss and voidness,
Swelling like water during the summer season.
This noble path was due to the kindess of the vajra vehicle,
O gurus you truly are extremely kind!
May I never be parted from this noble path,
In all my succession of future lives.

The Great Fifth Dalai Lama said that the gurus mentioned here unquestionably refer to Vajradhara Ngagrampa Gendun Tashi and Jetsun Bokharwa Metri Dhondup Gyaltsen.

Ngagrampa Gendun Tashi wrote tremendously beneficial treatises such as the above-mentioned *Clear Lamp, a Chanting Text of a Vajra Garland* and a liturgy for accomplishing the Four Vajra Seats. Furthermore, in Ü-Tsang and Do Kham he established many people from all

---

[47] The sphere of ultimate reality.

walks of life in the paths of ripening and liberation, and built a number of schools,[48] shrines, and monuments as fields for fortunate ones to accumulate merit.

After accomplishing greatly beneficial works, in 1559, an Earth Sheep year of the ninth Rabjung, he manifested the appearance of withdrawing his bodily manifestation into the *dharmadhatu* at Phende Monastery while on a journey from Gyal. Lama Choezepa and his disciples brought Vajradhara Ngagrampa's body back to Gyal, where it was cremated at his upper residence. His skull, teeth and many other relics were preserved in a newly built silver reliquary stupa, which was enshrined in the upper part of the Maitreya temple. He left a testament for Omniscient Sonam Gyatso requesting the Omniscient Master to find him in Dagpo Langdhar, where he would reincarnate. Consequently Jedrung Tenpa Gyatso, a reincarnation embodying great power, was born there, which clearly indicates that this master had attained very high realizations.

> I supplicate at the feet of Gendun Tashi,
> Whose wisdom pervaded the five fields of knowledge,
> Who elucidated teachings with the power of his
>   knowledge,
> Who opened doors to an ocean of mandalas such as deities
>   of the *Vajra Garlandi*!

---

[48] Temples which hold scriptures.

འཇེ་དྲུང་བསྟན་པ་རྒྱ་མཚོ།

VI. Tenpa Gyatso, the Third Lelung Jedrung Reincarnation

Jedrung Tenpa Gyatso was a reincarnation of great power and influence. He was born at Dagpo Ladar in 1560, an Iron Monkey year of the ninth Rabjung. The circumstances of his birth were exactly as described in the testament left for Gyalwa Sonam Gyatso at Zhingje Khar by his predecessor, Ngagrampa Jedrung Gendun Tashi. When he was three years old, he was recognized by the Omniscient Master, who presented him with a forty-pillar estate from the Upper Residence of Chokhor Gyal. At the age of five, he was invited by both Jampa Ling in Chamdo and many of the previous Jedrung Rinpoche's devoted disciples, to visit the monastery where his predecessor had served as abbot. He lived there for five years, extremely well provided for by the monasteries, monks and lay people connected to his predecessor.

When he was ten, Jedrung Rinpoche visited Central Tibet, where he offered Chokhor Gyal 140 copper plates for its golden roof and 500 tea packets.[49] In the following year he offered Sera, Drepung, and Ganden: butter tea, 300 tea packets, a total of 300 dzos[50] and mules, and other donations. With his remaining resources he renovated the Upper Residence at Gyal from its foundations upwards. Subsequently he became the chief spiritual guru of Depa[51] Lhapa.

Three years later he visited Kham, where he was given an excellent reception and was extremely well served and honoured. On his return to Central Tibet, he went as Gyalwa Sonam Gyatso's attendant to Chekar, Neudong, Rinpung, Gongkar Estate, and elsewhere, where he satisfied peoples' spiritual and material needs, and became a guru to all. During their visit to Kyishoe, while Omniscient Sonam Gyatso was giving him teachings on Four-Faced Mahakala, those present witnessed the sudden appearance of a Brahmin.[52] He also met Aku[53] Tashi from Ganden, who

---

[49] One packet contains sixteen small or four large tea bricks.

[50] Hybrids of cows and yaks.

[51] Regional governor responsible for the four districts of Lhasa.

[52] This would have been one of Mahakala's entourage.

43

became his patron, and they established a lama-disciple relationship. Jedrung Rinpoche then studied for five years at Jey College in Sera Monastic University.

When the Mongolian king Altan Khan invited the spiritual father and son[54] to visit his country, Jedrung Rinpoche went as Omniscient Sonam Gyatso's attendant to Chamdo in Kham. They visited Den Chokhor Ling at the invitation of Choeje Lung Rigpa and his disciples, and Sonam Gyatso left an extraordinary imprint of his foot on a rock, while Jedrung Rinpoche made a deep indentation in another by urinating on it. The Omniscient Master interpreted this as meaning Jedrung Rinpoche would have a son at the end of his life.

In 1584, a Wood Monkey year of the tenth Rabjung, they stopped at Drag Gya on their way to Blue Fortress in Mongolia. Gyalwa Sonam Gyatso had a remarkable dream about a rainbow pointing towards the roof of the house where they were staying. He prophesied that in the future, an authentic lama would contribute to the flourishing of the Kadampa doctrine in that region. Jedrung Rinpoche himself manifested in the form of Vajrapani and subdued several nonhuman negative spirits, notably a wily naga inhabiting a water spring below a giant rock shaped like an ogress's genitals. He caused the naga to be struck by lightning, and banished it to the depths of the valley.

In accordance with the Omniscient Master's prophecy, Oen Gyalse Rinpoche later founded the great monastery of Jampa Ling, one of the four illustrious northern monasteries in Amdo, from which arose numerous holy beings—like pearls on a rosary string—from the time of its foundation onwards. Along its path of circumambulation were thrones for Jedrung Tenpa Gyatso, the Great Fifth Dalai Lama, and the earlier and later Gyalse reincarnations, as well as the footprints of Karma Rolpa'i Dorje and Gyalse Losang Tenzin.

In Mongolia, both the spiritual father and son performed miracles beyond description and liberated many demonic spirits, burning their negativities. One such was Genghis Khan's minister Kerel Thu, who had been reborn as a powerful non-human spirit inhabiting a rock. He was appointed

---

[53] Governor of Lhasa.

[54] Gyalwa Sonam Gyatso and Jedrung Rinpoche.

by Jedrung Rinpoche to be the local deity and remained as a powerful protector called Oeden Gyatso, which is the Tibetan version of his name.

News of their illustrious accomplishments reached the Wanli emperor of China, the fourteenth emperor of the Ming Dynasty. He sent a delegation to invite them to his palace, but the Mongolian king refused to allow Gyalwa Sonam Gyatso to go. However, the Omniscient Master told them that Jedrung Rinpoche was a reincarnation of his own guru and in no way inferior to himself. With this commendation he sent Jedrung Rinpoche at the age of twenty-five to the Forbidden City in Beijing. The emperor decided to test him and ordered that he be served delicious food and drink for two weeks but not permitted to go outside to relieve himself. Only on the fifteenth day was he allowed to go to an open place, where he filled a whole pit with his bodily excretions. Astounded by this, the emperor developed faith in Jedrung Rinpoche and invited him to his palace, whereupon the syllables of Vajrapani appeared in the incense smoke. The emperor presented him with a red silk hanging brocade interwoven with the seal of Vajrapani. On the third day he gave Jedrung Rinpoche a throne to sit on, while he himself sat on a cushion.

Jedrung Rinpoche bestowed on the emperor, his queen, and their three sons, the permission blessing empowerment of the three lords of the buddha-families and a long-life empowerment. He also gave the princes privately a wrathful protection blessing. Before leaving, he accepted the emperor's gift offerings of gold and silver dishes and pots as well as 108 identical tables. However, he refused the many treasure houses he was offered, saying he would find them too mentally burdensome.

From there he went to Central Tibet and brought offerings to the monastic universities of Sera, Drepung and Ganden loaded onto 325 mules, 130 camels, and 200 dzos. He made copious offerings to the monks, each one receiving a roll of silk and brocade, a silk scarf with the eight auspicious symbols, a bundle of incense sticks and a large tea brick. He also gave tea offerings to the monastic assembly as a whole.

In the same year, Panchen Lama Losang Choekyi Gyaltsen became his disciple, who was then like a renunciate living in extremely humble circumstances. Nevertheless, Jedrung Rinpoche presented him with a complete set of high lama's robes, declaring with his clairvoyant insight that he would need them in the latter part of his life when he would be an eminent master. Jedrung Rinpoche lived at Ganden Phodrang[55] for three years, and gave wonderful tea offerings and generous donations to the monasteries of the three southern regions of Gyal, Oelkha and Dagpo, creating complete contentment.

In 1617, a Fire Snake year of the tenth Rabjung, Choepa Rinpoche Losang Tenpa Gyaltsen, a lama of Dechen Chokhor Ling Monastery in Ronpo, went to Central Tibet at the age of thirty-seven and received extensive teachings from Jedrung Rinpoche. Many other masters also came to him for teachings. These included Ngawang Gyaltsan, the head of Ne'u Mgo Pa Monastery, and Abbot Dragpa Shedrup, Ponlob Losang Rabten, the founder of the Tagtsang hermitage known as Jangchub Choeling, Tashi Choeling, and many other superior beings from Amdo, upholders of the holy Dharma. Most notably, he became the sacred tutor of Omniscient Yonten Gyatso,[56] who praised him as "a vajra holder able to summon Dharma protectors as his servants." He was also acclaimed by Panchen Lama Losang Choekyi Gyaltsen in these words:

> You do not merely masquerade as a learned master,
> You are free of the artifice of a phony realized master,
> Your holy conduct is worthy of praise from the holy—
> Therefore your qualities are reflected in the clear pool of
> my mind!

As this quotation shows, Jedrung Rinpoche's outer, inner and secret qualities rendered him supreme among great realized scholars. He became a master of the emperors of China and Mongolia and, in particular, completely satisfied the spiritual needs of Omniscient Yonten Gyatso and All-Seeing Panchen Lama Losang Choekyi Gyaltsen with his profound and extensive teachings. In 1625, a Wood Ox year of the tenth Rabjung, at the age of sixty-five, he had established many people in Tibet, China and Mongolia on the paths of ripening and liberation. Seeing there were no other direct disciples for him to teach, he manifested the appearance of dissolving his body and mind into the sphere of ultimate reality to

---

[55] Site of the original government of Tibet, later to become synonymous with the government itself.

[56] The Fourth Dalai Lama.

inspire with Dharma those who grasped at the permanence of their lives and possessions.

> I supplicate Gendun Tenpa Gyatso,
> Who gained perfection in the generation stage of
>   Manjushri Yamantaka,
> Lord of an ocean of power to summon spirits to his
>   service,
> Vajra-holding master and elucidator of Buddha's
>   teachings!

ཡེ་ཤེས་དངོས་གྲུབ་ཚོགས་རྒྱལ་དབང་ཕྱུག

VII. Gendun Choegyal Wangchuk, the Fourth Lelung Jedrung Reincarnation

Jedrung Gendun Choegyal Wangchuk was a master of spiritual accomplishments. He was born in 1646 on the fifteenth day of the eighth month, a Fire Dog year of the eleventh Rabjung in Ji Nyul. This is in the region of Chokhor Gyal, a place visited and blessed by many holy beings such as Machig Labdon, and close to Ae.[57] His birth was in accordance with the following prophecy by the great master Padmasambhava:

> On the border of Ae and Dagpo will appear
> An emanation of the mind of Vajrapani,
> Who will have the name of Dharma,
> And has been blessed by me Padmasambhava.
> He will be born in a Dog or a Boar year,
> With a white mole to the right of his navel;
> He will summon to his service all rahulas[58] and wrathful
> spirits.
> Everyone who makes a connection with him will go to
> Vajrapani's Pure Land of Changlojen,
> A clear prophecy and advice concerning this have already
> been given.

His father was called Ba Sonam Rinchen and his mother Atsug. His father belonged to the same Ba lineage as great holy beings such as Ba Ratna and Ba Yeshe Wangpo, who lived when Dharma first spread in Tibet, and also incomparable Yagde Panchen, Khedrup Sangye Yeshe and Omniscient Panchen Lama Losang Choekyi Gyaltsen at a later period. During the early dissemination of the Dharma, Ba Ratna was fully ordained by the great Abbot Shantarakshita and immediately attained five clairvoyant powers. King Trisong Deutsen bowed down at his feet and praised him as "the Jewel of Tibet," whence his name originated.[59]

---

[57] The district south of Lhasa.

[58] A class of beings linked with planetary influences.

[59] *ratna* means "jewel."

49

After the death of the great bodhisattva Abbot Shantarakshita, Ba Ratna, and Ba Yeshe Wangpo—who also achieved clairvoyance—were enthroned as his successors. While the latter was on retreat at Lhodrak Kharchu, a Chinese monk named Hashang Mahayana came to Tibet and spread his teaching on nothingness.[60] He declared that enlightenment could be attained by mere mental noncontemplation rather than by positive actions of the body and speech. This appealed to many Tibetans, and the altruistic practices of Buddha's teachings, such as generosity, fell into decline. The king was greatly concerned. He requested advice from Ba Yeshe, who said that the great abbot had told him on his deathbed that wherever Buddha's teachings flourished, they would be challenged by non-Buddhist teachers. In Tibet, however, there would be no such challenge due to the fact that Acharya Padmasambhava had entrusted the land to the twelve female protectors. However, a Chinese monk would come and propagate the path of sudden enlightenment, creating philosophical differences within the Buddhist community. When this happened, his disciple Kamalashila should be invited from India to deal with it and requested to refute these views with authentic reasoning. The king followed this advice, and in the ensuing debate the Hashang conceded defeat and returned to China. Thus Ba Yeshe Wangpo made a great and essential contribution to Buddha's teachings.

According to Abbot Losang Dhondup of Dagpo Monastery, at Jedrung Rinpoche's birth everyone witnessed a cascade of flowers and a rainbow like a dome over the roof. Moreover, in accordance with the prophecy about this reincarnation mentioned above, Jedrung Rinpoche's later attendants indeed saw a white mole on his right hip and marks like a tiger skin on the lower part of his body.[61] These authentic physical and external signs indicated that he was an unmistakable emanation of glorious Vajrapani. As soon as he started to talk, he spoke the names of his family home, servants, and animals from his previous incarnation through his power of recollecting previous lives. He also astounded everyone by reciting *Drenpa Nyamme*[62] during a tea offering despite never having learned it.

---

[60] *ci yang yid la mi byed.*

[61] Vajrapani is often depicted as wearing lower garments of tiger skin.

[62] *Praise to Buddha the Incomparable Teacher.*

His birth on the border of Ae and Dag and the fact that he was given the name Dharma—as he was called Chocgyal[63]—also accorded with the prophecy of Acharya Padmasambhava. Moreover, his birth sign was the dog, and the master had prophesied that the reincarnation would be either the dog or the boar. Furthermore, as already stated, he had unmistakable birthmarks like the mole to the right of his navel and imprints like a tiger skin, and he clearly identified the objects for identification, such as the scroll painting of Oechen Barma and the bell from his previous life. All of this led people to the deepest conviction that he was the reincarnation of Jedrung Gendun Tenpa Gyatso. The Panchen Lama Losang Yeshe[64] said of him:

> As a result of earnestly supplicating
> Gurus and deities over many lives,
> He had a recollection of his previous lives.
> This unbelievable brilliance immediately dispelled
> All the doubts of his disciples.

The Jedrung incarnation left with his followers for glorious Drepung via Kyishoe, along the Gyal route. There he offered the first cut of his hair at the lotus feet of the Glorious Omniscient Ngawang Losang Gyatso,[65] the lord of the people of the Land of Snows, who named him Gendun Choegyal Wangchuk. Afterwards he went to Oelkha Zhol and lived there for about four and half years, learning to read and write Uchen,[66] which he did extremely fluently and effortlessly. While memorizing a book of propitiation prayers to Palden Lhamo, he said that he dreamed of a lady offering him an auspicious scarf, which appeared to be a sign indicating his accomplishment of the activities of this deity. On another night, he dreamed of someone in a brahmin form talking to him at length, which was understood to be a manifestation of glorious Four-Faced Mahakala. He then spent about a year at Gyal, before leaving for Ngari Monastery

---

[63] *choe* is the Tibetan equivalent of the Sanskrit word *Dharma*.

[64] The fourth Panchen Lama.

[65] The Fifth Dalai Lama.

[66] One of the Tibetan scripts.

in 1660, the Male Iron Rat year, to attend the great anniversary of Lama Tsong Khapa.

In the winter of 1661, the Female Iron Ox year, when he had a slight skin rash, he dreamed of climbing a hill to the east. Seeing a fish in a stretch of water near the top, he generated himself into Vajrapani and kicked at it, thinking it was a naga. Immediately the rash disappeared, and he never again had a problem with his skin. Furthermore, during the summer retreat at Gyal he dreamed of signs indicating that great harm was being done by evil spirits. He became fearful, breaking into a sweat, and made a supplication to the great master Laykyi Dorje from Lhodrak. In a semi-conscious state he then saw this master in front of him. Going back to sleep, he proclaimed he was Padmasambhava from Oddiyana, who had bound under oath to protect the Dharma the eight categories of gods and demons and the twelve goddesses. It immediately occurred to him that he should bind the evil spirits in his dream in the same way. He arose in the form and attire of Padmasambhava, with his right hand lifting a vajra and the left pointing with a threatening gesture to the evil spirits, poised to launch himself into space. All these signs indicate that he was a human manifestation of both glorious Vajrapani, subduer of nagas and earth spirits, and the great master from Oddiyana, subjugator of the eight categories of gods and demons.

In the winter, while he was traveling from Zangri Monastery to Drepung, two women came to him in a dream and offered him a white and a black ball of thread in turn, saying these were his protectress Oechen Barma's weapons. This indicated that he had a strong karmic connection with the goddess, having cultivated her as his principal protectress in previous lives, and that she had always helped him. The women said he would have the power to bind her to his service, together with Rahula and other protectors, in order to destroy all the enemies of the Dharma.

During a study retreat at the Zangri district ruler's residence when he was twenty-three years old, he felt he had a problem with his foot, so one evening he offered ritual cakes to Yeshe Khyungtra.[67] That night in his dream he distinctly saw nagas appearing at their dwelling places around the district, but he experienced no harm from them. When he

---

[67] The multicolored Garuda.

subsequently questioned local people who knew where the nagas lived, to everyone's astonishment they confirmed what he had seen in the dream.

In 1668, on the fifteenth day of the eleventh month of an Earth Monkey year of the eleventh Rabjung, he entered into the Dharma completely, receiving full ordination from an august assembly. Ngawang Losang Gyatso,[68] a fully ordained human manifestation of Arya Avalokiteshvara and lord of the entire teaching of Buddha, performed the roles of both abbot and preceptor. Phabong Khapa Jey Jamyang Dragpa became his secret preceptor and several masters from Drepung completed the ordination quorum. Thus he became supreme among the monastic community.

Subsequently he received the following teachings from his precious secret preceptor: all four complete empowerments of the glorious Thirteen-Deity Yamantaka as well as the oral transmission of the commentary on their mandala, the two stages of generation and completion authored by Gomde Namkha Gyaltsen, and permission blessings and oral transmissions of numerous other practices such as Mahakala, Dharmaraja, and Palden Lhamo. He also completed meditational retreats on these teachings. Furthermore, during the long-life offering ceremony at Chokhor Gyal, he received the following teachings from the Omniscient Lord: permission blessings of White Heruka, Amitayus, and White Tara, and the oral transmission of an instruction on guru yoga based on the visualization of Amitabha. At that time the Dalai Lama also composed a biographical long-life prayer for him.

Later, in the sixth month of the Female Earth Bird year of 1669, he went to Oelkha Chuzang and served as head lama for six and a half years. While he was there, he had the following dream: first he saw a white rainbow, which gradually became five-colored and then circular in shape. In the center he saw a spontaneous appearance of the thirty-five Buddhas of Confession, each encircled by a five-colored rainbow. He said that after some time they all merged into a huge halo of light, which gradually diminished in size and then disappeared. Because of this he commissioned a thangka of the thirty-five Buddhas.

Subsequently, in the first month of the Female Water Ox year of 1673, he went to Riwo Serling Monastery, where he also took the position of abbot for twelve years. During this time, when monks from Ngari

---

[68] The Fifth Dalai Lama.

Monastery came for their annual summer debate session, he treated the assembly lavishly with tea and tsampa[69] for two or three days. He also commissioned nine thangkas of the lineage masters of Lamrim and a statue of Palden Lhamo the size of a fifteen-year-old along with her two retinues, in accordance with a standard oral instruction. Having consecrated them elaborately according to the glorious Vajrabhairava ritual, he offered them to the monastery.

Later, in the seventh month of the Male Earth Horse year of 1678, he visited Rinchen Gang, a monastery founded by Khaydrup Norzang Gyatso, and also Nyima Ling, which had been founded by Naytan Zangkyong, one of the eight pure disciples of the great master Jey Rinpoche. At Rinchen Gang, he conferred upon the great master Losang Wangpo and many others all four complete empowerments of glorious Guhyasamaja, and he commissioned a huge thangka of the deity. He also carried out excellent renovations to the chapel that housed a blessed image of Khaydrup Chenpo Norzang Gyatso, to which he offered the thangka. He subsequently served as Abbot of Nyima Ling for seven years.

Afterwards he went to Chokhor Gyal, a pilgrimage site that had been visited by the Dalai Lamas, the line of Omniscient Masters and protectors of the Land of Snows. On the night of his visit he dreamed that the entire sky was filled with gold letters. This auspiciousness is similar to a vision of Jey Rinpoche's, in which he saw lines from the mother-like Transcendent Wisdom Heart Sutras in gold letters.

On one occasion, while receiving an oral transmission of Buddha's teachings from Losang Dhondup, a master of Sutra and Tantra, he also wrote letters, gave audiences to some, blessed the cords and protection wheels of others, and gave advice as well. The master wondered how Jedrung Rinpoche could be receiving the oral transmission while engaged in these other activities. However, at the end of the transmission, he was able to tell Losang Dhondup that there were various parts missing. This indeed proved to be the case when another set of sutras was brought and they looked through them. Thus Tsang Pa master Losang Dhondup thought that Jedrung Rinpoche had internalized the complete sutras within his mind. He said that this generated devotion for Jedrung Rinpoche in his own mind and much greater faith in him. After

---

[69] Roasted barley flour.

receiving the oral transmission, Jedrung Rinpoche himself gave oral transmissions of these sutras, once to a gathering of many masters including Lama Drungpa from the white residence and Lama Drungpa Tsondru Gyatso, and subsequently on two or three other occasions. Jedrung Rinpoche said that this had been more beneficial for him than many years' solitary practice in a cave.

The fact that he put so much effort into giving and receiving these teachings indicates that he was endowed with all the qualities of a true Kadampa geshe as defined by Jey Rinpoche in the following anecdote. The master once asked the meaning of Kadam. When Chenga Rinchen Phel said it meant one understood there was not even one syllable of Buddha's teachings to be discarded and that it should all be taken personally as instructional advice, he responded with great delight, "That's right! That's right!"

In addition, Panchen Lama Losang Yeshe also praised Jedrung Rinpoche in these words:[70]

> From an ocean of authentic sutras and their commentaries,
> Atisha and Manjushri Tsong Khapa
> Excellently churned the essence of the path—a wish-
> fulfilling jewel.
> This you upheld, great master and guide to those wishing
> for liberation,
> A honey-like essence of extensive instructions from
> realized scholars of India and Tibet.
> You tasted it on your tongue through your knowledge and
> practice,
> Perfectly completing them through your skills in method
> and wisdom realizations,
> And swiftly attained a most elevated path!

While giving an oral transmission of the short, medium, and long versions of the mother-like Transcendent Wisdom Heart Sutras to about seventy monks at Gyal Legshe Ling monastery, Jedrung Rinpoche sent one of them away to publish the entire collected works of Omniscient Panchen Lama Losang Choekyi Gyaltsen. Some time later during an oral

---

[70] Of the previous quotation in this chapter.

transmission, Jedrung Rinpoche commented that he had seen a vision of this monk, whose name was Samten, being carried away by water in the Tsang valley. On Samten's return, he asked him if this had indeed happened, and the monk confirmed it. This indicates that Jedrung Rinpoche had unobstructed clairvoyance. Before retiring as the throne-holder of Gyal, he treated the monastic assembly lavishly with tea, tsampa and butter, and offered them gifts such as katas.[71] They themselves eagerly offered a long-life ceremony to Jedrung Rinpoche with pure devotion, during which he had a vision of great mahasiddhas such as Saraha, Shawari and Virupa in the sky.

Subsequently he gave empowerments, oral transmissions and instructions, satisfying the spiritual needs of the monks at Olkha hermitage and its main and branch monasteries. The following year he moved from Yulmon to Zateng, where he entered into a retreat. In the course of this, he dreamed that some monks put into his hand an opened text of what they said was *Guhyasamāja*, and he saw himself sitting on a throne facing the west and the assembly of monks sitting in rows performing a ritual. This is similar to an event in Jey Rinpoche's life when someone he believed to be omniscient Buton Rinpoche presented him with a *Guhyasamāja* text, and it may be understood as an auspicious sign of his empowerment as a master of Guhyasamaja. In fact Jedrung Rinpoche authored a great retreat guide to that glorious deity.

On one occasion he received a naked instruction on Avalokiteshvara practice according to the tradition of Mahasiddha Tsembu from his root guru, glorious Ngawang Losang Gyatso, the exceedingly kind Protector and Guide of the Land of Snows. Jedrung Rinpoche said that he had a pure vision of seeing his guru as Avalokiteshvara and that his guru's teaching was accurately and spontaneously reflected in his mind. The night after the teaching was completed, he dreamed of receiving from the Omniscient Master a conch shell with gold wings and many banners attached to it. This may have indicated that his fame would spread far and wide in Tibet, China, and Mongolia.

Subsequently Jedrung Rinpoche thought it would be most beneficial to use his devotees' offerings for spiritual purposes. He invested them in reproducing the precious collection of sutras and other worthwhile activi-

---

[71] Ritual scarves.

ties, and spent about 1,400 gold coins' worth on food, drink, wages and other expenses. Later, at the heartfelt request of several monks, he composed the following: a new Guru Yoga, a supplication while remembering the kindness of gurus, a liturgy of Secret Vajrapani clad in blue attire, and a prayer dedication for the harmony and prosperity of the monastic sangha. While he was at a summer retreat the following year, he gave teachings such as an empowerment of the Thirteen-Deity Yamantaka and the oral transmission of the *Togdun Tantra* to a gathering of about 300 monks. He also gave numerous teachings to the chant leader and monastic assembly of Ladrang Yomgon, such as the permission blessing of the Four-Armed Mahakala. Furthermore he bestowed the great Guhyasamaja and Thirteen-Deity Yamantaka empowerments as well as other permission blessings and oral transmissions upon about fifty monks at Lelung Monastery. He also invited a Nepali craftsman to come, and began a project to build an image of Maitreya. He commissioned the casting of a statue the size of a fifteen-year-old youth together with a throne and its back support, which he offered to Chokhor Gyal. Similarly, he commissioned an adult-sized silver stupa, which he donated to Ngari Monastery.

Jedrung Rimpoche reprinted many collections of texts, such as the entire works of Omniscient Gendun Gyatso and eleven volumes of the collected works of the Great Gyalwang Thamchad Khyenpa, the Fifth Dalai Lama. He also visited the new assembly hall of Ngari Monastery, where he offered tea and money to the monks and performed an elaborate fire offering ritual and consecration. He offered the monastery a victory banner made of brocades, eight stupas of Tathagatas made of medicinal clay and a statue of Buddha with his two attendants, as well as giving each monk a large brocade. From there he went on a pilgrimage to Tsari and then Upper and Lower Dagpo, where he gave teachings to the monastic community and laity and satisfied their spiritual needs. He also visited Gyal Residence and gave a subsequent empowerment of Amitayus and Hayagriva to its treasurer.

On his return to Lelung Monastery, he invited a number of accomplished artists to come, and commissioned them to make twenty-five thangkas depicting a hundred stories of Buddha's life, as well as a huge thangka of Vaishravana with a complete depiction of Changlojen, the Pure Land of Vajrapani. He also built a multi-storied temple to house these paintings. Panchen Lama Losang Yeshe wrote as follows about these actions:

> Heroes and yoginis of the past,
> And also buddhas, bodhisattvas and great arhats,
> Will show their smiling faces to you,
> Delighted with your deeds of body, speech, and mind.
> You built icons of Buddha's body, speech, and mind,
> You gave profound instruction to others,
> You practiced as you preached —
> O Guru, these were your three principal deeds!
> Through these three wheels of actions,
> You cared for monastic communities,
> Such as Choekhor Gyal and Oelkha in the east,
> You became the root and the branch,
> Saving the theory and practice of Buddha's teachings and
>   making them flourish!

Jedrung Rinpoche actualized the vajra body, which cannot be destroyed even by organic disease, negative spirits and epidemics. Nevertheless, he decided to manifest the appearance of taking on a sickness and passing away because most of his direct disciples of this life had come to an end, and he mainly intended to benefit those of his next reincarnation. On the night of his passing away, he performed an elaborate ritual cake offering in the presence of Omniscient Gendun Gyatso's main realization statue housed in Chokhor Gyal, saying that he had done this for a special purpose. Then he dissolved his form at dawn. This was in 1696, on the fifteenth day of the first month of a Fire Mouse year of the twelfth Rabjung, when he was fifty-one years old. Many auspicious signs appeared at that time such as a cascade of flowers falling like rain and also a rainbow. He emanated his wisdom body of subtle mind and wind energy from the heart, which instantly and unobstructedly dissolved into the heart of Vajrapani in his Pure Land of Changlojen beyond the three realms of existence.

I have recorded here a drop from the ocean-like collection of the deeds of Jedrung Gendun Choegyal Wangchuk, whose fame spread far and wide. Any reader wanting to know more can read a long biography of this master by Panchen Rinpoche Losang Yeshe called *Ocean of Delight for Realized Ones*.

Predicted by Padmasambhava you engaged in esoteric
     discipline,
You subdued the eight obstacles, you, a great yogi of Ba,
Purely endowed with the three higher trainings,
You non-conceptually actualized the nature of reality—
I pray at your feet Choegyal Wangchuk!

པཎ་ཆེན་བློ་བཟང་འཕྲིན་ལས་རྣམ་པར་བཞད་པའི་རྡོ་རྗེ།

VIII. Losang Trinley, the Fifth Lelung Jedrung Reincarnation

Glorious Pema Zhepai Dorje, also known as Jedrung Losang Trinley, was born at a small monastery near Zangri Kharmar, a practice site of Machig Labkyi Dronma,[72] in 1697, a Fire Ox year of the twelfth Rabjung. His father and mother were Kunga Gyaltsen and Gyalphur Choeden, both former monastics. People marveled at the many wonderful signs appearing at his birth, and his coming was foretold by Terton Rigzin Choeje Lingpa[73] in these words:

> One by the name of Tenpa—an emanation of Manjushri—
> Will in future appear at Dawa Thang in Domey.
> He will turn the wheel of Dharma and benefit many
>   beings.
> A wonderful Bodhisattva emanation of this emanation
> Will appear at the site of Zangri in Ngam Shod.
> He will do peaceful and wrathful retreats of
>   Avalokiteshvara,
> In order free beings from obstacles.

Terton Choeje Lingpa himself recognized the Lelung reincarnation, and through Gelong Namkha Gyaltsen presented the young Jedrung Rinpoche with a number of gifts. These included the prophetic revelation discovered in the region of Kongpo that was quoted above, a ritual text of Black Manjushri's meditative absorption, and longevity pills made from treasure-discovered pills displaying the syllable HRI. [74] At the age of two, the young reincarnation remembered his former life. He named articles that had belonged to the previous Jedrung, and also said, "Let's go to the monastery!" When asked where this was, he pointed to the east, where the Lelung monastery was indeed located, but being so young he pronounced

---

[72] A great female master (1055–1152) who finalized and set up the Choed lineage.

[73] The founder of Mindrolling monastery, one of the six main Nyingma monasteries of Tibet.

[74] *hri rgyal can las spel ba'i ril bu.*

its name "Ae-yung." He also had no difficulty recognizing many monks and benefactors from his previous existence. These recollections together with earlier prophecies and investigations by realized holy masters, and also clearer prophecies by Dharma protectors, led to one conclusion, and he was recognized as the unmistaken reincarnation of the previous Lelung. The monastic assembly and its benefactors invited him to his predecessors' estate monastery, where he was offered a wonderful enthronement ceremony.

Soon afterwards he visited the Potala Palace, the residence of Arya Avalokiteshvara in the Land of Snows, and had an audience with Gyalwang Tsangyang Gyatso,[75] a human manifestation of the deity, to whom he offered the first cut of his hair. The Dalai Lama gave him the name Tenpa Drubpay Gyaltsen after joking that he was going to call him Ani Tingting Drolma.[76] Thus he received the name prophesied by Padmasambhava in the previous quotation: "One by the name of Tenpa—an emanation of Manjushri..."

However, all the holy objects of his estate monastery, together with his personal residence and wealth, had been handed over to a certain Choezey, an avaricious individual from the Eastern Residence who had solicited them from the regent. In addition, some of his possessions had been taken by the government. As a result the young reincarnation had no suitable residence when he returned. He had to live in a ramshackle building and had difficulty acquiring food, clothing and other basic necessities. Despite this, Jedrung Rinpoche pursued his studies with great rigor and determination under the skilful encouragement of his paternal uncle. At times, however, he was greatly disturbed by the disruptive actions and behavior of some of those close to him.

Later he visited Tashi Lhunpo in Tsang to receive novice monk ordination from Panchen Rinpoche Losang Yeshe as Gyalwang Tsangyang Gyatso had given back his monastic vows. The Panchen Lama gave him the name Losang Trinley, highly praised him and rewarded him with material wealth. He also gave Jedrung Rinpoche vast and profound teachings and composed his biographical supplication and long-life prayer. On Jedrung Rinpoche's return, while receiving oral transmissions and

---

[75] The Sixth Dalai Lama.

[76] Sister Tingting Drolma.

commentaries from Dungkar Tulku, a speech emanation of Avalokiteshvara, he was appointed abbot of Chockhor Gyal. This monastery, Nga, and Dag were the three famous monasteries under the care of the line of the Dalai Lamas since their foundation by Omniscient Gendun Gyatso. While Jedrung Rinpoche served here as abbot, he completed with highest honors his studies in valid cognition, transcendent wisdom, the Middle Way, and ethical discipline. On one occasion he attended a gathering of great lamas in Lhasa and met Minling Terchen Rinpoche,[77] who was also attending the event.

On the occasion of Gelong Yeshe Gyatso's elevation to the Dalai Lama's throne[78] by King Lhasang Khan,[79] Gelong Yeshe Gyatso gave full ordination to a number of monks, having himself been fully ordained for ten years. For reasons of auspiciousness, the king wanted a great lama such as Lelung Rinpoche to be among the ordained, and Lelung was unable to refuse the request. He agreed to the king's wish, but was distressed to find that some members of the ordination faculty were unqualified, which made it an ordination in name alone.

As his old estate monastery of Lelung was so dilapidated, a magnificent new one was built and named Thegchog Namdrol Ling. This was completed with all its images in 1717, on the twenty-first day of the eleventh month of the Fire Bird year, when a new monastic community was established.

Subsequently Jedrung Rinpoche received many teachings on old and new secret Tantra from glorious Heruka Guru Damcho Zangpo. He also visited Orgyen Mindrol Ling, in accordance with a dakini's secret prophecy, and received teachings on Minling practice from Pema Gyurme Gyatso. Later he did many closed retreats, in particular one on the female Avalokiteshvara, Desheg Kundu Sangwa Yeshe, an embodiment of all the buddhas. This was in accordance with a prophetic revelation by Orgyen Terdag Lingpa, which foretold that he would be a holder of this teaching. Thereafter many miraculous signs indicating his realizations occurred, such as a cascade of auspicious scarves, which shortly afterwards

---

[77] Terton Rigzin Choeje Lingpa.

[78] He was mistakenly enthroned as Dalai Lama on the king's orders.

[79] 1705–1717.

turned to stainless white. Similarly, there were showers of fresh myrobalan arjuna plants,[80] with leaves attached and flowers with stems. Witnesses to these unimaginable miraculous signs were able to catch them in their hands. From then onwards, he had more and more inconceivable pure visions and he was showered with secret teachings from lamas and dakinis. Thus he generated bodhicitta altruism and did his utmost to be of immense benefit to the Dharma and sentient beings.

There was one occasion in particular when the Dzungar[81] chief professed to be protecting the Dharma, while [in fact] his evil intentions were just coming to fruition.[82] Lelung Rinpoche received various reports from Tagtser which gave him the impression that this man had a negative attitude towards Dorje Drak and Mindrolling.[83] He felt great concern, remembering Mindrolling's immense kindness in giving him the teaching lineage, and sent a letter to the Dzungar chief telling him to pay more care. The [chief] replied, "It was good to hear your great words through the messenger you recently sent to Drong Min," but [still he] had absolutely no awareness of what he himself was doing, like someone with a badly damaged nose who has no sense of smell. We do not know what effect this letter may have had. However, the mere fact that Jedrung Rinpoche did not hesitate to send it to this man who considered Nyingma spirituality demonic, clearly demonstrates his realization that there is no inconsistency between the four schools of Tibetan Buddhism.

On one occasion, the Dzungar leader unthinkably maligned Padmasambhava and the Great Fifth Dalai Lama in the presence of Jedrung Rinpoche. The following passage about this incident appears in his autobiography:

> The leader of the Dzungars once asked me to come to his residence at Tromzig Khang. He and a certain Choephel asked endless questions: about whether or not Padmasambhava was an authentic teacher, and about the

---

[80] Universal medicine.

[81] The Dzungars were western Mongolians who held power for some time in part of Tibet.

[82] Hostile to the Nyingma tradition, he completely eradicated it in the province of Ü-Tsang.

[83] The main Nyingma monasteries in Central Tibet.

Great Fifth Dalai Lama in general. In particular he questioned whether Ngawang Losang Gyatso[84] was the true reincarnation of Gyalwa Yonten Gyatso.[85] I replied, "How can people like us possibly know? However, he was unmistakenly recognized by the previous Omniscient Panchen Lama and other authentic realized masters." The Dzungar chief said that he did not think Panchen Rinpoche had given any such recognition. He maintained that Ngawang Losang Gyatso had resented the Zimkhang Gong Tulku's being regarded as the unmistakable reincarnation of Yonten Gyatso, and been vindictive towards him and unhappy with everyone related to him. He said that in his country they claimed Zimkhang Gong Tulku was the venerable Dalai Lama. "Even if Ngawang Losang Gyatso were considered the unmistakable reincarnation," he continued, "he had not remained celibate and later had to receive new lineage vows of celibacy, which was not a favorable sign; he had also been involved in discussions with soldiers about preparations for war." In particular he said it appeared that Desi Sangye Gyatso[86] was Ngawang Losang Gyatso's son, as the latter had spent a night in the lower town on his way to Phabongkhar. There he had had relations with Desi Sangye Gyatso's mother and given her gifts such as a garland of pearls and gold bracelets. He also claimed that Regent Zangriwa, the woman's husband, had been dismissed because of this.

I answered all these unimaginable questions to the best of my ability. I told him it was solely on account of the Omniscient Fifth Dalai Lama's great compassion and kindness that the teaching of the Riwo Gelug had spread far and wide, and gave my reasons for this assertion. At

---

[84] The Fifth Dalai Lama.

[85] The Fourth Dalai Lama.

[86] The Fifth Dalai Lama's regent.

the end of our conversation his face registered neither
pleasure nor displeasure, and he simply remarked that no
one else had told him such things. I heard later, however,
that he showed others he believed me.

During the civil war in U-Tsang, Lelung Jedrung was His Excellency
Sonam Topgyal's[87] priest, and as his spokesperson requested an audience
with Gyalwang Kalzang Gyatso, the Seventh Dalai Lama, to talk about the
difficulties between them regarding Nga-lum-jar-gsum.[88] He managed to
overcome these and gain an assurance for the Dalai Lama that the lives of
the senior ministers would be spared, for which he was rewarded. Later
he and Sonam Topgyal had an audience at the Dalai Lama's Sunshine
Residence, where Jedrung Tulku resolved the bad feeling between the two.
He finally sealed their pledge of friendship by placing on their heads several
holy objects: Tashi Dokarma, a representation of Jey Rinpoche, the second
Buddha; a treasure-discovered statue representing Guru Rinpoche; and
an image of Palden Lhamo.

From around this time, Jedrung Rinpoche primarily practiced Tantra,
fully engaging in both old and new secret Tantras exactly in accordance
with the authentic explanatory transmissions. In his autobiography *Festive
Joy for the Fortunate Ones* he responded to criticism about this in these
words:

I have developed immutable heartfelt faith in Dharma King
Manjushri Tsong Khapa. Having received into my heart
his blessings and inspiration and those of the venerable
guru Damcho Zangpo,[89] I see all holy masters of all
traditions as pure objects of refuge. Similarly, I partially
understand both the lack of contradiction between any
Dharma teachings from the different lineages and their
essential meaning as personal instructions. I have earned
no sweet titles such as Master of the Whole Teaching,

---

[87] The Tibetan prime minister.

[88] A case concerning three ministers—Ngaphod Dorje Gyalpo, Lumpa Tashi Gyalpo and
Jarra Lodoe Gyalpo—who had killed their colleague, Sonam Topgyal's father.

[89] Jedrung Rinpoche's root guru.

but nevertheless do my utmost to refrain from accumulating karma by abandoning the Dharma.[90]

All Jedrung Rinpoche's prophecies came true. In particular, he practiced the profound vital points of the unsurpassable Highest Yoga Tantra,
the speedy path to fulfilling the accumulations of merit and insight, and
actualizing the state of union. He thus actualized the exalted wisdom of
bliss and emptiness.

He reawakened to the path of unity[91] latent within himself, and
guided numerous fortunate disciples by this path, for which many people
with impure perceptions wrote to criticize him. However, in all the precious literatures of both old and new Tantras, this is explained as the
most excellent and speedy path. It was cultivated by many realized beings,
who actualized the state of union, so how can anyone find fault with it?
Jedrung Rinpoche had gained freedom and control over his psychic channels
and wind energy. Should anyone question whether all his disciples were
at a level to practice this path themselves, most had indeed attained control
over their own psychic channels. If one or two had not reached this stage,
it was they who were at fault and not the profound path of the Tantra, and
so it should not give rise to wrong views about this method. Ragra Tulku's
biography of the eminent scholar Gendun Choephel quotes him as saying
that one should practice Tantra exactly as Lelung Zhedor[92] had done.
However, Vinaya practitioners have criticized Jedrung Rinpoche for his
teachings and practice simply out of concern for the mainstream
approach[93] and the majority of practitioners.

Furthermore, according to Choeje Lingpa's autobiography, Rigzin
Tagsham Nuedan Dorje prophesied that people would gain enormous
benefit if Jedrung were given the *Drop of Dakini Mind Essence*, a special
method instruction that was one of Rigzin Tagsham Nuedan Dorje's
treasures. Through Jedrung Rinpoche's incredible power and miraculous

---

[90] See Appendix I for an explanation of this.

[91] The method of using a consort to achieve realizations.

[92] Lelung Zhepai Dorje.

[93] A reference to the Vinaya.

deeds he also manifested in a wrathful form[94] to uphold and maintain the precious Dharma.

Acharya Padmasambhava had prophesied that Jedrung would be a master of teaching, and indeed he authored twelve volumes of the major and secondary treasure texts regarding the teachings of Sangwa Yeshe.[95] These are widely known as The Lelung Cycle of Teachings. The Sakya Patriarch Dagchen Ngawang Kunga Lodoe wrote to Dege Zhechen Drungyig that he had initially had no faith in Jedrung Rinpoche, but having subsequently seen his *Collected Works*, now felt that there would be no greater realized scholar during the degenerate era. He had therefore confessed his error and still maintained his respect for the Wrathful One[96] and the Young Sun,[97] continuing to recite the mantra of Nyima Shönnu. Dege Zhechen Drungyig said the letter with the seal on it was still in his possession. Furthermore, many realized scholars have highly praised Jedrung Rinpoche's commentary on the root text of Heruka, taking it as their central practice. The biography of Gendun Choephel mentioned above reports the eminent scholar as saying that Lelung Zhedor was as rare as a daytime star, particularly with regard to his work on Heruka. He had not had time to read this carefully for its meaning, having been so mesmerised by the grammar and poetry, but he could see its language was absolutely incomparable. During one of my own audiences with His Holiness the Dalai Lama, he told me that Lelung Zhepai Dorje's commentary on the *Heruka Root Tantra* was written from personal experience and was thus a very blessed work.

The Jedrung also wrote many other treatises such as a commentary on *The Essence of Eloquent Explanation* and an appendix to the chapter in *Pramanavarttika*[98] on establishing the Buddha as [being the embodiment of] valid [knowledge]. Both of these are among the texts studied in On Ngari Monastery. He also composed numerous works from his pure vision, such as one on Guru Zijid Dorje, and also stories of the ocean of

---

[94] As the protector Tobden Drakshul Wangpo.

[95] The Secret Exalted Wisdom Dakini.

[96] The wrathful manifestation of Lelung.

[97] Nyima Shönnu a female Dharma protector, particularly of Dzogchen teachings.

[98] Dharmakirti's commentary on Dignaga's *Compendium of Valid Cognition*.

Dharma protectors. In short, he wrote many treatises to benefit both general and particular aspects of Buddha's teaching, of which I have been able to collect thirty volumes. About ten others, all handwritten, are housed in a library at Otani University in Kyoto. Some of his writings are probably in Mongolia, but I have not been able to get hold of them. Numerous works are still in existence, such as a 127-page catalogue of the Narthang edition of the Precious Kangyur[99] called *The Sole Ornament and Miraculous Chariot Beautifying the Three Worlds.* However, many have been dispersed due to the changing times and I am trying to trace them.

Some scholars criticized many of Jedrung's works on the grounds that he mixed old and new Tantras, to which he responded in *Festive Joy for the Fortunate Ones.* He first justified his work with a quotation from the *Samvarodaya Tantra,*[100] beginning "Whichever particular action you are doing with this ...," and continuing as follows:

> Everyone who believes in Guhyasamaja, Heruka, Yaman
> taka and the Circle of the Black Trinity as deities and
> Dharma protectors should already know these pith in
> structions of the Father's teachings. However, most of
> those who wear the yellow hat[101] will not have heard of
> them previously, but should now understand them through
> these teachings. Some biased scholars have alleged that I
> have given teachings mixing old and new Tantras to
> gether. If they simply mean that I combined them,
> without contradicting their intended meanings, that was
> indeed my intention. However, there has been no mixing
> of specific approaches that conflict with each other. I have
> extensively quoted from the *Samvarodaya* and the
> *Heruka Root Tantra* because these have also been accepted
> and quoted by authentic realized scholars of Nyingma. I
> ask all presumptuous scholars of Gelug and Nyingma to
> show me a single piece of evidence proving that I should

---

[99] The translated words of Buddha Shakyamuni.

[100] *Source of Vows.*

[101] Worn by monks of the Gelug school.

not unashamedly combine these Tantra treatises with Sangwa Yeshe's teachings.

These words of the Jedrung shed light on what it would mean to mix up Dharma. His heart disciple Rigzin Yunggon Dorje, an emanation of Dreu Lha, also continued these teachings, contributing numerous works including a number from his pure vision.

Jedrung Rinpoche was undoubtedly a great holy master of both old and new Tantras. In order to propagate the precious lineages he gave many profound Tantric teachings to his disciples, who included many holy beings of Nyingma, such as Dodrak Rigzin Kalzang Pema Wangchuk, and also many great Gelug masters such as the well-known Phurchog Ngawang Jampa and Zhog Dhonyoe Khedrup.

In 1740, when he was forty-four years old and had no more direct disciples to teach, Jedrung Rinpoche manifested the appearance of dissolving his form into the sphere of ultimate reality on the twentieth day of the eighth month of the Iron Monkey year. For a time he dissolved himself directly into Vajrapani's heart in northerly Changlojen. Even today, his beneficial deeds shine out among all the four great traditions of Tibetan Buddhism.

> As a result of pursuing Sutra and Tantra—precious jewels
> of the universe—
> You directly realized the vast and profound Sutra and
> Tantra [teachings],
> Like the rays of the sun and moon you spread them in all
> directions—
> I pray to you great master Rigzin Zhepai Dorje!

འཇེ་དྲུང་བློ་བཟང་ཕྱུན་གྲུབ་འཕྲིན་ལས་རྒྱན་མཆན།

IX. Losang Lhundrup Trinley Gyaltsen, the Sixth Lelung Jedrung Reincarnation

Jedrung Rinpoche Losang Lhundrup Trinley Gyaltsen was born in Dagpo Shongyul in 1741, an Iron Bird year of the twelfth Rabjung. At the age of three, in the Wood Rat year, he was recognized by Gyalwang Kalzang Gyatso[102] as the reincarnation of the previous Jedrung. He subsequently offered the first cut of his hair to the Omniscient Master, who named him Losang Lhundrup Trinley Gyaltsen and ceremoniously presented him with an image of Vajradhara and a platter full of delicious foods as an auspicious cause for him to become a realized scholar and benefit Buddha's teachings. In 1749, an Earth Snake year, the young reincarnation received novice monk ordination from Kalzang Gyatso at the great Potala Palace, and in 1750, in the fourth month of the Iron Horse year, the Dalai Lama bestowed upon him an empowerment of the Three-Faced and Six-Armed Vajrapani. Gyalwang Kalzang Gyatso also presented both Jedrung Rinpoche and Sempa Tulku[103] with monastic robes and other necessities for their spiritual education at the glorious monastic university of Drepung, reminding them that their predecessors had been holy masters who made great contributions to the Dharma in general and particularly to the teachings of Manjushri Lama Tsong Khapa. In view of this, he advised them to diligently complete their education and generate good intentions and observe good conduct in order to bring honour to Buddha's teachings. After much advice of this kind, the two young incarnations left for Drepung.

This sixth Lelung Jedrung was the first of his line to enter the glorious Drepung monastic community, and he and the subsequent reincarnations were renowned as extraordinary high lamas of the monastery. In 1752, on the fifteenth day of the third month of a Water Monkey year, Jedrung Rinpoche received from the Seventh Dalai Lama, like nectar poured from one vase into another, a Shri Kalachakra empowerment and the four

---

[102] The Seventh Dalai Lama.

[103] Another of the Three Principal Reincarnations of Tibet. Cf. Chapter 3.

complete empowerments of Shri Chakrasamvara with sixty-two deities according to Luyipada, based on a cloth-painted mandala.

After completing his monastic education, Lelung Jedrung received the title of Geshe and then joined glorious Gyuto Datsang Monastery, a large community of secret Tantric practitioners, where he completed his Tantric education. Later he also served as abbot of Gyuto Datsang for some time, though his name does not appear in the lineage of its abbots. It is possible that he did not complete his tenure, but this is unclear and needs further investigation. Jedrung Rinpoche often rigorously performed long-life rituals for the Dalai Lama's life to benefit both the general and particular aspects of Buddha's teaching. His unsurpassable intention to maintain Buddha's teachings led him to do his utmost to create causes for the flourishing of the Dharma and the happiness of sentient beings.

During his abbotship Jedrung Rinpoche returned his monastic vows and cultivated a relationship with a consort. There were several reasons for this. First, in his previous lives he had had extensive experience of the generation and completion stages. Furthermore, among his disciples were many holy beings from different traditions, as unquestionably great as the sun and the moon. In addition, in his current life he cultivated as his spiritual masters the Seventh Dalai Lama, a human manifestation of Chenrezig and master of Sutras and Tantras, and many others universally accepted as realized scholars. Finally, he was confident in his experiences and realizations, having thoroughly studied both Sutra and Tantra and practiced them correctly. It was therefore not inappropriate for him to cultivate a consort. Rather, it augmented his practice of the paths of the Buddha's general and specific teachings, and was thus an ornament for those who uphold the parasol of practice. In *Solar Illumination of the Hidden Meanings of Shri Chakrasamvara* he states:

> The special profound path of the Highest Yoga Tantra involves sensual pleasure being taken onto the path. Nevertheless, great yogis who have actualized the view of ultimate reality and meditation are censured these days when they cultivate secret consorts. Their critics are [either] people presumptuously assuming themselves to be great masters of Vinaya monastic discipline, who attend closely to the three sets of vows, or also those in our monasteries [...] who break their vows [...]. They criticize merely

because they see slight differences between their own viewpoint and realizations and those of these great beings. I observe many hypocrites posing as outwardly gentle and peaceful and inwardly noble and virtuous with no attachment or sexual craving, who even refuse to eat the evening tsok substances. They attempt practices that are too difficult for them while discarding those which are permitted, like a person who disregards the juicy part of a fruit but holds on to the peel. These people are a long way from Vajradhara's tradition, and I see the negative karma they carelessly create.

Anything is possible when method is conjoined, he continues. Without method, however, "[to be a monk] in appearance only fulfills no purpose." Thus I feel that those who are interested in Dharma should point their fingertip back towards themselves and give deep thought to these matters.

In 1811, an Iron Sheep year of the fourteenth Rabjung, when he was seventy-one years old and had no more direct disciples to teach, Jedrung Rinpoche temporarily dissolved his mind into the sphere of reality.

You internalized all the texts and traditions of the Dharma,
Studied and taught at institutions such as great secret
  Gyuto,
Attained high experiences and realizations and thus took
  the path of discipline—
I pray at your feet Losang Lhundrup!

འཇིག་རྟེན་དབང་ཕྱུག་དབང་བསྟན་འཛིན་རྒྱ་མཚོ།

X. Losang Ngawang Tenzin Gyatso, the Seventh Lelung Jedrung Reincarnation

Oelkha Jedrung Rinpoche Losang Ngawang Tenzin Gyatso was born in 1812, a Water Monkey year of the fourteenth Rabjung, in the Ae region of Lhokha. His father's name was Rabten. He was recognized as the true reincarnation after a divination in which his name was placed in a gold vase with that of another local child who was also considered a prospective candidate. He was later ordained, and studied at glorious Drepung. When Omniscient Tsultrim Gyatso, the Tenth Dalai Lama, was placed on his golden throne in 1822, a Water Horse year, Jedrung Rinpoche attended the ceremony and offered a silk kata scarf and some gifts.

At dawn on the first day of Losar in 1825, Gyalwang Tsultrim Gyatso together with the assembly of his personal monastery performed an elaborate ritual invocation of Palden Lhamo, the protectress of the three worlds, and a Losar ritual cake offering. This was in a Wood Bird year. Afterwards, on his way to the great assembly hall, the young Omniscient Master was given offerings by Jedrung Tulku, and privately some [more gifts] by Ngaphoe at the Sunlit Stairway, and he gave them a hand blessing and Losar presents. In the great hall, he enjoyed the spiritual and secular celebrations, commenting to those nearby on the sacred dances and monastic debates, and sharing in a number of the dishes.

In 1827, on the eleventh day of the fifth month of a Fire Boar year of the fourteenth Rabjung, Lelung Tulku and Drepung Lhopa Lama together with 300 monks were given the Nine-Deity Amitayus empowerment according to the ear-whispered Lhodrak lineage by Vajradhara Jangchub Choephel. This master was a great successor to the throne of the second Buddha, Manjushri Lama Tsong Khapa. On the fourteenth and fifteenth days of the eleventh month, he also gave a Heruka empowerment of the Luipada tradition and a profound empowerment of the Ngam Zong ear-whispered lineage to Lelung Jedrung and many other reincarnations and geshes. These included Geshe Gendun Dhargye of Gyuto, Tatsag Tulku, Tagphu Tulku, Odzer Tulku, Gyalron Tritul of Drepung, and Phaggo Tulku. In addition, in 1829, on the fourteenth and fifteenth days of the Earth Ox year, Lelung Rinpoche was one of a large gathering that received from Vajradhara Jangchub a great empowerment of Guhyasamaja and profound explanations in the Ramoche assembly hall of glorious Gyuto Tantric University. Also present were Tachog Tulku, Dragyab Tulku, Mili Tulku, Drupkhang Tulku and many other devotees, including the abbot of the monastery.

In the same year, when the Tenth Dalai Lama went to study at glorious Drepung, he was offered a long-life mandala by Jedrung Rinpoche. Furthermore, in 1831, in the fourth month of the Iron Hare year, Vajradhara Ganden Tri Rinpoche on a visit to Drepung was glad to accept Jedrung Rinpoche's invitation to his residence. During a subsequent visit to Drepung two years later, the Vajradhara gave Tenling Tulku and Jedrung Rinpoche permission blessings of Solitary Green Tara and the Twenty-One Taras in the first month of the Water Snake year.

In 1835, on an auspicious day of the fourth month of the Wood Sheep year, Great Vajradhara Trichen Jangchub Choephel, a lord of all the buddha families and regent of Manjushri Lama Tsong Khapa, presided as abbot over the full ordination ceremony of Lelung Jedrung Rinpoche and twenty other ordinands. Jangtse Choeje Ngawang Namgyal was the assistant preceptor and Shartse Yeshe Norbu the secret preceptor. Thus, Jedrung Rinpoche became like Arhat Upali, a shining example to the monastic community. In the same year he received empowerments and mantra recitations of Solitary Yamantaka and Guhyasamaja Manjuvajra. In 1836, in the second month of the Fire Monkey year, Jedrung Rinpoche had the fortune to receive teachings such as the explanatory transmission of mahamudra followed by the mahayana bodhicitta precepts from Trichen Dorje Chang. These teachings were regularly attended by devotees such as Agya Huthukthu, Gyalse Tulku, Sharpa Choeje, and Ling Tulku as well as over 2,000 other reincarnations and geshes.

At the end of the year, Lelung Jedrung Rinpoche's tutor Trichen Dorje Chang advised him to do a retreat of Yamantaka Victor over Negative Beings at Chuzang. Jedrung completely absorbed himself in this. When his tutor subsequently manifested the appearance of illness, Lelung Rinpoche often visited him and requested him to live longer, but after he finally indicated his wish to pass away, Lelung Rinpoche devotedly followed the procedures for his funeral. Seven days after the cremation, Lelung Jedrung and Tagphu Yongzin opened the stupa, collected all the bone relics and conveyed them to the lama's residence with the utmost respect. Here they made offerings to them and performed a ritual purification.

In 1845, a Wood Snake year, the Eleventh Dalai Lama, Omniscient Khedrup Gyatso, reached the age of eight. Kunzig Panchen Rinpoche was invited at Losar to go from the eastern chambers of Potala Palace to the Omniscient Master's bedchamber. Here they met and together performed an invocation to Palden Lhamo, the female protector of the desire realm. Afterwards they went to Potala's assembly hall for Losar celebrations and, seated on their thrones, greeted and gave a hand blessing to the Dalai Lama's tutor Tatsag Ngawang Losang Tenzin Gyaltsen, Lelung Jedrung, Sempa Tulku, ministers and high ranking government officials, and reincarnations and monastic officials of Sera, Drepung and Ganden.

In 1849, around the twentieth day of the sixth month of the Earth Bird year, Lelung Jedrung Rinpoche invited Gyalwang Khedrup Gyatso for the midday meal and they dined together at Lhundrup Gatsel, the Miraculous Garden of Joy. In 1852, in the seventh month of the Water Rat year, the Omniscient Master went to visit Rinchen Gang Monastery, a great practice community in the south. On his way he stayed at the Yargyud Residence, where Lelung Jedrung gave him a huge amount of offerings at a great feast, together with a mandala offering and its explanation. On the eighth day of the month, Lelung Tulku made him a smoke offering on the hilltop of Khartag, where he hung fortune flags. He also escorted the Dalai Lama up to the Lhalung tea stop, where Gyari Tripa, Zhapad Samdrup Phodrang, and others in the welcoming party with him offered the Omniscient Master katas and invited him to Zangri Khamar. Eight years later, in the Iron Monkey year, Lelung Jedrung took part in the enthronement ceremony of Gyalwang Trinley Gyatso, the Twelfth Dalai Lama.

It is unclear how long this Jedrung Rinpoche lived. He must have survived for more than 48 years because of his participation in the enthronement. However, he does not appear to have done so for very long afterwards as there is no subsequent mention of his presence in the Dalai Lama's biography. Further research is needed into this question.

> From a young age you activated your bodhicitta,
> Showed your love for sentient beings,
> And merged your mind with the line of the Dalai Lamas,
> You accomplished services for the Omniscient Masters—
> I pray to you Losang Tenzin Gyatso!

པོ་ཏོ་དུང་བསྐལ་བཟང་བསྟན་འཛིན།

XI. Kalsang Tenzin, the Eighth Lelung Jedrung Reincarnation

> At the supreme pilgrimage site of Manjushri Tsong Khapa,
> You realized all Sutras and Tantras as personal
>   instructions—
> To the realized master scholar Kalsang Tenzin,
> I pray to you to bless my mindstream!
> *(from a lineage master prayer in a supplement to the*
>   *liturgy of glorious Gargyi Wangchuk Sangwa Yeshe)*

This next reincarnation of Lelung Jedrung must have been born after 1860. We know this because in the Water Rat year of 1852, his previous life had offered the Eleventh Dalai Lama a mandala with its explanation, and attended the Twelfth Dalai Lama's enthronement ceremony in the Iron Monkey year eight years later. Some documents indicate that he died from an ulcer before he could complete his education, which would mean that he could not have lived for more than about twenty years. However, his own reincarnation was not born until 1905, over forty years after his presumed birth. Consequently, if his life span had only been only about twenty years, there would have been another twenty or so when no reincarnation was alive. Otherwise he must have lived for over thirty years. The matter might be resolved if we could clearly trace and authenticate the source of the statement about his passing away before his education was complete. Unfortunately, however, due to the changing times and situations it is difficult to find experts in this history, and many documents are unavailable to me.

There is no absolute certainty even as regards the eighth Lelung Jedrung's real name and one might ask how I have identified him as Kalsang Tenzin. In 1999, I went to Nagchu to look for the cycle of Lelung teachings. At a nunnery that for centuries has practiced Zhepai Dorje's teaching cycle, I was able to obtain a text entitled *A Written Supplement to the Speedy Path Liturgy of the Secret Exalted Wisdom Dakini*[104] and a *Side Ornament of the Deity's Activity Manual*. This shows that until quite

---

[104] Sangwa Yeshe.

81

recently there were lineage masters of Sangwa Yeshe and that the lineage was held alternately by the line of Lelungs and other lamas. If he is among these lineage masters, about which I cannot be certain, his name must be the one given in the opening stanza of this chapter, where he is mentioned as a great scholar who completed his education.

Historians interested in this subject should consider the oral history and research authentic sources carefully and impartially. If they find a definitive answer, I would ask them to write an appendix to this chapter.

> At the supreme pilgrimage site of Manjushri Tsong Khapa,
> You realized all Sutras and Tantras as personal
> instructions.
> To the realized master scholar Kalsang Tenzin,
> I pray to you from my heart with immutable faith!

འཇེ་དྲུང་བསྟན་འཛིན་ཆོས་ཀྱི་དབང་ཕྱུག

XII. Tenzin Choekyi Wangchuk, the Ninth Lelung Jedrung Reincarnation

Oelkha Jedrung Rinpoche Tenzin Choekyi Wangchuk was born at Tsal Gungthang in 1905, a Wood Snake year of the fifteenth Rabjung. His parents were Tsering Dhondup and Tsering Dolma. Tsal Gungthang is in the central division of Happy Valley, which is one of the four divisions of Ü-Tsang, a province renowned for spirituality and one of three in Tibet—the land and people under the care of the Lotus Holder. Tsal Gungthang was the birthplace of Zhang Drolwai Gonpo Yudrakpa, the founder of Tsalpa Kagyu, who established a monastery here in which study and debate flourished. It was one of the six great well-known monasteries of Central Tibet known as Sang De Gung[105] and Ga Kyor Zul,[106] before Manjushri Tsong Khapa established Ganden Monastic University.

Jedrung Rinpoche was the youngest of three children, the eldest of whom was Kyabje Trijang Rinpoche Losang Yeshe Tenzin Gyatso, who later became the Fourteenth Dalai Lama's junior tutor. The middle child was a girl named Jampal Choetso. After being recognized as Jedrung Rinpoche's reincarnation, he manifested the appearance of passing away at the age of four while preparing for his enthronement ceremony. This must have been for a positive purpose, and to avert some negativity. His life could not have been harmed by gods, nagas or arrogant demons, unlike that of ordinary persons with no power over their own life and death. In general, it is wrong to believe in concepts arising from discursive thinking created by one's impure thoughts. These are no different from Devadatta's[107] wrong views about Buddha Shakyamuni, which arose from his own impure thoughts. It would therefore be better to be neutral about this matter.

---

[105] A group of three monasteries.

[106] A group of three others.

[107] A cousin of Buddha Shakyamuni's whose jealousy led him to make three attempts on the Buddha's life; when these failed, he tried to split the sangha by creating an order with stricter rules to justify his claims to be purer than the Buddha.

85

I pray to Choekyi Wangchuk, the miraculous
    manifestation,
Who came as a reminder of impermanence,
For us who always cling to permanence.
He was sent out as a momentary embodiment then
    gathered back in,
By the secret-holder Vajrapani from his Pure Land.

འཇེ་དུང་ཐུབ་བསྟན་ཡུང་རྡོགས་ཚོས་ཀྱི་དཔལ་ཕུག

XIII. Thubten Lungtok Choekyi Wangchuk, the Tenth Lelung Jedrung Reincarnation

Olkha Jedrung Rinpoche Thubten Lungtok Choekyi Wangchuk was born in 1909, an Earth Bird year of the fifteenth Rabjung. He was recognized as the reincarnation of the previous Jedrung Rinpoche by the Great Thirteenth Dalai Lama, who composed a long-life prayer for him entitled *Miraculous Marks and Signs*. According to the former abbot of Gomang Ngawang Nyima, he completed his education at glorious Drepung, gaining the fourth highest place within the Geshe Lharampa category. Afterwards he went to Gyuto Tantric University, where he took his Tantric debate examination, and then returned to his monastery, as I was informed by his treasurer, Norbu. Subsequently he engaged in retreats and also gave extensive teachings to monks and lay people.

Shortly before the tragic events in Tibet, Jedrung Rinpoche jokingly told Norbu that he should dig a pit in the debate courtyard. When Norbu asked why, he pointed to some young monks and said he wanted to bury them in it and build a black stupa above. Those children subsequently became the monastery's main destroyers. At a later date, when Jedrung Rinpoche distributed his possessions among the monks and laity, the treasurer was disappointed to receive only an incense pot and a large soft mattress, in spite of his long and dedicated service to the great master. However, Norbu was stripped of his possessions during the Cultural Revolution, when he was designated a feudal lord by the Chinese communists, and these were the only objects he was allowed to keep. Norbu therefore maintained that Jedrung Rinpoche must have been clairvoyant, which was undoubtedly true.

Jedrung Rinpoche attended a conference just before he passed away, where he recited verses of auspiciousness and dependent arising on behalf of the various religious traditions of China and Tibet. He urged the participants to cherish the Dharma, abandon negativity in everyday life and cultivate positive actions. Jedrung Rinpoche gave clear indications that he was soon going to depart this life and, at the political assembly's dinner banquet that same day, made a prayer reciting the Gyaltsen Tsemo verse. The circumstances made it difficult for him to clarify his exact intentions, but the prayer was in fact a dedication for the flourishing of

89

the Dharma and the wellbeing of sentient beings. In particular it was for the Dalai Lama—that he should enjoy a long life, succeed in rekindling the fire of the precious Buddha Dharma and be enthroned as a Dharma king wherever he went.

After the banquet, when Jedrung Rinpoche got near Dondrak in Tsethang, he manifested the appearance of illness. With great unsteadiness he reached his residence at the local political assembly chamber, and at nine o'clock that night dissolved his form into the sphere of reality. This was in 1962, when he was 53 years old. The regional council and local governor took upon themselves the responsibility of taking care of Jedrung Rinpoche's funeral. The rites were entrusted to lamas and tulkus from various monasteries of Lhokha who were resident in Tradruk, and to an organization known as The Religious Rights of Monks. In a procession led by monastics and Chinese officials carrying funeral wreaths, Jedrung Rinpoche's body was brought to Sheldrak, where it was consigned to the flames.

> The precious Dharma, source of benefit and happiness,
> Was spread by you through teachings and practice.
> Master who taught with unfailing determination,
> I pray to you Thubten Lungtok!

Dedication

The incredible deeds of the buddhas' three secrets,
Are the exclusive domain of the buddhas themselves,
They are beyond the domain also of bodhisattvas,
Therefore undescribable by someone like myself.

But through the fortune of seeing these Jedrung
      Rinpoches' life stories,
With immutable faith in them, and appreciation,
I—bearing the name of these reincarnations—wrote this,
Without poetic elaboration and with honest words.

You among the ranks of experts and scholars,
It is not your eyes that I hope to attract,
I wish to benefit you that share a fortune similar to mine,
Enjoy this work written with an unbiased attitude.

By the power of these virtues, may His Holiness
Live long and his deeds reach in all directions;
May other Dharma upholders also live long,
May a golden age radiate from the Land of Snows!

By the blessings of kind spiritual teachers,
May I become a servant of the mother sentient beings,
May I live until samsara ceases to exist,
May I become an agent to spread benefit and happiness!

Only through the unsurpassable kindness of my root spiritual guru,
His Holiness the Dalai Lama, have I been able to compile these life
stories of the line of Jedrung Rinpoches. He is a human manifestation of
Arya Avalokiteshvara, the embodiment of all the buddhas' compassion,
clothed in monastic robes, and holding the three sets of vows. His
kindness is unmatched in this entire world. He is an inestimably precious
ambassador for peace, endowed with the three kindnesses and possessing
supreme compassion and omniscient wisdom. Having taken refuge with
him, through his grace I have had the opportunity to join great monastic
communities of the Arya Sangha. In the presence of excellent spiritual
teachers I have been able to humbly engage in study and contemplation of
Dharma teachings, whose worth cannot be measured by all the precious

jewels in the three realms.[108] Though my intelligence is weak, through their kindness I have been able to receive in my heart a drop from their ocean-like blessings. I have thus understood the need to cultivate regularly the precious mind of cherishing others.

We should all nurture such bodhichitta within our hearts, by following the footsteps of undisputed holy beings of the past. We should remember their kindness and become worthy of it. However, because of the changing times, their great biographies remain on the shelves unread. Consequently I have tried to compile life stories of a reasonable length, neither too short nor too long, considering the fast pace and constant busyness of society today. May this be a dew-drop-sized fulfilment of one of His Holiness the Dalai Lama's innumerable wishes for the benefit of us sentient beings.

With a strong intention to benefit both myself and others, I took a considerable time out of my hectic married life from 1997 to 2002, the Fire Ox to the Water Horse year of the seventeenth Rabjung. I endeavored to carry out careful research based on many authentic sources. By virtue of my compiling these biographies with sincere faith, may His Holiness the Dalai Lama live long and may his wishes be speedily fulfilled without obstacles. May we recognize the ripening on ourselves of virtues accumulated over many aeons in the past as well as in our present lives. May we also be able to taste the nectar of the speech of our patron deity, His Holiness the Dalai Lama, so that our precious human lives of this degenerate era do not become wasted. May this virtue contribute to opening the door to the great path that will make meaningful the long succession of our future lives. May we be able to return before long to our homeland and be together with His Holiness at his celestial palace on the hilltop of Potala.

Sarvamangalam[109]

---

[108] The realms of celestial beings above, human beings on the earth and nagas below.

[109] A customary ending to Tibetan works meaning "May everything conclude completely auspiciously."

Appendixes

Appendix I. Lelung Pema Zhepai Dorje's Advice Concerning Old and New Translation Tantras

Below is an extract from Pema Zhepai Dorje's biography. I feel the point made here is extremely useful for all Dharma students, particularly in countries where Buddhism is spreading rapidly, and above all for new students, who might be confused about the different traditions of Tibetan Buddhism.

Some controversial teachers spread confusion by claiming Old Translation Tantra teachings (Nyingma) are more important than New Translation teachings (Sarma), or vice versa. As a consequence, students unfamiliar with the background might start to criticize other Buddhist schools. This would be very harmful for them and equivalent to forsaking the Buddha Dharma, which carries some of the heaviest negative karma. Having entered the Dharma to create peace and positive karma, they would end by accumulating negative karma, like someone who goes into business to make a lot of money but ends up drowning in debt because of one unwise decision. In fact, all genuine teachings contain the Buddha Dharma. If you have wrong views and reject any, the Dharma will never grow in your heart however hard you practice it, and you will go through hundreds of lifetimes before you discover it again.

Some time ago I was given all kinds of advice by many great geshes close to me. They stressed that it was crucially important to maintain pure tradition in order to benefit the Dharma. Later, I had to make ritual offerings to avert epidemics and so on and practice the meditation and recitation of peaceful and wrathful deities from a terma revelation. I also needed to create images of the deities according to prophecies revealed secretly to me.[110] This was for the good of the Dharma and all beings generally, and in particular to benefit myself and the many people connected to me. However, it upset some people, who claimed that because of these rituals I had altered my tradition and brought great disgrace upon the Dharma.[111]

---

[110] These rituals belong to Nyingma, the Old Translation School.

[111] Believing Lelung Rinpoche to be a holder of pure Gelug teaching, they thought he should not perform Nyingma Tantra practices.

There were many intelligent and sincere monks and lay people on my side who accepted that I needed to do these things in accordance with secret prophecies. However, even they lovingly urged me to carry them out unobtrusively. They feared that otherwise I might be obstructed in fulfilling my altruistic intentions as there were many people with wrong views.

In my view, however, when it comes to distinguishing between Old and New Translation Tantra, even the most learned scholars appear to have had difficulty drawing a clear dividing line between them. Most early scholars designated teachings translated after Pandita Smirti and Lotsawa Rinchen Zangpo as New Translation and those before their era as Old Translation. On that basis, however, several of what are currently considered New Translation teachings, such as the Manjushri Root Tantra,[112] would become Old Translation because they were translated during the reign of King Trisong Detsen. Similarly the many cycles of Nyingma teachings that arose from the pure visions of great holy beings after Lotsawa Rinchen Zangpo's time would become New Translation Tantra. Some might object that the latter would not belong in this category as the lotsawas did not translate them. However, they would then have to concede that even the cycle of teachings given by Manjushri to Dharma King Tsong Khapa would be neither New nor Old Translation Tantra. They would need to be considered as belonging to a new third category. Moreover, many vital points widely practiced in New Translation teachings but not currently well-known in Nyingma—such as the five stages of the path and the six preliminary secondary practices—were in fact mentioned in an early translation of *Heruka Kapala Tantra*.

How can a clear distinction be made between Old and New Translation Tantra when these terms did not exist in India? It might be easier if Nyingma teaching could be dismissed as inauthentic, but it cannot be false. If it were, Acharya Padmasambhava could not be accepted as a genuine teacher. However, he is repeatedly mentioned as verifiably authentic by numerous universally recognized Buddhist masters such as precious Atisha, Buton the omniscient, Drupchen Laykyi Dorje, Choeje Sakya Pandita, and many other great beings from earlier traditions, as well as the five Omniscient Masters and also the earlier and later incarnations of Panchen Lama Choekyi Gyalpo and other lamas, all of whom

---

[112] *'jam dpal rtsa-rgyud.*

were universally recognized as holders of great Dharma King Tsong Khapa's teaching. These masters are the crown jewel, the victory banner and the triumphal conch of our Ganden tradition. It would be absurd to think they could have been confused in accepting Padmasambhava as an authentic teacher.

Nevertheless, at the beginning of *The Great Treatise on the Stages of the Path to Enlightenment*,[113] great Dharma King Tsong Khapa states that while Acharya Padmasambhava and Abbot Shantarakshita established the Dharma in Tibet, the teaching of the Dzogchen view was not effective for that time. He had two reasons for saying this. He wanted to put an end to many wrong views that had been introduced under the name of Dzogchen, and also to elucidate the realistic view of emptiness that was falling into great decline, because it is so difficult to understand. This was like the approach of the great Indian panditas such as Bhavaviveka and Chandrakirti, who used valid reasoning and scriptural authority to refute the mistaken views of others and clearly establish effective philosophical positions.

Furthermore, these words by Lama Drima Medpa appear in the Kadam Legbam[114]:

> After this life without taking rebirth elsewhere,
> Out of compassion go to Tibet where the people are in
>   great need of a protector.
> Tibetans trust the words of their kings—
> Be born as a king and lead them peacefully.
> As I told you in Oddiyana,
> I too will go there and subdue the demons,
> Another of my emanations will go to Nepal,
> A third to northeastern Tibet,
> And a fourth to the great pilgrimage sites of India.

The words: "I too will go there and subdue the demons" refer to his manifestation as Acharya Padmasambhava, who indeed came to Tibet, where he subdued many demons. The phrase "a third to north eastern

---

[113] *Lam rim chen mo.*

[114] The scriptures of the Kadampa Father and Son Teachings.

Tibet" refers to his manifestation as Dharma King Tsong Khapa, "a fourth to the great pilgrimage sites of India," refers to his manifestation as Atisha; and "another of my emanations will go to Nepal," refers to his manifestation as Nepali Padma Vajra. This proves that Lama Drima Medpa, Atisha, Acharya Padmasambhava, Lama Tsong Khapa and Nepali Padma Vajra all shared the same mental continuum. Moreover, Omniscient Gendun Gyatso[115] declared:

> Salutation to the one who displays multiple emanations,
> Padmasambhava, the powerful lord of Tantra,
> Atisha, crown jewel of the five hundred panditas,
> And Vajradhara Losang Drakpa,[116] the glorious one!

Many other passages stating that Padmasambhava and Tsong Khapa shared the same mental continuum appear in various chapters of the works of the Omniscient Fifth Dalai Lama and in the writings of the earlier and later Panchen Lama incarnations, notably at the beginning of the *Commentary on the Three Principal Paths*[117] by the present Panchen Lama.

Furthermore, Sakya Pandita praised Acharya Padmasambhava as follows:

> Abbot Shantarakshita embodies pure monastic vows,
> Padmasambhava embodies yogic discipline,
> And Kamalashila embodies wisdom—
> They are the second Buddhas of this degenerate age.

These words are in his own handwritten notes, which can still be found in the middle corridor on the top floor of Samye Temple.

More importantly, Padmasambhava was accepted as an authentic teacher by the great Tantric master Karma Vajra[118], who was great Dharma King Tsong Khapa's ultimate guru and gave him Lamrim teaching combining the two lineage streams.[119] As he was repeatedly praised by great

---

[115] The Second Dalai Lama.

[116] Jey Tsong Khapa.

[117] *lam gyi rtso bo rnam gsum gyi rnam bshad.*

[118] The first Lelung, Drupchen Laykyi Dorje.

[119] Cf. Chapter IV page 7.

Lama Tsong Khapa, we must all accept him as a genuine teacher. In his account of inner meditative stabilization, he describes Padmasambhava as follows when recounting his birth in the land of demons:

> The land appeared as white as a crystal floor, the mountains and rockfaces as jewels, and the forests and other features of the landscape as in a pure land by the power of great Padmasambhava's compassion and prayer. In the morning he manifested as a young boy of eight years old adorned with jeweled ornaments, mesmerizing in his beauty and fascination, and gave Dharma teachings. In the evening he subdued demons and eliminated their five poisons. He then manifested as an old sage of 120 years, and gave Dharma teachings to the demons. At dusk and dawn he gave Dharma teachings to the demons according to their individual needs, and completely enthralled them.

During his thirteenth year, which was an obstacle year, Karma Vajra practiced virtuous activities undistractedly every single day, and one evening when he was circumambulating the stupa of Drowa Monastery, locals declared that they saw fire encircling it. Around this time an Acharya[120] came to him, who said he had come from the presence of Gyalsey Togmey[121] and, while prostrating many times, requested teaching on visualization for removing obstacles. Karma Vajra taught him how to practice the visualization of Akshobhya, saying that one could not remove true obstacles through visualization motivated by hatred. Rather, it had to be done in the form of a wrathful deity king and from the unwavering pure altruistic mind of enlightenment. The sage told Karma Vajra that he would delight him with faith and respect, and requested further teaching. Wishing to teach him *The Summary of the Essentials of the Two Truths of the Middle Path,*[122] as well as *The Absence of Conceptual Fetters and*

---

[120] Wandering sage.

[121] Also known as Gyalsey Ngülchu Togmey Zangpo (1295–1369), a master of the Sakya tradition famous for his *Thirty-Seven Practices of a Bodhisattva.*

[122] *dbu ma bden gnyis kyi de nyid bsdus pa.*

Liberation,[123] Karma Vajra began discussing the nonduality of mind and wind energy.[124] Thereupon the acharya immediately suggested they go westwards to Oddiyana for the feast offering as he himself needed to receive some teaching there. Karma Vajra wished fervently for the joy of meeting great Padmasambhava, in whom he generated tremendous faith and respect. He replied that his companion did not seem to be ordinary and requested his care and guidance as he himself did not have any miraculous power to go to Oddiyana. The acharya said that in the land of Zali Besha there were foods blessed by precious dakinis, and he gave him many blessings and discourses on the *Three Roots* and the *Hung Liberation*. [125] He also gave him a skull cup filled with nectar, and instructed him to look up at the sky unbound by the rope of ordinary conceptual thoughts, hopes or doubts.

Immediately the sky was filled with heroes and heroines, dakas and dakinis, who came in different forms. Some unfurled silken walkways, while others covered these with rainbow parasols. Some gave gifts of jewels and flowers, and some displayed single or multiple emanations of wrathful male and female deities. Some unrolled a white silk scarf towards Karma Vajra. At the end was a throne of a halo of light, where he was asked to sit. As they were speaking, from the sky came many sounds of "URURU TOLOLO," and he went towards the northwest. He saw landscapes of red coral. Flowers of different colors blossomed and there were three cool waterfalls of liquid gold. In the south of this land were beautiful cities populated by many lay men and women, and in the center stood a red mountain with an inconceivable celestial palace on its peak. Above it was a lotus with petals made of the five precious jewels, on which was a throne of seven-colored rays of light. Here great Padmasambhava sat, encircled by numerous dakinis making him many different types of offerings such as songs and music.

Large numbers of male and female adepts were engaged in disciplined conduct.[126] Padmasambhava himself appeared in the form of a

---

[123] *don 'ching grol med pa.*

[124] *rlung sems gnyis med.*

[125] *rtsa gsum hum grol.*

[126] *brtul zhug kyi spyod pa.*

great pandita, discussing and debating in tones loud as thunderclaps the intended meanings of the three pitakas with many arhats of the disciple[127] vehicle. Innumerable celestial beings, nagas, and yakshas were making offerings of all kinds in their native songs and listening to his teaching. Numerous wisdom dakinis and offering goddesses made inconceivable offerings of all kinds: the fivefold outer offering, the fivefold inner offering, the fivefold secret offering, and the fivefold offering of reality. One hundred and eight kinds of wonderfully delicious food and drink for the feast offering were blessed many times in rituals of purification, regeneration, and enchancement and were distributed and enjoyed by all.

Then Padmasambhava declared, "Secret Tantra is vitally important to benefit the pitiful short-lived people of this universe. As these four great classes of Tantra empowerments are remarkable and unsurpassed, you should realize pure perception and not hold impure perceptions in your mind at any time." He then conferred the empowerments one by one. Meanwhile dakinis conducted the mandala rituals, Tantric teachings and pith instructions took place and the feast offerings were enjoyed. Afterwards he proclaimed the following six lines, which he thoroughly elucidated:

> Whatever appears look at your own mind!
> Understanding the nature of mind,
> The intrinsic meaning of all the Tantra teachings,
> The bodies of the buddhas and their Pure Lands,
> And the empowerments of the two stages and the nine
>   vehicles —
> Realization of any one of these brings realization of all!

Then he gave a number of teachings including *The Ocean of Secret Nectar: A Quintessential Instruction on the Four Tantras*.[128] The *Precious Vase of Four Empowerments*,[129] and *Spontaneous Liberation: The Perfection Stage*.[130]

---

[127] Śhrāvakayāna.

[128] *gsang ba rgyud sde bzhi'i man ngag gsang ba bdudr tsi'i rgya mtsho.*

[129] *wang bzhi rin chen bum pa.*

[130] *rdzog rim ye grol lhun drup.*

Furthermore, in the ear-whispered lineage of Vajrapani,[131] it is said that Yamantaka, the Lord of Life,[132] and the Goddess of Mantra Protection[133] were directly given teaching cycles by deities. Moreover, the following words appear in the *Root Vajra Verses of Dropping Nectar*,[134] transmitted to Karma Vajra by Vajrapani:

> Clear light of primordial pristine awareness
> Appears in the form of a deity.

Thus many matters in accord with the vital points of Dzogchen were taught by Vajrapani, and both Dzogchen and Padmasambhava were authenticated by Karma Vajra throughout the ear-whispered lineage.

The previous Panchen Lama, King of Dharma, states in his great autobiography that he received many Nyingma teaching cycles such as Red Yamantaka, the Lord of Life; the *Complete Secret Teachings of the Eight Deities*,[135] and the empowerment and oral transmission of *The Assemblage of Sugatas* from a secret acharya. This master also quotes the following lines from the *Oral Autobiography* of the great Yungton in his biography of that lama:

> By the power of activating karmic remnants from my past
> life,
> I have encountered the ultimate definitive meaning of
> Dzogchen.
> Having seen the enlightened nature of mind,
> I have no need to seek Buddha elsewhere.

The authenticity of both Dzogchen and Padmasambhava have been established by numerous authoritative sources like those above, and it is doubtful that these great holy masters would have done anything to bring shame on the Dharma. The line of omniscient lords, the Dalai Lamas, and the Panchen Lama, King of Dharma, all make the same point. If you

---

[131] *gsang dag rnyan rgyud.*

[132] *gshin rje'i tshe bdag.*

[133] *ngag gsum pa.*

[134] *bdud rtsi thing pa'i rdor rje'i rtsa tshig las.*

[135] *bka brgyad.*

think these glorious holy beings have brought disgrace to great Manjushri Tsong Khapa, who else do you believe has made a contribution to his tradition? Furthermore, apart from Acharya Padmasambhava and the discovered treasures of Dzogchen Tantras, one can find no other authoritative sources to rely on for meditational deities and Dharma protectors such as the Secret Practice of Hayagriva, Palden Lhamo, and Begtse Chamsing, which are commonly accepted as authentic by all Gelugpas. One might therefore have to accept that all Gelugpas have converted to the Nyingma tradition! How can one possibly take up the challenge of differentiating clearly between the two schools? Rather, instead of trying to make such precise distinctions, consider as a service to the Dharma any spiritual practice that becomes an antidote to one's delusions and benefits the Dharma and sentient beings. Many tenets and traditions have been taught by previous authentic teachers. What difference does it make which of these one takes as the basis for one's practice?

There have been a number of lamas, however, who have abandoned their own tradition and sat prominently among the pratitioners of another tradition with raised heads. I do not think there is much point in this. When I took on board practices from different traditions, I did not do so blindly or before I had become as firmly established in my own as a peg stuck in mud. I have developed immutable heartfelt faith in Dharma King Manjushri Tsong Khapa. Having received into my heart his blessings and inspiration and those of the venerable guru Damcho Zangpo,[136] I see all holy masters of all traditions as pure objects of refuge. Similarly, I partially understand both the lack of contradiction between any Dharma teachings from the different lineages and their essential meaning as personal instructions. I have earned no sweet titles such as Master of the Whole Teaching, but nevertheless do my utmost to refrain from accumulating karma by abandoning the Dharma. Through the compassion of these two spiritual mentors, I have practiced the meditation and recitation of peaceful and wrathful deities, eradicating adverse conditions, and other methods to benefit the Dharma and beings according to secret prophecies. However, I did not rush out whenever drums were beating and smoke

---

[136] Jedrung Rinpoche's root guru.

billowing,[137] deferential to all and sundry, in the naïve belief that all initiations given were authentic.

If you understand the essence of this issue, you will see there is no point in my keeping these practices secret, particularly as I have no guilty sense whatsoever that I might be holding or propagating tenets harmful to the teachings of our own great Lama Tsong Khapa. I do not believe I need to hide any practice that I carry out, according to prophecy, in order to benefit the Dharma and sentient beings, whichever tradition it might come from.

There are very many Nyingmapas and holders of other tenets who in their turn have criticized and held wrong views about Dharma King Manjushri Tsong Khapa. They have committed serious errors through misunderstanding the vital points about the Dharma explained above. Their eyes have been blinded by sectarianism and they have not engaged in deep study and contemplation of their own traditions. The truth of this can be seen in the following passage from *Gyalpo Kathang*:[138]

> Therefore, during the twenty-fifth assembly an arya[139] will
> appear,
> In a huge miraculous temple which is the environment of
> Shakya,
> He will be a Bodhisattva benefiting sentient beings
> through his pure prayers,
> And will become supreme among the assembly.

Also, Thangyig Lugchig states:

> In the sublime solitude of Ganden,
> There will appear a person with the names of Lob and
> Sang,
> A supreme scholar well versed in Sutra and Tantra,
> An emanation of Vajradhara who will teach secret Tantra,

---

[137] A reference to the village custom of beating drums and making smoke offerings to mark the arrival of a lama.

[138] *The Chronicle of the Kings*—one of five chronicles recording the dynasties of prominent Tibetan families.

[139] A sublime transcendental being.

A leader and guide of sentient beings—
His secret name will be Lasrab Dorje, Giver of Bliss

This passage clearly indicates great Lama Tsong Khapa's name, Losang, and his secret name, Donyoe Dorje. Furthermore, Pema's testament contains the following passage:

The upholder of Sutra and Tantra known as Losang
    Drakpa—
An emanation of Manjushri—will lead beings.
He will teach secret Tantra widely for eight generations,
After leaving this world he will go to the presence of
    Maitreya.
Whoever upholds his lineage will become a Buddha in a
    single lifetime.
During the self-arisen great kalpa,
He will undoubtedly become a supreme arhat.

Moreover, the following passage appears in *A Dedication of Prophecy*, discovered by Choeje Gonpo Rinchen, who took it from Zangyak Rockface in Tsona:

Losang, an emanation of Manjushri,
Will marvellously spread the teaching.

Also, a treasure text discovered by Choewang Rinpoche states:

Losang Drakpa, an emanation of Manjushri,
Will be a marvellous master who will spread the teaching
    far and wide.

Furthermore, several discovered treasure texts contain this prophecy:

Compassionate Vairo, my (Padmasambhava's) heart
    emanation,
From a portion of your light
Will arise one body with many emanations.
One of these
Will appear at Ganden in Central Tibet,
He will be known as the bodhisattva Losang

In addition, according to Ratna's *Great General Prophecy:*[140]

> An emanation of Manjushri will hold the teaching of secret
>   Tantra,
> He will be known as Lodoe Tobjen.[141]

All these passages say the same thing. Therefore if Jey Rinpoche were not authentic, Acharya Padmasambhava too would become a great sack of lies, and all Nyingmapas and Gelugpas would be in the same predicament.

The great master Nyida Sangye had a pure vision of Great Padmasambhava in which he told Guru Rinpoche that Jey Rinpoche was very well-known in Tibet and asked where he had generated bodhichitta and where he would go in his future life. Padmasambhava replied:

> He generated bodhichitta in the presence of Buddha
>   Shakyamuni,
> In a single prayer, he benefits sentient beings in all his
>   lives.
> Those who criticize him become objects of his
>   compassion.
> Fearless one who makes meaningful everyone karmically
>   connected to him,
> Surrounded by followers upholding the baskets of teaching,
> He will protect and spread the Dharma during this
>   degenerate age.
> He should beware of evil spirits, defilement and
>   contagions.
> Obstacles may appear that could threaten his life.
> He should practice protectors such as Ushnisha Vijaya,
> As an antidote to dispel these obstacles.
> After being in the presence of Buddha Maitreya for some
>   time,
> He is destined to go to the Pure Land of Sukhavati,
> He will be known as Bodhisattva Golden Flower.

---

[140] *Rat na'i chi lung chen mo.*

[141] Losang.

In addition, in the biography of the master Karma Vajra, it is stated that a deity made the following prophecy:

> Four men will come with a letter from an emanation of Buddha Maitreya, one of whom will be a man who has the karma to realize Ekajati. You should give him the blessing and oral transmission of that protector as well as the empowerment of Vajra Vidarana.[142]

The following day four men indeed came with a letter, which Karma Vajra said appeared to be from the virtuous Lama Losang Drakpa. Furthermore Vajrapani's prophecy to the followers of Karma Vajra stated:

> Losang Drakpa is absolutely incomparable,
> He generated bodhichitta in the presence of Shakyamuni.
> In Tibet he will spread Sutra and Tantra.
> When he departs this life he will go to Tushita.
> This son of Maitreya
> Will soon become a fully enlightened Buddha!

One of the twenty-six chapters of the Kadampa Father's precious teaching refers to Dromtönpa's great offering and contains the following prophecy:

> One of my sublime emanations
> Sometimes manifests as a fully ordained monk.
> He will guide that land.[143]
> Sometimes he manifests as a child,
> Sometimes as a destitute beggar,
> Sometimes as an animal such as a bird or a dog,
> Sometimes he manifests as the sounds of prayer,
> And sometimes as the shapes of mantra syllables.
> He will be a fully ordained monk known as Drakpa.
> He will appear again and again for as long as the Dharma
>   remains,
> His lineage will carry out activities precisely as he did.

---

[142] Vajra Subjugator.

[143] Tibet.

Through the blessings of this holy monk,
Of all the three types of practitioners who seek
    enlightenment,
Only one hundred will truly understand.
In that land they will cultivate concentration.
They may be slightly harmed by certain views,
Demons of sensual pleasures will attack them,
Their meditation will be disturbed by attachment and hatred.
However by the blessings of this emanation,
They will become worthy recipients of offerings,
And unquestionably deserving objects of praise.
In short in that excellent land,
There will first be a community of four monastics,
Which will come to number three thousand five hundred
    monks—
Shakya sons endowed with the three higher trainings—
They will be guides to all beings.
From every direction and sub-direction in that land,
Innumerable monks will gather in a huge assembly,
Some will go in the ten directions to serve those
    karmically connected,
They will be just like the oceans out there,
Which hundreds of rivers cannot fill up,
Nor hundreds of channels deplete.

Furthermore, the twenty-sixth chapter of the precious Kadampa manuscript contains the following prophecy:

Eventually the Dharma embers
Will be rekindled by one named Drakpa.
He will bring benefit and happiness to many,
Also that will be a sublime and excellent land.

Karmapa Mikyoe Dorje criticized Jey Rinpoche in his youth, but he later came to regret it and declared in one of his spiritual songs:

In the Snowy Land of Tibet,
When Vinaya-holding was a mere outward show,
A person named Losang Drakpa truly observed monastic
    vows,

In the manner of Buddha Shakyamuni.
His followers upheld the victory banner of monasticism,
Just like Shariputra in the past,
And covered many nations on this earth.
In whom would one have faith if not in him?
I confess the negativity of past sectarianism,
And having been unwittingly influenced by negative
    friends,
I confess my errors due to ignorance.
Please guide me over successive rebirths!

Thus everyone must accept for themselves, and not just on my account, that these sources are authentic, as are many others which most clearly honor and praise Dharma King Jey Tsong Khapa. So abandon all thoughts of sectarianism. It is largely a matter of individual choice whether to practice view, meditation or conduct, but it is wrong to ignorantly criticize these sublime authentic masters. I urge everyone to point their fingertip back towards themselves and seriously reflect on these issues.

As has been established through scriptural quotation and logical reasoning, both the spiritual Father and Son,[144] and many holy and sublime beings of today, share the same mental continuum in the sphere of exalted wisdom. Aryas work to benefit sentient beings according to their fortunes and abilities. Therefore it is senseless to cultivate attachment and hatred based on sectarianism, as many appear to do these days. I feel this may greatly harm all Tibet and so beg you to avoid it.

In discussing these issues, I have used a variety of sources and arguments which seem most important for benefitting the Dharma and sentient beings. You may or may not be pleased by my words, but I have been completely sincere.

I feel we truly need to keep this advice of Jedrung Rinpoche's in our hearts during the twenty-first century. I have reproduced it exactly as it appears in this master's autobiography, "A Festive Joy for the Fortunate Ones: The Story of Vajra Master Losang Trinley."[145]

    — Lelung Tulku Tenzin Phuntsok Loden

---

[144] The Dalai Lama and the Panchen Lama.

[145] Pages 308–315 of the Delhi Edition (1985).

Appendix II. Bibliography of the Collected Works of Lelung Pema Zhepai Dorje[146]

VOLUME ONE

> *rig pa 'dzin pa blo bzang 'phrin las kyi rtogs pa brjod pa skal bzang dga' ston la/*

> *Festive Joy for the Fortunate Ones: A Biography of Tantric Master Losang Trinley* (pp. 1–747)

VOLUME TWO

KA

> *rje btsun bla ma dam pa dam chos bzang po dpal bzang po'i rnam par thar pa ngo mtshar rgya mtsho'i snying po la/*

> *An Essence of the Marvellous Ocean: A Biography of Eminent Holy Guru Damcho Zangpo Pal Zangpo* (pp. 1–76)

KHA

> *bdag nyid chen po kun mkhyen dharma'i mtshan can gyi rtogs pa brjod pa ngo mtshar rol mo la/*

> *Enchanting Music: A Biography of the Sublime Omniscient Master Named Dharma* (pp. 77–138)

GA

> *dpal 'khor lo sdom pa'i zab don 'ga' zhig gi gnad 'grol ba sbas don yang gsal nyin byed la/*

> *A Solar Illumination of Hidden Meanings: Elucidating Some Vital Points of the Profundity of Glorious Chakrasamvara* (pp. 139–227)

---

[146] Most of these works are not available in English but their titles are translated for the reader's convenience.

NGA

gnod sbyin chen po beg tse lcam dral gyi bskang ba mchod bstod kyi rim pa srog bdag rol mtsho la/

An Ocean of Life: Propitiation and Praises to Great Yaksha Begtse Camdral (pp. 229–289)

CA

lha mchog tshangs pa chen po'i mdos kyi 'phrin las kyi cho ga nyin byed snang ba la/

Solar Radiance: A Dhos[147] Offering to Special Protector Great Tsangpa (pp. 291–390)

CHA

rgyal po chen po rnam thos sras kyi mdos kyi lag len gsal byed yid kyi srog 'dzin la/

Sustaining Mental Life: An Elucidation of Great King Vaishramana's Dhos Practices (pp. 391–399)

JA

gsang bdag snyan brgyud kyi nang tshan rgyal po chen po rnam thos sras kyi mdos chog nor 'dzin mdzes rgyan/

An Ornament of Wealth: A Dhos Ritual of Great King Vaishramana Belonging to the Ear-Whispered Lineage of Vajrapani (pp. 401–429)

NYA

legs ldan tshogs rje chen po'i mchod sprin las bzhi'i bang mdzod la/

A Treasure of the Four Activities of the Excellent Protector Legden Tsog Jey (pp. 341–519)

---

[147] A representation made of crossed threads of a person and their dwelling used to attract special attention from higher beings or divert harmful attacks from demonic beings.

TA

dmag dpon chen po jo bo rgyal mtshan pa'i gsol mchod btsan rgod rnam rol la/

A Festive Celebration of Tsangoe: A Supplication and Offering to Great Commander Jowa Gyaltsen (pp. 521–542)

THA

khra tshal mgon gyi gzhis bdag gi gsol mchod mdor bsdus la/

A Short Ritual of Supplication and Offering to the Local Deity of Tratsal Monastery (pp. 543–551)

DA

stag sher rje btsan pa'i gsol mchod mdor bsdus/

A Short Ritual of Supplication and Offering to Tagsher Jetsanpa (pp. 553–566)

NA

zhing skyong tshe ring ma'i sgos sgrub dge legs myur du 'gugs pa'i pho nya la/

A Messenger for the Quick Gathering of Virtues and Excellence: A Zhing Kyong Blessing Practice Specifically of Tsering Ma (pp. 567–580)

VOLUME THREE

PA

rdo rje g.yu sgron ma'i phyi nang gsang gsum gyi bsnyen yig 'dod 'jo'i yang snying yid bzhin dbang rgyal la/

A Wish-Fulfilling Majestic Gem: A Retreat Manual of the Outer, Inner and Secret Practices of Dorje Yudron (pp. 1–29)

PHA

dpal ldan lha mo e ka dza Ti'i baM skongs dpag bsam ljon 'bras la/

A Fruit of the Wish-Fulfilling Tree: Gratifying Palden Lhamo Ekajati (pp. 31–64)

BA

rnam sras mdung dmar can gyi sgrub thabs dang 'brel bar thugs dam bskang ba byed pa nor bu'i do shal/

A Garland of Jewels: A Gratifying Propitiation Combined With A Sadhana of Vaishramana Holding A Red Spear (pp. 65–75)

MA

lha mchog dri za'i rgyal po'i sgrub phrin khyer bde'i gsal byed shel bum zab yangs la/

A Fine and Spacious Crystal Vase: A Convenient Practice and Entrusting of One's Purpose to the Supreme Divine King of the Gandharvas (pp. 77–107)

TSA

ging chen srog gi bdag po'i sgrub phrin tshangs chen srog gi nying khu la/

Great Brahma's Life Essence: A Sadhana Practice of Gingchen Sogdag (pp. 109–122)

TSHA

bon skyong lha'i rgyal po'i gsol mchod dbyings kyi rnga chen la/

A Great Meditative Drum: A Petition Offering to the Protector Bonkyong Lhagyal (pp. 123–147)

DZA

dregs pa'i yang rje gnod sbyin tsit+ta dmar po mched bdun gyi srog btad kyi rim pa rdo rje'i 'khrul 'khor/

A Vajra Miracle: A Rite of Entrusting Oneself to the Seven Siblings of Yaksha Tsita Marpo, Lord of Wrathful Ones (pp. 149–174)

WA

rgyal gsol legs tshogs rgyas byed la/

Enhancing Prosperity: A Petition Offering to Gyal Po (pp. 175–186)

ZHA

ging chen rdo rje Od ldan dkar po'i gsol mchod 'phrin las kyi le lag ging chen dgyes pa'i dga' ston/

Festive Joy for Gingchen: A Secondary Practice of Supplication and Offering to Gingchen O'd De Karpo (pp. 187–200)

ZA

klu rgyal mal gro gzi can gyi mchod sprin rdo rje'i nyin byed/

A Vajra Illumination: A Cloud of Offering to Naga King Medro Zican (pp. 201–223)

'A

bla ma'i rnal 'byor gsol 'debs zhabs brtan smon lam bslab bya dkar chag dang snyan dar kha byang bris thang rgyab yig sna tshogs sogs la/

A Miscellaneous Collection: Guru Yoga, A Supplication, Long-Life Prayers, Aspiration Prayers, A List of Advice, Nyen Dar Addresses and Poems for the Backs of Thangkas (pp. 225–352)

YA

tshad ma grub pa'i le'u'i zur rgyan gzhan phan rgya mtsho/

An Ocean of Benefit to Others: An Annotation to the Chapter on Establishing Buddha As Valid (pp. 353–439)

RA

gnyen po lha gsum gyi nyams len snying po dril ba la/

An Integrated Practice of the Three Authoritative Deities (pp. 441–487)

LA

thun drug gi rnal 'byor bya tshul la/

How to Practice Six-Session Yoga (pp. 489–524)

SHA

gcod yul gyi gdams pa 'khor 'das mnyam sbyor/

An Instruction on the Focus of Choed: Equalizing Samsara and Nirvana (pp. 525–552)

SA

yang zab 'khor ba rgyun gcod kyi bsreg pa'i man ngag gam bha ra ho la/

Gambha Raho: A Profound Quintessential Instruction That Severs the Continuation of Samsara (pp. 553–575)

HA

srad rgyud lugs kyi dmigs brtse ma'i bla ma'i rnal 'byor dga' ldan lha brgya mar grags pa'i khrid yig ngo mtshar dga' ston la/

Marvellous Festive Joy: A Guide to Ganden Lhagya and Migtse Ma Guru Yoga According to the Sedgyu Tradition (pp. 577–590)

A

zab don gyi legs bshad yungs 'bru nam mkha' la/

A Mustard Seed With Infinite Meanings: An Excellent Explanation of Profound Reality (pp. 591–596)

VOLUME FOUR

KI

khyung nag gi bzlas dmigs bya tshul gdengs can mthar byed la/

The Elimination of Nagas: How to Practice the Visualization and Recitation of Black Garuda (pp. 1–9)

KHI

'jig rten gsum gyi mgon po rdo rje rgyal po dpal phag mo gru pa'i rnam par thar pa ngo mtshar snying po la/

A Marvellous Essence: A Biography of Glorious Dorje Gyalpo Phagmo Drupa, Guide to the Three World Systems (pp. 11–30)

GI

zhabs brtan dang gsol 'debs kyi rim pa 'ga' zhig la/

A Collection of Long-Life Prayers and Supplication (pp. 31–44)

NGI

bde mchog gi cho ga spro bsdu'i gsal byed 'jug bde'i sgron me la/

A Clear Lamp: An Easy Guide to Heruka's Rite for Emanating and Withdrawing Deities (pp. 45–71)

CI

dri lan blta ba'i mig yangs la/

A Panoramic View: Questions and Answers (pp. 72–208)

CHI

thos bsam dar rgyas gling gi srung ma rgyal smyon pa'i gsol kha bshan pa rnam rol sogs mang bar/

A Collection of Petition-Offering Rites to Gyal Nyon, Dharma Protector of Thosam Dhargye Ling Monastery (pp. 209–234)

JI

e se bo'i yul lha dar ma bkra shis kyi gsol mchod sprin phung rgya mtsho la/

An Ocean of Clouds: Supplication and Offering to Dharma Tashi, A Local Deity of Ae Se Wo (pp. 235–244)

NYI

hum bsgrub dang 'brel ba'i bla ma'i rnal 'byor gyi rim pa/

A Guru Yoga Rite Combined with Hung Practice (pp. 245–262)

TI

dgongs 'dus las gsungs pa'i grib sel gyi lag len gsal byed yan lag brgyad ldan la/

Water Possessing the Eight Qualities: An Elucidation of the Practice of Purifying Obscurations from Gongdus (pp. 263–292)

THI

sgrol dkar tshe sbyin yid bzhin 'khor lo'i sgrub 'phrin dang 'brel ba brtan bzhugs 'bul tshul gyi cho ga 'chi med rdo rje'i pha lam kun dga'i 'dod 'jo la/

An Indestructible Vajra Diamond Fulfilling All Wishes: A Long-Life Rite Combined with White Tara (pp. 293–324)

DI

sa skyong rgya ri ba chen po'i zhabs brtan 'chi med 'dod 'jo sogs mang bar/

A Long-Life Prayer of Great Governor Gyari and Other Prayers (pp. 325–332)

NI

snyan dar zhal byang gi rim pa sna tshogs la/

A Succession of Wishing Verses for Silk Offering Scarves (pp. 333–338)

PI

snyan dar zhal byang sna tshogs la/bod kyi dkar chag nang ñdi med/

A Miscellaneous Collection of Wishing Verses for Silk Offering Scarves (not in the Tibetan Catalogue (pp. 339–354)

rdo rje g.yu sgron ma'i phyi nang gsang gsum gyi sreg chog la/ 'di bod kyi dkar chag nang (pi)

A Fire Offering Ritual of Dorje Yudonma Related to Her Outer, Inner and Secret Practices (pp. 1–6)

PHI

bdud mgon mched gsum gyi rten mdos rgyun khyer gyi cho ga brngam brjid rol ba la/

A Ferocious Play: A Convenient Daily Practice of Tendos of Dudgon's Three Brothers (pp. 355–357)

BI

bla ma mchod pa'i cho ga dngos grub yid bzhin 'dren pa'i shing rta la/

A Chariot-Harbinger of Attainments: A Rite of Lama Choedpa (pp. 359–394)

MI

gsang 'dzin las kyi rdo rjer gsol 'debs smon lam/

A Prayer Supplication to Laykyi Dorje, Holder of Secrets (pp. 395–452)

TSI

rje tsong kha pa chen po/kun mkhyen blo bzang ye shes/rje btsun sgrol ma/dngos sogs thun mong la gsol 'debs dbyig gi phreng ba la/

A Garland of Common Prayers to Great Jey Tsong Khapa, Omniscient Losang Yeshe and Eminent Tara etc. (pp. 453–520)

VOLUME FIVE

TSHI

rnam dkar phyogs la bskul ba'i bslab bya lam don gsal byed la/

A Clear Illumination of the Meaning of the Path: Inspirational Advice to Engage in Virtuous Actions (pp. 1–48)

DZA

drang ba dang nges pa'i don rnam par 'byed pa'i bstan bcos legs bshad snying po'i dgongs don gsal bar byed pa blo bzang dgongs gsal la/

A Clear Illumination of Jey Rinpoche's Thought: Elucidating the Intended Meaning of an Essence of Eloquent Explanation that Thoroughly Distinguishes the Concepts of Definitive and Interpretative Discourses (pp. 49–152)

WI

'dod khams dbang phyug e ka dza Ti'i bskang ba mchod bstod kyi rim pa 'dod 'jo'i bang mdzod la/

A Wish-Fulfilling Treasure: Propitiation, Offering, and Praises to Ekajati, Empress of the Desire Realm (pp. 153–205)

ZHI

gong sa rgyal ba'i dbang po bskal bzang rgya mtshor phul ba'i zhu yig dang gzhan zhu yig khag bcas la/

A Collection of Appeal Letters such as Those Addressed to Gyalwang Kalzang Gyatso (pp. 207–248)

ZI

bsam yas su byams pa gtsor gyur gyi gos sku gsar bzhengs kyi dkar chags la/

A Catalogue of Costumes including Those Offered to Maitreya at Samye (pp. 249–301)

'I

snyan dar zhal byang sogs 'dod gsol sna tshogs la/

A Collection of Wishing Verses for Silk Offering Scarves and Request Prayers (pp. 303–341)

rta mgrin gsang sgrub kyi rgyan khyer mdor bsdus la/'di gsung thor bu khongs min nam snyam yang dpyad/

A *Short Daily Practice of Secret Hayagriva* (This may belong to "Miscellaneous Discourses," but requires further examinination) (pp. 343–344)

YI

rdo rje gces 'phreng gi las byang dang byin rlabs kyi lhan thabs don gnyis mdzes rgyan la/

A *Beautiful Dual Ornament: Appendices of Blessings and Sadhana Instructions of Dorje Chetreng* (pp. 345–369)

RI

bdud mgon rong lha rgya mtshan gyi bskang ba mchod bstod kyi rim pa zhing skyong dga' skyed la/

Delighting the Local Guardians: Propitiation, Offering, and *Praises To Dudgon Ronglha Gyaltsen* (pp. 371–396)

LI

dra po gsum dril gyi sgrub thabs gsal ba'i me long/

A *Clear Mirror: A Sadhana of Three Wrathful Ones* (pp. 397–421)

SHI

gsang ba bsam gyis mi khyab pa'i brgyud 'debs smon lam dang bcas pa gsang 'dzin myur lam la/

A Speedy Sacred Path: Prayers to the Inconceivable Sacred Lineage *and Wishing Prayers* (pp. 423–442)

SI

snying po don gsum gyi 'khrid kyi sngon 'gro'i brgyud 'debs la/

A Preliminary Lineage Supplication for Teaching on the Three Core *Concepts* (pp. 443–467)

HI

(dpe ma rnyed)

[text missing]

I

(dpe ma rnyed)

[text missing]

VOLUME SIX

KU

bcom ldan 'das dpal gar gyi dbang phyug gsang ba ye shes kyi mkha' 'gro ma'i cho ga'i rnam bshad snying po'i mchog sbyin legs bshad rgya mtsho la/

An Ocean of Excellent Explanation that Grants the Supreme Essence: A Commentary on the Rites of the Glorious Bhagavati of the Dance, the Enlightened Secret Wisdom Dakini (pp. 1–99 in Tibetan page numbering—short manuscript size)

KHU

(dpe ma rnyed)

[text missing]

GU

(dpe ma rnyed)

[text missing]

NGU

(dpe ma rnyed)

[text missing]

CU

btsan rgod dar ma rgyal mtshan gyi gsol mchod 'dod yon 'khyil ba la/

A Pool of Sensual Resources: Offering and Supplication to Tsangoe Dharma Gyaltsen (pp. 1–16)

CHU

(dpe ma rnyed)

[text missing]

JU

lha chen gyi bsnyen yig bde 'byung mchog sbyin la/

Granting Supreme Bliss: A Retreat Manual of Mahadeva (Ishvara) (pp. 17–40)

NYU

(dpe ma rnyed)

[text missing]

TU

gsol 'debs zhabs brtan gyi rim pa la/

A Collection of Supplications and Long-Life Prayers (pp. 41–62)

THU

e pa drung yig ngag dbang phun tshogs la gdams pa dri lan phun tshogs nyin byed la/

Solar Illumination: Answers to Questions from Ngawang Phuntsok, Secretary of Aepa (pp. 63–88)

DU

byad grol gser gyi lde mig gi man ngag gi gnad lhug par bkral ba lag len gsal byed la/

A Clear Practice Guide Elucidating Vital Points of the Golden Key Quintessential Instructions for Setting Oneself Free from Harmful Powers (pp. 89–146)

NU

rta mchog pad+ma dbang chen gyi tshogs mchod la sogs pa la/

A Tsok to Tachog Pema Wangchen Hayagriva and Others (pp. 147–154)

PU

sha brgya zan brgya'i cho ga nag 'gros su spel ba snyigs dus phan byed la/

A Benefit for the Degenerate Time: An Orderly Guide to the Shagya Zangya Ritual (pp. 155–166)

PHU

zhal gdams zab don gyi snying po la/

A Testament: The Essence of Profound Meaning (pp. 167–172)

BU

nam mkha'i bcud len bdud rtsi'i thur ma la/

An Ambrosia-Like Spoon to Extract the Essence of Space (pp. 173–176)

MU

snyan dar zhal byang 'dod gsol gyi rim pa la/

Request Prayers and Wishing Verses for Silk Offering Scarves (pp. 177–180)

TSU

mgur gyi rim pa thol byung rdo rje'i glu la/

Vajra Song: A Spontaneous Outburst of Spiritual Euphoria (pp.
181–186)

TSHU

shis brjod phan bde'i lam bzang la/

A Beneficial Path: Auspicious Verses (pp. 187–190)

DZU

*'jam dbyangs chos skor gyi nang tshan khros nag gi las byang
zab don snying po'i rgya mtsho la/*

An Ocean of Profound Quintessential Meaning: Sadhana Instructions of Tronag as Included in the Cycle of Manjushri Discourses
(pp. 191–228)

WU

bden tshig bcud len snying po la/

The Essence of Extracting the Core of Truthful Words (pp. 229–
246)

ZHU

*lcags khyi lo rnam grol gling du sman sgrub chen mo bgyis pa'i
dkar chag bdud rtsi'i gar mkhan la/*

A Nectar-Bestowing Dancer: A Catalogue of Great Medicine Ritual
Accomplishments at Namdrol Ling Monastery in the Iron Dog
Year (pp. 247–266)

ZU

sman sgrub mdor bsdus bya tshul gcig chog sman gyi thig le la/

A Medicine Drop: A Short Version of Medicine Ritual Accomplishments (pp. 267–282)

'U

> *(dpe ma rnyed)*
>
> [text missing]

YU

> *(dpe ma rnyed)*
>
> [text missing]

RU

> *(dpe ma rnyed)*
>
> [text missing]

LU

> *(dpe ma rnyed)*
>
> [text missing]

SHU

> *rgyal ba'i bka' 'gyur ro cog gi gsung par rin po che srid gsum rgyan gcig rdzu 'phrul shing rta'i (snang thang bka' 'gyur)*
>
> *The Jewel Ornament of the Three Realms and A Miraculous Chariot: A Catalogue of Blocks of All the Buddha's Teachings Translated into Tibetan (the Narthang Kagyur)* (127 pages in Tibetan page numbering; pp. 1–127)

SU

> *(dpe ma rnyed)*
>
> [text missing]

HU

> *(dpe ma rnyed)*
>
> [text missing]

U

(dpe ma rnyed)

[text missing]

KE

bla ma bde chen dbang phyug gi brgyud 'debs smin grol myur lam la/

A Quick Path and Liberation of the Ripened Ones: Lineage Prayer to Guru Dechen Wangchuk (pp. 283–286)

KHE

'jam dpal nag po'i rgyun khyer nyung gsal la/

A Clear and Short Daily Practice of Black Manjushri (pp. 287–288)

KHE

skyabs sems sngon 'gro la/bod rtsis shog bu/ *(dpe ma rnyed)*

A Preliminary Practice of Refuge and Bodhicitta (1 page in Tibetan page numbering—text missing)

KHE

'jam dkar gyi sgrub thabs rgyun khyer snying po bsdus pa la/

A Short Essential Daily Sadhana of White Manjushri (pp. 289–294)

GE

rnam 'joms kyi khrus chog bdud rtsi'i gter bum la/

A Nectar Vase: An Ablution Rite of Vidhyara (pp. 295–300)

NGE

rdo rje rnam 'joms kyi sgrub thabs la/

A Sadhana of Vajra Vidhyara (pp. 301–304)

CE

> *seng ldeng nags sgrol gyi sgrub thabs la/*

> A Sadhana of Tara Sengdeng Nagdrol (pp. 305–308)

CE

> *seng ldeng nags sgrol gyi rgyun khyer nyung bsdus la/*

> A Short Daily Practice of Tara Sengdeng Nagdrol (pp. 309–310)

CHE

> *thugs rje chen po 'jigs rten dbang phyug gi dbang gi brgyud 'debs byin rlabs myur 'jug la/*

> A Quick Blessing: A Lineage Prayer for an Empowerment of Great Compassionate Avalokiteshvara (pp. 311–314)

> *thugs chen chen po phyag bzhi pa'i sgrub thabs la/*

> A Sadhana of Four-Armed Avalokiteshvara (pp. 315–318)

JE

> *gsang bdag bdud rtsi thigs pa'i rjes gnang gi yi ge smin byed bdud rtsi'i yang snying la/*

> An Innermost Essence of Nectar: A Permission Blessing of Nectar-Dropping Vajrapani (pp. 319–340)

NYE

> *gsang bdag gtum po me 'bar gyi sgrub thabs la/*

> A Sadhana of Blazing Wrathful Vajrapani (pp. 341–354)

TE

> *gsang bdag gtum po'i sgrub thabs yang gsang bdud rtsi'i bcud thigs la/*

> An Innermost Essential Drop of Nectar: A Sadhana of Blazing Wrathful Vajrapani (pp. 355–358)

THE

gsang bdag gtum po me 'bar gyi sgrub thabs la/

A Sadhana of Blazing Wrathful Vajrapani (pp. 359–362)

DE

gsang bdag bdud rtsi thigs pa'i rgyun khyer la/

A Daily Practice of Nectar-Dropping Vajrapani (pp. 363–366)

NE

phyag na rdo rje 'gro bzang lugs kyi rgyun khyer la/

A Daily Practice of Vajrapani According to the Drozang Tradition (pp. 367–368)

phyag rdor dang rdor sems kyi sgom bzlas rgyun khyer dngos grub bum bzang la/

A Noble Vase of Attainments: Daily Practices of Vajrapani and Vajrasattva's Meditation and Recitation (pp. 369–372)

PE

gsang bdag gtum po'i me 'bar gyi zhi ba'i sbyin sreg gi cho ga gzhan phan rgya mtsho la/

An Ocean of Benefit to Others: A Peaceful Fire-Offering Ritual of Blazing Wrathful Vajrapani (pp. 373–386)

PHE

rta mgrin gsang sgrub kyi sgrub 'phrin rgyal gdon sog gi spu gri la/

A King Demon Killing Razor: An Activity Accomplishment of Secret Hayagriva (pp. 387–392)

BE

dbang chen thugs rje bskul ba'i sgrub 'phrin nyin byed Od snang la/

A Solar Radiance: A Sadhana Practice Invoking the Compassion of Hayagriva (pp. 393–400)

ME

bcom ldan 'das 'khor lo bde mchog dril bu lha lnga'i dbang gi brgyud 'debs grub rigs dga' bskyed/

Delighting Practitioners: A Lineage Prayer for an Empowerment of the Five-Deity Heruka Chakrasamvara according to the Gandhapada Tradition (pp. 401–404)

TSE

rnam sras kyi mnga' gsol gnod sbyin yid 'gul/

Capturing the Heart of Yaksha: An Enthronement of Vaishramana (pp. 405–408)

TSHE

khyung nag me'i spu gri'i bsnyen yig mdor bsdus 'khyer bde la/

A Short Convenient Retreat Guide to Black Garuda's Fire Sword (pp. 409–417)

VOLUME SEVEN

DZE

khyung nag gi sgrub thabs 'khyer bde la/

A Convenient Sadhana of Black Garuda (pp. 1–4)

WE

rgyal sras khyung gi sgrub thabs gdon gsum mthar byed/

Liberation from the Three Demons: A Sadhana of Garuda, Son of the Buddhas (pp. 5–8)

ZHE

khyung nag gi rjes gnang gi cho ga la/

A Permission Blessing Ritual of Black Garuda (pp. 9–12)

ZE

khyung nag gi sgrub thabs la/

A Sadhana of Black Garuda (pp. 13–16)

'E

snyan brgyud kyi nang tshan gsang ba bsam gyis mi khyab pa'i khrus chog la/

An Inconceivably Secret Ablution Rite from the Ear-Whispered Lineage (pp. 17–22)

YE

sngags kyi rtsa ltung dang/sbom po'i sdom tshig don gsal la/

A Clear Elucidation of the Verses on Root and Secondary Transgressions of Tantra (pp. 23–28)

RE

bsangs kyi cho ga 'dod dgu'i mchog sbyin la/

Fulfilling Supreme Wishes: Rites of Incense Offering (pp. 29–44)

LE

lho sgo'i cho ga thugs rje'i dpyang thag la/

A String of Compassion: Rites of the Southern Gate (pp. 45–54)

SHE

thugs rje chen po rtsa gsum 'dus pa'i brgyud 'debs mchog gi myur lam la/

A Quick Path for Supreme Attainment: A Lineage Prayer to Avalokiteshvara, the Embodiment of the Three Roots (pp. 55–58) *'di gsung thor bu khongs min nam snyam yang dpyad/dregs pa'i ded dpon rgyal mtshan pa'i mnga' gsol bstan srung dgyes pa'i sgra dbyangs la/*

An Echo Pleasing the Dharma Protector: The Enthronement of Gyaltsen Pa, Leader of the Wrathful Ones (pp. 59–62 [This may belong to a volume of miscellaneous discourses but needs further examination])

SE

khra 'brug chos skyong chen po'i mchod bstod tshangs pa'i dgyes skong la/

Delighting Brahma: Offering and Praises to the Great Dharma Protector of Tradruk Temple (pp. 63–74)

HE

tshangs pa dung thod can dpon blon gyi rten mdos kyi cho ga snang srid zil gnon la/

Overpowering Phenomena: Tendos[148] Rites of Conch-Crowned Brahma and His Ministers (pp. 75–80)

E

lha mo/dpal lha/beg tse/rgyal mtshan pa rnams kyi gtor 'bul rgyun khyer bsdus pa la/

A Short Daily Practice of Ritual Cake Offerings to Palden Lhamo, Pel Lha, Beg Tse, and Gyaltsen Pa (pp. 81–86)

KO

lha chen tshangs pa chen po'i mnga' gsol srid gsum zil gnon la/

Overpowering the Three Realms: Enthronement of the Great Protector Maha Brahma (pp. 87–94)

---

[148] A representation of a dwelling place.

KHO

tshangs pa'i drag bskul brngam pa'i gad rgyangs zhes bya ba la/

Roaring Laughter: Strongly Invoking Brahma's Wrathful Actions (pp. 95–98)

KHO

tshangs pa dung thod can gyi 'dod gsol la/

Fulfilling Conch-Crowned Brahma's Wishes (pp. 99–100)

GO

sprul pa'i chos skyong chen po'i 'phrin las 'dod pa'i re bskong la/

Fulfilling Hopes: Activities of a Great Dharma Protector's Manifestation (pp. 101–104)

NGO

khra 'brug tshangs pa chen po'i bka' sdod bse sku ba'i bskang ba mchod bstod kyi rim pa 'phrin las myur 'grub la/

A Quick Accomplishment of Actions: Propitiation, Offering, and Praises to Seku Wa, Commander of Maha Brahma, Protector of Tradruk Temple (pp. 105–110)

CO

ging chen tshangs pa'i bka' sdod gnod sbyin chen po'i bskang ba mchod bstod kyi rim pa bshan pa rol mtsho/

An Ocean of Enjoyment for Butchers: Rites of Proppitiation, Offering and Praises to Maha Yaksha, Commander of Maha Brahma (pp. 111–116)

CHO

lha chen gyi bsnyen pa bya tshul mdor bsdus la/

A Short Retreat Guide to Great Protector Ishvara (pp. 117–120)

JO

> ***lha chen dbang phyug chen po'i me mchod dge legs myur 'gugs la/***
>
> *A Swift Gathering of Virtue and Excellence: A Fire Offering to Great Protector Ishvara* (pp. 121–126)

NYO

> ***dam can sde bdun gyi bskang ba 'khyer bde la/***
>
> *A Convenient Propitiation of the Seven Damchan* (pp. 127–136)

TO

> ***gsang bdag snyan brgyud kyi bka' bsrung dam can sde bdun gyi gtor 'bul 'khyer bde la/***
>
> A Convenient Ritual Cake Offering to the Seven Damchan, Protectors *of the Ear-Whispered Lineage of Vajrapani* (pp. 137–140)

THO

> ***rtsa gsum dam can rgya mtsho'i bskang ba 'dod dgu'i bang mdzod la/***
>
> *A Wish-Fulfilling Treasure House: Propitiation of an Ocean of Damchans, Protectors of the Three Roots* (pp. 141–148)

DO

> ***chos srung spyi'i 'phrin bcol bsam don lhun grub ma la/***
>
> *A Spontaneous Fulfilment of Wishes: Entrusting One's Purposes to the General Dharma Protectors* (pp. 149–152)

NO

> ***gtor 'bul nyung ngur bsdus pa ro 'dzin dga' bskyed la/***
>
> *Delighting the Taste Buds: An Abbreviated Version of a Ritual Cake Offering* (pp. 153–158)

PO

mtshams mtho bskyed chog la/

Rites for Planting Retreat Boundary Markers (pp. 159–162)

PHO

mgon po phyag drug pa'i thugs dam bskang ba'i rim pa yid kyi re skong la/

Fulfilling Hopes: Rites of Fulfilling the Wishes of Six-Armed Mahakala (pp. 163–170)

BO

gnod sbyin tsi'u dmar po'i mnga' gsol sde brgyad zil gnon la/

Overpowering the Eight Classes: the Enthronement of Yaksha Tse'u Marpo (pp. 171–176)

MO

gnod sbyin chen po'i mchod pa'i 'phrin las dam can dgyes pa'i sprin phung la/

A Cloud of Delights for Damchan: An Activity of Offering to Maha Yaksha (pp. 177–188)

TSO

sngags srung ma'i gtor 'bul 'khyer bde la/

A Convenient Ritual Cake Offering to Ngagsung Ma, Ekajati (pp. 189–192)

TSHO

rdo rje'i chos srung spyi sgos la 'phrin las bcol ba mi slu'i don 'grub la/

An Unfailing Accomplishment of Purpose: Entrusting One's Purposes to the Activities of the General and Particular Vajra Dharma Protectors (pp. 193–198)

DZO

Ol dga'i yul lha gzhi bdag rnams kyi gsol mchod nyung bsdus la/

A Very Short Supplication and Offering to the Local Deities and Spirits of Olga (pp. 199–204)

WO

zhal bram gzugs kyi bstod pa log 'dren zil gnon/

Overpowering Mahakala in the Form of a Brahmin (pp. 205–208)

ZHO

'bur dong dgon gzhis bdag dpon blon gyi gsol mchod la/

Supplication and offering to the Local Spirits, Both Leader and Retinue, of Burdong Monastery (pp. 209–214)

ZO

'phrin bcol 'dod 'jo'i dpal ster la/

Wish-Granting Rites of Entrusting one's Purposes to the Protectors (pp. 215–218)

O

rgyal ba'i sras kyi rnam par thar par 'jug pa'i smon lam rgya mtsho phyogs kyi sprin chen la/

Oceans of Clouds: Aspirational Prayers to Engage in the Liberating Deeds of Bodhisattvas, Children of the Buddhas (pp. 219–354)

YO

rgyal chen sku lnga'i gtor 'bul 'khyer bde dang gtor bsngo phrin bcol nyung bsdus la/

A Convenient Ritual Cake Offering Rite of Gyalchen Ku Nga and A Very Short Ritual Cake Dedication and Rite of Entrusting One's Purposes to the Protectors (pp. 355–358)

RO[*]

gser skyems bzhugs so/'di ni (ro)

Golden Libation Offering Rituals

RO[*]

dmag dpon rgyal mtshan pa'i mnga' gsol chos srung dgyes pa'i rol mtsho la/

An Ocean of Delight for the Dharma Protector: The Enthronement of Commander in Chief Gyaltsenpa (pp. 361–362)

RO[*]

rdor legs kyi gtor 'bul 'khyer bde la/

A Convenient Ritual Cake Offering Rite of Protector Dorje Legpa (pp. 363–364)

RO[*]

yam shud dmar por 'dod gsol la/

A Request Prayer to the Protector Red Yam Shud (pp. 365–366)

RO[*]

rgyal mtshan par gnyer gtad bgyis pa'i 'phrin tshig

Verses of Entrustment to Gyaltsen Pa (pp. 367–368)

LO

bskang ba'i rim par gzhol ba yi//blo gsal gzhon nu'i tshogs dag la//bzang po'i bslab bya ston pa'i 'phrin//legs bshad las ongs 'di nao//

This Chapter contains Heartfelt Advice for Intelligent Young People Who Engage in Propitiation rituals (pp. 369–378)

---

[*] Some of these five texts labelled 'ro' may belong to a work of miscellaneous pieces; this needs further examination.

SHO

gsang 'dzin las kyi rdo rje la brten pa'i bla ma'i rnal 'byor nyung gsal la/

A Clear and Short Guru Yoga Practice of Relying upon Tantric Master Karma Vajra Drupchen Namkha Gyaltsen (pp. 379–386)

SO

chab shog gi rim pa mchog dman la bsrings ba la/

Letters to People of High and Ordinary Rank (pp. 387–396)

HO

me lug zla tshes nang du gong sa mchog la phul ba'i zhu chings la/

A Letter Written to the Seventh Dalai Lama in a Fire Sheep Year (pp. 397–406)

O

mkha' spyod 'grub pa'i smon lam 'phrul gyi zhags pa/

A Mystical Lassoo: An Aspiration Prayer to Actualize the Pure Dakini Land (pp. 407–414)

VOLUME EIGHT

KA

mkha' spyod kyi gnas yig la/

A Guide to the Pure Dakini Land (pp. 1–33)

KHA

gnas mchog zangs mdog dpal ri'i gnas bshad kyi gtam la 'jug pa'i mtshams sbyor bklags pas yid ches la/

A Trust-Inspiring Introduction: A Preface to a Description of the Supreme Pilgrimage Site of Zangdog Pelri (pp. 35–55)

GA

gnas chen zangs mdog dpal ri'i gtsug lag khang gi gnas bshad ngo mtshar rab gsal la/

A Clear and Marvellous Guide to the Temples of the Great Pilgrimage Site of Zangdog Pelri (pp. 57–65)

NGA

lha gcig zhing skyong mched gnyis spyan drangs pa'i lo rgyus rin po che ngo mtshar dad pa'i me long la/

A Precious and Marvellous Mirror of Faith: Accounts of Inviting the Two Zhingkyong Sisters (pp. 67–108)

CA

gnas chen zangs mdog dpal ri'i gnas rten gyi bkod pa las 'phros pa'i lo rgyus rags rim ngo mtshar dad pa'i ljon shing la/

A Marvellous Tree of Faith: A General History of the Environment and the Inhabitants of the Great Pilgrimage Site of Zangdog Pelri (pp. 109–147)

CHA

gnas chen zangs mdog dpal ri'i cha shas las 'phros pa'i gnas ri rnams kyi lo rgyus DA ki dgyes pa'i glu dbyangs la/

A Song Delighting Dakinis: Histories of Holy Mountains Connected to Branches of the Great Pilgrimage Site of Zangdog Pelri (pp. 149–210)

JA

mkha' 'gro rdo'i mchod rten gyi lo rgyus DA ki'i lam yangs la/

A Vast Path to the Land of the Dakinis: A History of a Dakini's Stone Stupa (pp. 211–218)

NYA

g.yung drung 'khyil pa'i gsang phug rnyed pa'i lo rgyus ngo mtshar 'khor lo la/

A Wonderful Circle: An Account of the Discovery of a Secret Cave of Swirling Swastikas (pp. 219–224)

TA

sa sprel zla brgyad 'tshes lnga kyi nyin la glang po sna'i ljongs su bskyod pa'i gnas tshul la/

A Record of a Visit to Elephant Trunk Valley on the Fifth Day of the Eighth Month of an Earth Monkey Year (pp. 225–232)

THA

mtsho mgor bgrod tshul gyi lam yig nyams dga' nyung gsal la/

Very Brief and Enjoyable Directions to Tsogo (pp. 233–245)

DA

gzi can dang u ma'i pho brang gsar du rnyed tshul gyi lo rgyus Od 'bar snang gsal la/

A Radiant Blaze of Illumination: Accounts of the Newly Discovered Palaces of Uma and Zecan (pp. 247–254)

NA

ma gcig tsiN+Di ka 'bar ma dbang gi gdong pa can gang du spyan drangs pa sogs kyi lo rgyus rin po che Od zer stong gi dra ba la/

A Jewel Radiating a Network of Thousands of Rays: Accounts of Machig Chandrika Barma Wanggi Dongpa Can, including Places where He was Invited (pp. 255–279)

PA

srid gsum zil gnon gyi gnas bshad la/

Directions to the Pilgrimage Site of Silsum Zilnon (pp. 281–326)

PHA

gnas thor bu rnams kyi lo rgyus ltad mo'i grong khyer la/

A City of Entertainment: Histories of Scattered Holy Places (pp. 327–371)

BA

ham lung gsang chen bkod pa'i gnas su bgrod tshul gyi lam yig la/

Directions to the Great Secret Ham Valley, Kongpo (pp. 373–388)

MA

gnas mchog pad+mo bkod du bgrod pa'i lam yig dga' byed bden gtam la/

Pleasant and truthful Words: Directions to the Supreme Pilgrimage Site of Pema Koe (pp. 389–493)

TSA

rdo lung rdo rje gling gi gnas gsar du rnyed pa'i lo rgyus go bde drang gtam la/

True Words that are Easy to Understand: Annals of the Newly Discovered Holy Place of Dolung Dorje Ling, Pema Kod (pp. 495–518)

TSHA

spro lung dbang phyug gling gi gnas sgo gsar du phye ba'i lo rgyus rab snyan sgra dbyangs la/

A Marvellously Melodic Tune: An Account of the Inauguration of the Holy Place of Trolung Wangchuk Ling, Kongpo (pp. 519–546)

VOLUME NINE

DZA

l+wa ba pa'i gzims phug dang /dpal lha dang /jag me'i gsang phug sogs ngo 'phrod pa'i lo rgyus dran pa'i me long la/

A Mirror of Memory: An Introduction to the History of Lawa Pa's *Residence, the Secret Caves of Pal Lha and Jagma* (pp. 1–27)

WA

mkha' 'gro'i 'du gnas gri gug gsang lam gyi lo rgyus me tog 'phreng mdzes la/

A Garland of Beautiful Flowers: A History of Drigug Sang Lam, Meeting Place of Dakinis (pp. 29–33)

ZHA

pho brang chen po lta na sdug gi gnas bshad la/

A Guide to the Great and Magnificent Palace of Tana Dug (pp. 35–44)

ZA

don mthun 'dus pa'i tshom bu du mar ngo mtshar ba'i ltad mo mthong ba'i lo rgyus rig rtsal sgyu 'phrul dra ba la/

An Illusory Emanation Net of Mental Power: An Account of Witnessing the Marvellous Spectacle of Many Groups Assembled for one Purpose (pp. 45–79)

'A

lcags khyi lo lha gcig nyi ma gzhon nu'i dus ston chen mo bgyis pa'i lo rgyus ma sbas drang gtam bklags pas kun shes la/

All-Revealing Truthful Words: Accounts of Holding the Great Festivity of Lhacig Nyima Zhonnu on an Iron Dog Year (pp. 81–183)

YA

yid bzhin gyi nor bu bde ba gdung sel dang btsan rgod kha la me 'bar gyi bla rdo rnyed tshul gyi lo rgyus yid ches zangs thal la/

Mebar: Accounts of the Discovery of the Spirit Rock of Tsangos Khala Mebar and the Wish-fulfilling Jewel Dewa Dungsel (pp. 185–201)

RA

ltal chung mkha' 'gro'i dga' tshal gyi gnas sgo gsar du phye ba'i lam yig bden pa'i zungs ldan la/

Spirit of Truth: Directions to the Newly Discovered Joyous Holy Garden of Talchung Dakini (pp. 203–219)

LA

ltal chung mkha' 'gro'i dga' tshal gyi gnas yig dran pa'i gsal byed la/

A Clear Reminder: A Guide to the Joyous Garden of Talchung Dakini (pp. 221–226)

SHA

gsal dwangs ri bo che'i gnas zhal gsar du phye ba'i lo rgyus mngon sum snang byed mig gi dbang po la/

A Clear Visual Faculty: Annals of the Inaugaration of the Holy Site of Saldang Riwo Che (pp. 227–252)

SA

gsal dwangs ri bo che'i gnas yig 'jug bde'i 'phreng ba la/

A Convenient Entry: Directions to the Holy Site of Saldang Riwo Che (pp. 253–270)

HA

yid bzhin gyi nor bu rat+na tA re'i lo rgyus mthong na kun dga' la/

A Sight of Universal Joy: Accounts of the Wish-Fulfilling Jewel Ratna Tara (pp. 271–278)

A

mi dbang bsod nams stobs rgyas rnam grol gling du byon pa'i lo rgyus ngo mtshar 'bum snang la/

A Million Marvellous Light Rays: Accounts of Miwang Sonam Topgyal's Visit to Namdrol Ling Monastery (pp. 279–359)

KI

lcags pho khyi'i lo 'gal rkyen gyi g.yul las rgyal ba'i lo rgyus sgyu 'phrul rgyan gyi me long la/

A Miraculous Mirror Ornament: Accounts of Victory Over Adverse Conditions in an Iron Dog Year (pp. 361–469)

KHI

lha gcig rdo rje skyabs byed kyi 'khrungs khang du dam can rgya mtsho'i bsti gnas gsar du bskrun pa'i deb ther rin po che'i 'phreng ba la/

A Garland of Jewels: Accounts of the Construction of Damchan Gyatso's New Dwelling at the Birthplace of Lhacig Dorje Kyab (pp. 471–483)

GI

dam can snyon kha chen po spyan 'dren mdzad pa sogs kyi lo rgyus rin po che ut+pal la'i chun po la/

(pp. 485–497)

4

dag snang gsang bdag bla ma'i phyi nang gsang gsum gyi rnal 'byor dang rgyun khyer la/

A Daily Practice and Guru Yoga of the Outer, Inner and Secret Dimensions of the Sandak Lama—from Pure Vision (pp. 59–71)

5

rigs ldan ma rnams la gsol ba gdab pa'i gdung tshig dga' bzhi'i bang mdzod la/

A Treasury of Four Joys: A Fervent Prayer Petition to Dakinis (pp. 73–88)

6

rigs ldan ma mchod pa dang bdud rtsi mchod pa'i gsal byed la/

An Offering to Dakinis and an Elucidation of the Nectar Offering (pp. 89–94)

7

rigs ldan ma rnams mchod bstod kyi rim pa las bzhi lhun grub la/

A Spontaneous Accomplishment of the Four Activities: Offering Rites and Praises to Dakinis (pp. 95–99)

8

bdud mo nyi shar me long gi sgos sgrub srog gi spu gri la/

A Sword of Life: A Personal Sadhana of Dudmo Nyishar Melong (pp. 101–105)

9

dag snang mkha' 'gro'i thugs bcud las/khyung btsun gung rgyal sgrub bskor la/

A Circle of Practices of Khyungtsun Gunggyal Belonging to the Heart Essence of the Dakinis—from Pure Vision (pp. 107–109)

10

jo mo kha rag dang /gung rgyal gyi sgrub skor 'phrul gyi me long la/

A Miraculous Mirror: A Circle of Practices of Jomo Kharag and Gunggyal (pp. 111–117)

11

srog sgrub rang byung rgyal mo/dung skyong ma/bdud mo re ma ti gsum gyi srog gtad bya tshul 'jug bde'i lam bzang la/

A Convenient Noble Path: How to Entrust Oneself to Sogdrub Rangjung Gyalmo, Dungkyong Ma and Dudmo Remati (pp. 119–125)

12

dag snang rigs ldan ma rnams kyi sgrub thabs dang sgrub thabs kyi zur rgyan la/

A Sadhana of Dakinis—from Pure Vision, and Appendices to the Sadhana (pp. 127–135)

13

dag snang tshangs pa dang Od ldan dkar po'i sgrub thabs/ye shes grags pa'i rna mnyan/rgyal po las la bskul pa'i phan byed dag snang rgyal rdzongs kyi le'u mtshan la/

Sadhanas of Tsangpa and Odden Karpo—from Pure Vision, an Ear-Adornment of Yeshe Dragpa and a Chapter on Sending Off Gyalpo: The Benefit of Requesting Gyalpo to Perform the Necessary Activities—from Pure Vision (pp. 137–145)

14

dag snang lha chen gyi sgrub skor las tshogs rdzogs rim gcig chog srog sdud chen po la/

A Great Gathering of Life Energy: Combining the Completion Stage, Tsok and Practices of Lhachen from Pure Vision (pp. 147–152)

15

drang srong gi yum duk+ti ka'i sgrub rim gu h+yaO/

Stages of Practices of Dugti Ka, Mother of the Black Wrathful Brahmin (pp. 153–158)

16

dag snang drang srong gi sgrub skor las bzhi'i 'byung gnas la/

Source of the Four Activities in the Practice of Drang Song—from Pure Vision (pp. 159–171)

17

gsang bdag drang srong lok+t+ri zhi khro'i bsnyen yig gces nor mthar thug la/

A Most Precious Resource: A Retreat Manual of a Peaceful and Wrathful Deity, the Secret Lord Brahmin Loktri (pp. 173–326)

18

drang srong khro gtum nag po'i bskang ba la/

A Propitiation Rite of the Black Wrathful Brahmin (pp. 327–330)

19

drang srong khro gtum nag po'i rgyun khyer dang /dag snang drang srong gi las bzhi chig dril gyi dbang chog

A Rite of Empowerment Integrating the Four Activities of the Black Wrathful Brahmin—from Pure Vision, and a Daily Practice of the Brahmin (pp. 331–337)

20

nA ga rak+sha Og gdon mthar byed kyi bsnyen sgrub las gsum gyi rnam gzhag gsal bar byed pa dug sel bdud rtsi'i snying po la/

An Essence of Nectar for Eliminating Poison: An Elucidation of the Retreat, Practice and Activities of Naga Ragsha to be Freed from the Underground Demon Nagas (pp. 339–425)

25

zhing skyong ma'i las mtha' drag po'i 'phrin las gnam lcags ur mo'i khang bu la/

An Iron House: Wrathful Beneficial Activity of Zhingkyong Ma's Concluding Action (pp. 25–32)

26

dag snang srog bdud ma mo'i le lag gi las phran nyams su blang tshul la/

How to Practice Auxiliary Activities of the Retinue of Sogdud Mamo—from Pure Vision (pp. 33–52)

27

dag snang srog bdud ma mo'i chos skor gyi le lag las las phran sgrub thabs skal bzang 'jug ngogs la/

Entry of the Fortunate Ones: A Sadhana of Auxilary Activities of the Retinue, Belonging to the Secondary Discourses of Sogdud Mamo—from Pure Vision (pp. 53–60)

28

dpal ldan dmag zor rgyal mo'i las tshogs do shal mdzes rgyan la/

A Beautiful Ornamental Garland: A Host of Activities of Glorious Palden Magzor Gyalmo (pp. 61–68)

29

zhing skyong ma mo lang+ka'i dbang phyug gi sgrub thabs gnam lcags spu gri ngar ma la/

A Sharp Sword of Meteoric Iron: A Sadhana of Zhingkyong Mamo Langka Wangchuk (pp. 69–85)

30

dag snang du byung ba'i zhing skyong ma mched gnyis kyi gsol mchod la/

A Supplication and Offering to the Two Sisters of Zhingkyong Ma Who Appeared in Pure Vision (pp. 87–90)

31

zhing skyong ma mched gnyis kyi mchod 'phrin bde chen myur lam 'dod dgu'i rgya mtsho la/

A Fulfilling Ocean and Quick Path to Great Bliss: Offering and Propitiation to the Two Sisters of Zhingkyong Ma (pp. 91–102)

32

zhing skyong ma phyi nang gsang gsum gyi srog gtad rdo rje'i bdud rtsi dang dag snang tsaN+Di ka'i srog gtad la/

Vajra Nectar: Entrusting Oneself to Zhingkyong Ma's Outer, Inner and Secret Dimensions, and to Chandika—from Pure Vision (pp. 105–109)

33

lha gcig nyi ma mun sel gyis gnang ba'i man ngag 'khyer bde gsum dril la/

A Convenient Collection of Three Quintessential Instructions of Lhacig Nyima Munsel (pp. 111–114)

34

zhing skyong ma gsang sgrub kyi sgrub skor sbrang rtsi'i bum bzang la/

An Excellent Vase of Nectar: Practices for Accomplishing Secret Zhingkyong Ma (pp. 115–121)

35

zhing skyong mas dag snang du stsal ba'i man ngag (skor tsho lnga'i)

A Vital Essence of Vajra: Quintessential Instructions (Five Sets of Pith Instructions Given by Zhingkyong Ma in Pure Vision (pp. 123–133)

36

dag snang btsan rgod kyi sgrub skor la/mkha' 'gro phyi nang gsang gsum gyi sgrub thabs la/

A Sadhana of Dakinis' Outer, Inner, and Secret Dimensions from the Set of Practices of Tsangoe—from Pure Vision (pp. 135–144)

37

zhing skyong nyi ma mun sel gyi sgo nas tshe sgrub srog bcud 'gug byed dang dag snang bsu bzlog la/

Longevity and Enriching the Life Essence through the Rite of Zhingkyong Nyima Munsel, and Eliminating Obstacles—from Pure Vision (pp. 145–155)

38

mkha' 'gro phyi nang gsang gsum btsan rgod dang bcas pa'i las tshogs don gnyis mchog stsol la/

Granting the Dual Supreme Purpose: A Host of Activities of Dakinis' Outer, Inner, and Secret Dimensions, and of Tsangoe (pp. 157–177)

39

thabs mchog dpa' bo'i gsol 'debs la/'di'i sho bu gsum pa'i rgyab par chad 'dug

A Supplication to Thabchog Pawo (the reverse side of page 3 of this text is blank) (pp. 179–186)

40

dag snang rigs lnga'i mkha' 'gro'i mdos chog dgyes skong mchod sprin la/

A Cloud of Delightful Offerings: A Crossed-Thread Ritual Offering to the Dakinis of the Five Buddha Families—from Pure Vision (pp. 187–199)

41

dag snang mkha' spyod ma dkar mo'i man ngag rnams kyi gsal byed phan bde'i srog stsol la/

Bestowing Benefits and Happiness in Life: A Commentary on the Quintessential Instructions of White Vajrayogini—from Pure Vision (pp. 201–227)

42

dag snang rigs lnga'i mkha' 'gro'i sgrub thabs dbang chog dang bcas pa Od lnga'i tshom bu mchog bde'i myur lam la/

A Quick Path for Supreme Bliss and a Halo of Five Colored Lights: A Sadhana and Rites of Empowerment of the Dakinis of the Five Buddha Families—from Pure Vision (pp. 229–243)

43

lha gcig nyi ma gzhon nu'i bka' drin rjes dran gyi rnam bshad skal bzang rgya mtsho'i khang bzang la/

An Ocean-Side Mansion of the Fortunate Ones: A Detailed Explanation of Remembering the Kindnesses of Lhacig Nyima Zhonnu (pp. 245–427)

44

legs ldan tshogs rje chen po'i zor gyi las mtha' thog mda'i bu yug ces bya ba la/

Lightning and a Blizzard: Malign Torma Activities of Legdan Tsogje Chepo (pp. 429–449)

45

lha gcig nyi ma gzhon nu'i bskang gso rgyas pa 'phrul gyi sgo 'byed la/

Opening the Door to Miracles: A Long Version of the Propitiation Rites of Lhacig Nyima Zhonnu (pp. 451–489)

46

rdo rje g.yu sgron ma'i phyi nang gsang gsum gyi sreg chog dag byed rgya mtsho'am srid gsum yid 'gul du 'bod pa la/

Purifying an Ocean or Delighting the Three Realms: A Fire Offering Ritual of Dorje Yudon's Outer, Inner, and Secret Dimensions (pp. 491–501)

VOLUME TWELVE

47

dag snang ge sar gyi gtam rgyud le'u la/

Chapters of Narrative about Gesar—from Pure Vision (pp. 1–9)

48

ge sar rgyal po dpon blon gyi gsol mchod dus mtha'i dbugs 'byin la/

Relief at an Era's End: A Supplication and Offering to King Gesar and His Ministers (pp. 11–19)

49

dag snang ge sar gyi man ngag skor tsho gsum pa la/

The Third Set of Quintessential Instructions of Gesar—from Pure Vision (pp. 21–27)

50

dag snang dmag zor ma'i las tshogs nor bu'i do shal la/

A Garland of Jewels: A Host of Activities of Magzorma—from Pure Vision (pp. 29–32)

51

gter bdag chen po rdzong btsan pa'i bskang ba rgyas pa gang 'dod mchog stsol la/

Granting Supreme Wishes: A Long Version of the Propitiation Rites of Dzong Tsan Pa, the Great Lord of Treasure (pp. 33–58)

52

lha mchog srid gsum gyi bdag po tshangs pa chen po'i bskang gso chen mo las bzhi'i rgya mtsho la/

An Ocean of the Four Activities: Great Propitiation Rites of Great Tsangpa, the Supreme Protector and Lord of the Three Realms (pp. 59–96)

53

zhing skyong 'bar ma srog bdud nag mo'i gtor bzlog gi las rim mngon spyod 'phrul mdzod la/

A Miraculous Treasure of Fierce Activities: Black Zhingkyong Barma Sogdud's Ritual Cake Activity Rites for Removing Obstacles (pp. 97–122)

54

drag sgrub 'phrul gyi lding khang gi lhan thabs la/

Appendices to a Sadhana of the Wrathful Aspect of the Miraculous Hanging House (pp. 123–130)

55

dag snang gnod sbyin chen po'i sgrub skor mtshon brgya'i 'khrul 'khor la/

A Wheel of 100 Weapons: Practices of Maha Yaksha—from Pure Vision (pp. 131–142)

56

skrag med nyi shar gyi srog gtad kyi cho ga 'jug bde'i mtshams sbyor la/

A Convenient Engagement: Rites of Entrusting Oneself to Tragme Nyishar (pp. 143–152)

57

dag snang btsan rgod las la bskul ba'i rim pa dang cig car dmar po'i gsol kha la/

A Propitiation of Red Chigchar and Procedure for Motivating Tsangoe to Act—from Pure Vision (pp. 153–160)

58

gnod sbyin chen po'i gsol bskul dag snang ma la/

A Propitiation of Maha Yaksha—from Pure Vision (pp. 161–166)

59

dag snang HUM sgrub kyi rgyun khyer la/

A Daily Practice of Actualising Hung—from Pure Vision (pp. 167–169)

60

bzhad pa'i rdo rje'i gsang sgrub snying por dril ba la/

The Essence of Integrating the Secret Practice of Zhadpai Dorje (pp. 171–175)

61

bzhad pa'i rdo rje'i phyi nang gsang gsum gyi sgrub skor/

Regarding Practices of the Outer, Inner, and Secret Dimensions of Zhadpai Dorje (pp. 177–179)

62

dag snang mkha' 'gro'i thugs bcud las/lnga ldan Od lnga'i lam bzang la/

The Noble Path of the Five Possessions of the Five Lights from the Heart Essence of Dakinis—from Pure Vision (pp. 181–192)

63

dag snang bla ma rdo rje thod pa rtsal gyi rgyun khyer/dag snang yang dag he ru ka'i sgrub thabs/sman gyi bla ma'i sgom bzlas dag snang rgyun khyer la/

A Daily Practice of Lama Dorje Thodpa Tsel—from Pure Vision, A Sadhana of Perfect Heruka—from Pure Vision, and a Daily Meditation and Recitation of the Medicine Buddha—from Pure Vision (pp. 193–200)

64

dag snang gsang bdag gtum po gtso 'khor gsum pa'i sgrub thabs la/

A Sadhana of Wrathful Vajrapani and his Two Principal Attendants —from Pure Vision (pp. 201–206)

65

dag snang mkha' 'gro'i chos bskor las/gsang bdag gtum po'i sgrub thabs la/

A Sadhana of Wrathful Vajrapani from the Collection of Discourses of Dakinis—from Pure Vision (pp. 207–210)

66

dag snang 'chi med dpal ster gyi dbang chog tshe bcud sbrang rtsi la/

A Shower of Life Essence: Rites of Empowerment of Amitayus— from Pure Vision (pp. 211–218)

67

mtsho rgyal 'gro ba kun 'dul gyi byin rlabs kyi cho ga skal bzang snang byed dang zhing skyong gi man ngag la/

Illumination for the Fortunate Ones: Rites of Blessing of Tsogyal Drowa Kundul and Quintessential Instructions of Zhingkyong (pp. 219–226)

68

bde ldan ma'i sgrub tāhabs byin rlabs rgyun khyer 'phrin las kha skong 'jug bde la/

A Sadhana of Deden Ma: A Daily Blessing and Appendix of Con- venient Activities (pp. 227–239)

69

lha gcig gi dril sgrub rtsa gsum thig le'i bsnyen yig snang ba'i sgo 'byed la/

Opening a Door to the Light: A Retreat Manual of the Essence of the Three Roots Combined Sadhana of Lhachig (pp. 241–260)

70

zhing skyong ma nyi gzhon gur kum gyi rigs gtad kyi cho ga la/

Rites of Knowledge Entrustment of the Lineage of Zhingkyong Ma Nyishon Gurkum (pp. 263–270)

77

dag snang lha gcig nyi ma gzhon nu'i dril sgrub rtsa gsum thig le'i dbang chog la/

Rites of Empowerment of an Essence of the Three Roots Combined Sadhana of Lhachig Nyima Zhonnu—from Pure Vision (pp. 317–324)

78

mthong grol sku rten rnam gnyis la brten pa'i don gnyis sgrub tshul dgongs gter snying po la/

An Essence of Thought Treasure: How to Accomplish the Dual Purpose Relying upon the Liberating Visions of Two Precious Statues[149] (pp. 325–350)

79

gcod kyi gdams pa snying por dril ba mnyam nyid blo bde la/

Equal Satisfaction: An Essence of Cutting through Instructions (pp. 351–361)

80

lha gcig gi dag snang du stsal ba'i thabs lam nyi zla'i bcud len dang brgyud 'debs la/

A Skilful Path of Extracting the Essences of the Sun and the Moon Presented in a Pure Vision by Lhachig, and a Lineage Supplication (pp. 363–370)

---

[149] The statues of Guru Rinpoche and Yeshe Tsogyal.

81

zhing skyong ma nyi ma mun sel gyi pra 'bebs dang Od gsal gyi gdams pa las tshogs nye lam mchog gcig las tshogs thor bu la/

A Divination of Zhingkyong Nyima Munsel and a Miscellaneous Collection of Activities of the Swift and Supreme Path, from Instructions on Clear Light (pp. 371–384)

82

sde brgyad gnod bzlog phan bde'i dga' ston la/

A Beneficial and Joyous Festivity: Warding Off the Eight Classes of Demons (pp. 385–388)

83

dag snang bstan srung rgya mtsho'i rten rdzas bca' thabs kyi man ngag gsal bar byed pa gcig shes kun grol la/

Liberation from Knowing One Point: An Elucidation of the Quintessential Instructions on how to Prepare the Holy Ingredients for an Ocean of Dharma Protectors—from Pure Vision (pp. 389–412)

84

sgos kyi bstan srung rgya mtsho rnams la gser skyems 'bul ba'i rim pa/

Procedures for Making Golden Libation Offerings to an Ocean of Personal Dharma Protectors (pp. 413–416)

85

lha gcig nyi ma mun sel gyi gnang ba'i 'khrul pa rtsad gcod kyi man ngag rnam rtog 'ur 'ded la/

Chasing away Discursive Thoughts: Quintessential Instructions for Cutting Through Misconceptions, Given by Lhachig Nyima Munsel (pp. 417–422)

86

lo skor bcu gnyis la brten pa'i bsu zlog tshe sbyin yid bzhin nor bu la/

A Wish-Fulfilling Jewel of Longevity: Getting Rid of Obstacles Related to the Twelve Birth Signs (pp. 423–434)

87

bstan srung rnams la zhabs brtan 'bul tshul gyi cho ga srog bcud rgyas 'debs la/

Enhancing Life Energy: Rites of Requesting Dharma Protectors to Remain for a Long Period (pp. 435–439)

88

zhing skyong lha mos man ngag skor tsho lnga pa dang lhan cig tu gsungs pa'i them byang chen mo la/

Instructions Given by Zhingkyong Lhamo along with the Five Sets of Quintessential Instructions (pp. 441–445)

89

zhing skyong 'bar ma chen mo'i mdos bskang bka' srung dgyes byed la/

Delighting Protectors: Crossed-Thread Propitiation Rituals of Great Zhingkyong Barma (pp. 447–451)

90

mthong grol sku rten rnam gnyis kyi las tshogs dgongs gter yang gsal la/

The Ultimate Elucidation of a Host of Activities of the Two Precious Statues (pp. 451–483)

91

mtsho rgyal 'gro ba kun 'dul gyi phyi sgrub thabs mchog myur lam la/

A Supreme and Speedy Path: Accomplishing the Outer Sadhana of Tsogyal Drowa Kundul (pp. 485–506)

92

dag snang btsan rgod kyi las mtha' las bzhi'i phrin las gang sgrub kyang shin tu myur ba'i zab lam gsal byed me long la/

A Magnifying Mirror: A Profound and Very Speedy Path for Accomplishing Any of the Four Activities of Tsangoe—from Pure Vision (pp. 507–516)

93

lha gcig gi dril sgrub rtsa gsum thig le'i zur 'debs/

Appendices to an Integrated Practice of the three Roots Combined Sadhana of Lhachig (pp. 517–524)

94

dag snang seng gdong ma dmar mo'i las tshogs srid zhi'i mchog ster dang dbang chog dpyid kyi pho nya la/

A Spring Messenger: An Empowerment of the Red Lion-Faced Dakini and her Host of Activities Known as "Granting the Best of Samsara and Nirvana"—from Pure Vision (pp. 525–530)

95

dag snang mkha' 'gro'i chos skor las/seng gdong ma dmar mo'i sgrub skor la/

Regarding the Practice of the Red Lion-Faced Dakini from the Collection of Discourses of Dakinis—from Pure Vision (pp. 531–535)

96

seng gdong dmar mo'i bsnyen sgrub kyi gsal byed nyi ma'i Od zer la/

Rays of Solar Illumination: A Commentary on Retreat Practices of the Red Lion-Faced Dakini (pp. 537–543)

97

gter bdag 'bar ba spun bdun gyi las tshogs rdo rje'i gsang tshig la/

Secret Vajra Words: A Host of Activities of the Seven Siblings of Treasure Lord Barwa (pp. 546–566)

98

btsan rgod 'bar ba spun bdun gyi bsreg pa me'i las sbyor gyi cho ga reg 'joms me zhun la/

Consuming Flames: Fire Offering Activity Rituals of the Seven Siblings of Tsangoe Barwa (pp. 567–584)

99

rkyen ngan lam khyer gyi man ngag thar lam rab gsal/

A Clear Illumination of the Path of Liberation: A Quintessential Instruction on Taking Adverse Conditions into the Path (pp. 585–592)

100

dbang bzhi bdud rtsi bum pa'i dbang chog dang 'bras bu bdun pa'i khrid yig snying dril la/

Integrated Essence: An Explanatory Commentary on the Seven Results and Rites of the Four Empowerment Nectar Vase (pp. 593–604)

106

bskang ba thol byung dgyes skongs snyan pa'i glu dbyangs dang zhing skyong sgrol ma lha mdzes dmar bshal ma'i gsol kha la/

A Spontaneous and Delightfully Enchanting Propitiation and Petition Offering to Zhingkyong Red Dolma Lhaze (pp. 57–62)

107

dag snang lha gcig nyi ma gnyon nu'i nor sgrub la/

A Wealth Accomplishment of Lhachig Nyima Zhonnu—from Pure Vision (pp. 63–67)

108

zhing skyong nyi gzhon gur kum ma'i man ngag gam+b+hi ra la/

A Quintessential Instruction of Zhingkyong Nyima Zhonnu Gurkum Ma (pp. 69–70)

109

dag snang tshe sgrub nyi zla'i srog 'dzin la/

Harnessing Life Energy from the Sun and Moon: Longevity Rites —from Pure Vision (pp. 71–86)

110

zhing skyong 'bar ma srog bdud nag mo'i sgrub skor byung tshul gyi lo rgyus ngo mtshar mdzes rgyan la/

An Account of the Origin of the Practice of Black Zhingkyong Barma Sogdud (pp. 87–96)

111

rgyud sde thams cad kyi mthar thug Od gsal rdzogs pa chen po'i man ngag gi yang bcud mkha' 'gro yang tig gi dbang chog mtha' yas 'gro phan la/

Limitless Benefits for Sentient Beings: Rites of Empowerment of Dakini Yangtig, the Innermost Essence of the Quintessential

> Instruction on the Great Completion of Clear Light—the Ultimate Tantra (pp. 97–467)

112

> *dgra lha'i rgyal po gnod sbyin tsi'u dmar po ya ba skya bdun gyi bskang gso chen mo 'dod dgu'i nyin byed la/*

> *A Wish-Fulfilling Sun: Extensive Propitiation Rites of the Seven Siblings, including Red Yaksha Tse'u, King of Dralha* (pp. 469–511)

113

> *rgyo 'dod skeus bu'i gdung sel/*

> *Eliminating the Desire of Lustful Individuals* (pp. 1–13 in Tibetan page numbering)

114

> *khros nag gi las byang zab don snying po'i rgya mtsho/dpe ma rnyed/*

> *An Ocean of Profound and Essential Meaning: Sadhana Instructions of Tronag* [text missing]

115

> *las tshogs thor bu rnams/dpe ma rnyed/*

> *A Collection of Miscellaneous Activities* [text missing]

116

> *gsang bdag bla ma'i phyi nang gsang gsum gyi rnal 'byor dang rgyun 'khyer/dpe ma rnyed/*

> *A Daily Practice and Outer, Inner, and Secret Yogas of Sangdag Lama* [text missing]

117

> *rje drung blo bzang 'phrin las kyi don bdun cu/*

> *Jedrung Losang Trinley's Texts on the Seventy Topics* [pages missing]

118

gnas yig dang lo rgyus dpar du 'khod pa rnams kyi dkar chag bkod pa/

A Catalogue of Published Guides to Pilgrimage Sites and their Histories (pp. 1–2)

119

rdo rje 'dzin pa che mchog 'dus pa rtsal gyi rnam thar las 'phros pa byung ba brjod pa gdung ba'i mun sel/

Eliminating Agonizing Darkness: Events from the Life Story of Vajra Master Chechog Duspa Tsel

120

lha mi'i ston pa shAkya'i rgyal po'i rnam thar mdor bsdus/

A Short Biography of Buddha Shakyamuni, Teacher of Gods and Humans

121

lha mo gtad dkar 'gro bzang ma'i mchod phrin kun bzang 'dod yon zur rgyan dang bcas pa la/

A Samantabhadra Sensory Enjoyment Offering: Offering and Invocation Rituals of Goddess Tedkar Drozang Ma along with an Appendix (34 pages)

122

lha mo'i gtor sgrub kyi zin bris lag len 'khrul med la/

An Authentic Note-Commentary to Engage in Attaining Palden Lhamo by Offering Ritual Cakes (16 pages)

123

'jam dpal nag po'i rjes gnang la/

A Permission Blessing Ritual of Black Manjushri (10 pages)

Appendix III. Lamp of Universal Illumination: A Catalogue of Scriptures on Khandro Sangwa Yeshe[150]

VOLUME KA

KA

dkar chag kun gsal sgron me la/

A Catalogue Entitled "Lamp of Universal Illumination" (6 pages)

KHA

gter gzhung rtsa ba'i lo rgyus la/

Accounts of Root Treasure Texts (2 pages)

GA

gter gzhung rtsa ba'i sgrub thabs la/

A Sadhana from a Root Treasure Text (6 pages)

NGA

gter gzhung rtsa ba'i byin rlabs la/

Blessings from a Root Treasure Text (3 pages)

CA

gter gzhung rtsa ba'i bstod bskul la/

Praises from a Root Treasure Text (2 pages)

CHA

gter gzhung rtsa ba'i me mchod la/

A Fire Offering from a Root Treasure Text (2 pages)

---

[150] *Sang ye'i par gyi kar chag kun sel dron me zhes ja wa zhug so.*

JA

gter gzhung rtsa ba'i dam tshig gnad thems la/

Vital Points of Samayas from a Root Treasure Text (2 pages)

NYA

gter gzhung rtsa ba'i rnal 'byor rim bzhin la/

The Four Stages of Yoga from a Root Treasure Text (5 pages)

TA

rigs sras 'gyur med rgya mtshos mdzad pa'i gsang ye'i rgyun khyer snying po la/

An Essential Daily Practice of Sangwa Yeshe by the Gyurme Gyatso Son of the Mindrolling Lineage (3 pages)

THA

des mdzad pa'i bsnyen yig grub gnyis gter mdzod la/

A Treasure House of Two Accomplishments: Retreat Manual by the Son Gyurme Gyatso Lineage (9 pages)

DA

dge slong khrid gnyer pas mdzad pa'i rdzogs rim kyi 'khrid mkha' spyod bde ba'i dpal ster la/

Granting the Glory of Vajrayogini's Pure Land: A Commentary on the Completion Stage by Bhikshu Trid Nyer (21 pages)

NA

ngag rtsoms bskyed rim gyi rnam bshad snying po'i mchog sbyin legs bshad rgya mtsho la/

An Ocean of Excellent Explanation Granting the Supreme Essence: *A Commentary on the Generation Stage by Lelung Zhepai Dorje* (99 pages)

PA

rdzogs rim rnal 'byor bzhi'i rnam bshad rdo rje'i gsal byed la/

A Vajra Elucidation: A Commentary on the Four Yogas of the Completion Stage (203 pages)

VOLUME KHA

PHA

gzhi lam 'bras gsum gyi rnam bshad rdo rje'i sgron me la/

Vajra Light: A Commentary on the Ground, Path, and Fruition (75 pages)

BA

dbang chog nag po 'gro shes su bkod pa go sla don gsal/

Clearly Comprehensible Meaning: An Orderly Guide to Rites of Empowerment (176 pages)

MA

sgrub pa'i khog dbug chu zla'i gar mkhan la/

A Performance of Moon Reflections on Water: A Sadhana Framework (72 pages)

CA

sman sgrub kyi ngag 'don bklags pas kun shes la/

Understanding All through Reading: A Medicine Buddha Sadhana (24 pages)

TSHA

dud 'gro shi gson la phan pa'i man ngag ngan song dag byed la/

Purifying the Lower Realms: Quintessential Instructions for Bene-fiting Living and Dead Animals (11 pages)

DZA

las bzhi'i man ngag gcig shes kun grol la/

Knowing One Liberates All: A Quintessential Instruction on the Four Activities (14 pages)

WA

dmigs skor byed tshul nyams bzhes gsal byed la/

A Clarification of Visualization Practice (9 pages)

ZHA

sngags kyi rgyas bsdebs 'khrul 'khor thig le la/

A Drop of a Magic Wheel: An Explanation that Goes with the Mantra (17 pages)

ZA

bsnyen sgrub la mkho ba'i chos tshan la/

Required Texts for Intensive Retreat Practice (7 pages)

(Ga)

'A

rigs drug gnas 'dren gyi cho ga khams gsum dong sprugs la/

Shaking The Tree of the Three Realms: Rites of Liberating the Six Classes of Beings (32 pages)

YA

phrin las kyi le lag srog gi skyabs gcig la/

The Sole Refuge of Life: Auxiliary Practices of Beneficial Activity (57 pages)

RA

'chi blu srog gi bcud len la/

Extracting the Life Essence: Saving Life (7 pages)

LA

phrin las kyi le lag ngal bso'i bang mdzod la/

A Treasure of Relief: Auxiliary Practices of Beneficial Activity (24 pages)

SHA

gnas lung gi rnam bshad mkha' spyod snang ba'i mdzes rgyan la/

A Beautiful Ornament Presenting Dakini Land: A Commentary on Pilgrimage Sites (34 pages)

SA

gnas lung gi cho ga mkha' spyod snang ba la/

Viewing Dakini Land: Pilgrimage Site Rituals (13 pages)

HA

bsnyen yig dran pa'i gsal byed la/

Clear Remembrance: A Retreat Manual (4 pages)

A

grib sel rdo rje'i bum bzang la/

A Noble Vajra Vase: Eliminating Obstacles (41 pages)

KI

byad 'grol chang khrus ma'i man ngag la/

A Quintessential Instruction on Cleansing with Beer: Liberation from Black Magic (4 pages)

KHI

sde brgyad kyi dug dbyung byed tshul rdo rje'i snying po la/

Vajra Essence: How to Eliminate the Poisons of the Eight Harmful Agents (23 pages)

GI

phrin las kyi le lag mngon shes mkha' 'gro lnga skor la/

Discourses on Five Types of Clairvoyance Achieved through the Five Dakinis: Auxiliary Practices of Beneficial Activities (8 pages)

NGI

lo dgra'i 'jigs pa srung thabs sprin phung rgya mtsho la/

An Ocean of Clouds: Methods to Protect Oneself from Adversaries for the Year (32 pages)

CI

char 'bebs sprin phung snying po la/

An Essence of Clouds: A Downpour of Rain (9 pages)

CHI

char 'bebs pa'i man ngag gi mde'u gnad kyi snying po la/

Hitting the Target: A Quintessential Instruction to Bring about Rainfall (13 pages)

JI

sad bsrung ba'i man ngag sprin gyi gur khang la/

A Dome of Clouds: A Quintessential Instruction on Protecting Crops from Cold Climatic Conditions (8 pages)

NYI

ser bsrung nyi ma'i dkyil 'khor la/

A Sun Disc: Protection from Hailstorms (8 pages)

TI

chu bsgyur gyi man ngag rdo rje'i chu lon la/

A Vajra Dam: A Quintessential Instruction on Diverting Water (7 pages)

THI

res gza' btson 'dzin dang rmu sgab gtong tshul gza' bdun mchod thabs drang srong tshim byed rnams la/

Delighting the Brahmins and Making Offerings to the Seven Planets: Binding the Planets and also Performing Sorcery (9 pages)

DI

glud chog gtong tshul la/

How to Conduct the Rite of Discarding an Effigy (8 pages)

NI

sbyin sreg zur rgyan dus me'i khang bu la/

End of the World Conflagration: Appendices to the Fire Offering Rituals (17 pages)

PI

las bzhi'i sbyin sreg mthong bas kun grol la/

Liberation through Seeing: Fire Offering Rituals of the Four Activities (20 pages)

VOLUME NGA

PHI

rab tu gnas pa'i cho ga tshangs pa'i rnga sgra la/

The Sound of Brahma's Drum: Rites of Consecration (19 pages)

BI

skra chog dag byed bdud rtsi la/

Nectar: Purifying Activities through Hair Rituals (6 pages)

MI

bskang bshags rgyas 'bring gnyis la/

Extensive and Medium-Sized Versions of Confession and Propitiation Texts (22 pages)

TSI

bskang bshags bsdus pa la/

A Short (Version of) Propitiation (4 pages)

TSHI

dam tshig gi rnam bshad rdo rje'i rgyud mang la/

Multiple Vajra Strigs: A Commentary on Commitments (14 pages)

DZI

las bzhi'i kha bsgyur dgos 'dod snying po la/

A Core of Wishes: Transformation through the Four Activities (22 pages)

WI

mi kha khrom bsgyur gyi las mtha' bdud rtsi'i rgyun 'bab la/

A Stream of Nectar: An Activity to Clear Away People's Verbal Attacks (7 pages)

ZHI

las byang nag 'gros mkha' spyod lam bzang bklags chog tu bkod pa la/

A Straightforward Presentation of the Rites of the Activities of Vajrayogini's Noble Path (34 pages)

ZI

'pho ba dpag chen 'phrul mdzod la/

A Miraculous Treasure: Speedy Transference of Consciousness (3 pages)

'I

bslab bya gdung sel sgron me la/

A Lamp of Advice to Dispel Mental Agony (9 pages)

YI

bde thabs kyi man ngag gsal bar byed pa 'dod dgu'i gter chen la/

A Wish-Fulfilling Treasure: Clarification of a Pith Instruction for Attaining Happiness (49 pages)

RI

bla blu nor bu'i snying po la/

An Innermost Jewel for Life Energy (27 pages)

LI

dam tshig gi snang brnyan bzhengs tshul kun gsal sgron me la/

Universal Light: How to Paint a Samaya Deity's Image (13 pages)

SHI

bdag 'jug len tshul bya sla 'khyer bde la/

An Easy and Portable Practice: How to Receive Self-Empowerment

SI

dkyil chog gi lhan thabs mkha' spyod gsang lam bklags chog tu bkod pa la/

A Straightforward Presentation of Vajrayogini's Secret Path: Appendices to Mandala Rituals (9 pages)

HI

thugs rje chen po bde gshegs kun 'dus kyi gtor dbang bskur tshul bgrod bde'i lam bzang la/

A Convenient and Noble Path: How to Bestow the Empowerment of the Ritual Cakes of Avalokiteshvara, Embodiment of all the Buddhas (10 pages)

I

klu gta' bsdam pa'i cho ga bdud rtsi'i char 'bebs 'chi med lam yangs la/

A Showerl of Nectar and a Spacious, Immortal Path: Rites to Bind Nagas to Oath (29 pages)

KU

klu'i gdon 'grol bya tshul bdud rtsi'i rgyun 'bab la/

A Nectar Stream: How to Recover from a Naga's Negative Actions (21 pages)

KHU

char 'bebs kyi mde'u klu'i me long la/

A Naga's All-Seeing Mirror: An Arrow-Like Ritual to Cause Rainfall (4 pages)

GU

ldang ba'i rnal 'byor rdo rje'i snying po la/

Vajra Essence: A Yoga for the State of Waking (5 pages)

NGU

phreng ba'i de nyid srid zhi'i mun sel la/

Eliminating the Darknesses of Samsara and Solitary Peace: Vital Points of the Garland (22 pages)

CU

thun drug gi rnal 'byor bya tshul gnad 'gag kun 'dus la/

A Compendium of All Vital Points: How to Practice Six-Session Yoga (2 pages)

CHU

de'i gsal byed rgyus can drang po la/

Honest Spiritual Expertise: Elucidation of a Compendium of all the Vital Points of Six-Session Yoga (4 pages)

VOLUME CA

JU

skyabs 'gro'i rnam bshad rgyal ba'i dgongs bcud la/

An Essence of Buddha's Thought: A Commentary on Taking Refuge (440 pages)

VOLUME CHA

NYU

zab khrid kyi stong thun blo gsal mig 'byed la/

Opening the Eyes of Intelligent Ones: A Profound Commentary with Thousands of Meanings (4 pages)

TU

me 'brug khrid chen mo'i sngon 'gro rdo rje'i stong thun la/

A Thousandfold Vajra Session: A Preliminary to the Great Commentary of the Fire Dragon Year (64 pages)

THU

bskyed rim gyi rtsa tshig dang po'i zungs 'dzin la/

Cherishing the Primordial Essence: Root Verses of the Generation Stage (2 pages)

DU

bskyed rim gyi sa bcad mdor bsdus gti thug mun sel la/

Eliminating Thick Darkness: A Short Outline of the Generation Stage (4 pages)

NU

bskyed rim gyi dmigs rkang ngos 'dzin lus gnad gsal sgron la/

A Clear Lamp of the Essential Physical Points: Identification of the Vital Focus of the Visualization of the Generation Stage (19 pages)

PU

rnal 'byor rim bzhi'i man ngag gsal sgron la/

A Clear Lamp of the Quintessential Instruction on the Four Stages of Yoga (74 pages)

PHU

rdzogs rim gyi sa bcad mdor bsdus srog 'dzin snying por/

Cherishing the Life Essence: A Short Outline of the Completion Stage (3 pages)

BU

rdzogs rim gyi dmar khrid gnas lugs nyima la/

The Sun of Ultimate Meaning: An Experiential Commentary on the Completion Stage (14 pages)

MU

rdzogs rim gyi mtha' gcod sems kyi mun sel la/

Eliminating the Darkness of the Mind: A Final Analysis of the Completion Stage (7 pages)

TSU

a ti'i khrid yig klong chen yang rtse la/

A Pinnacle of Vastness: A Guide to Ati Yoga (38 pages)

TSHU

rdzogs rim dum dum gyi man ngag Od gsal 'khor lo la/

A Circle of Light: A Quintessential Instruction on the Vital Points of the Completion Stage (5 pages)

DZU

'dod chags sel thabs ltas ngan bzlog sgyur la/

The Transformation and Abandonment of Bad Omens: A Method of Eliminating Attachment (27 pages)

WU

zhe sdang lam khyer stong srog gcig 'joms la/

The Destruction of Innumerable Negativities at One Fell Swoop: Taking Anger into the Path (14 pages)

ZHU

bskyed rim gyi gsal byed snying por dril ba zab gsang sgo 'byed/

Opening the Door to Profundity and Integration: An Essence of Elucidations of the Generation Stage (12 pages)

ZU

brtag ril bsgril tshul dwangs shel rgya mtsho la/

A Crystal Ocean: How to Prepare Dough-Ball Divination (10 pages)

VOLUME JA

'U

sman sgrub gyi gsal byed zag med bcud 'dus la/

A Collection of Uncontaminated Tastes: An Elucidation of Blessed Medicine Accomplishment (77 pages)

YU

sman sgrub bya tshul tshig gcig don 'bum la

One Single Word but a Thousand Meanings: How to Accomplish Blessed Medicine (9 pages)

RU

bdud rtsi'i las tshogs zag med rgya mtsho la/

An Ocean of Uncontaminated Bliss: A Host of Activities with Nectar (25 pages)

LU

rak+ta'i las tshogs dmar chen rgya mtsho la/

A Red Ocean: A Host of Activities with Rakta (37 pages)

SHU

sin+ng+hu ra sgrub tshul gyi cho ga rdo rje'i bcud len la/

Extracting the Vajra Essence: Rites to Accomplish Sindhur (11 pages)

SU

b+h+ru rlung gi man ngag srog gi zungs 'dzin la/

Holding the Vitality of Life: A Quintessential Instruction on Hrulung (A Way of Holding Wind Energy)

HU

dza b+hir rlung khrid kyi gsal byed srog bcud bum bzang la/

A Noble Vase of Life Essence: An Elucidation of a Guide to Zabhir's Way of Holding Wind Energy (15 pages)

U

las tshogs za Og gur lding dpe ris dang bcas pa la/

A Host of Activities of ZaOg Gurding (A Hanging Silk Brocade Tent (with Accompanying Illustrations)

KE

bsu bzlog dang gdan bzhugs bya tshul rdo rje'i srog sbyin la/

Granting Vajra Life: How to Practice Eliminating Obstacles Causing Separation from the Protectors Combined with a Long-Life Ceremony (64 pages)

KHE

bsu bzlog bya tshul rdo rje'i ka chen la/

A Great Vajra Pillar: Eliminating Obstacles Causing Separation from the Protectors (40 pages)

GE

> ***bag chags stobs sbyong gi khrus chog rgya mtsho'i bcud thigs la/***
>
> *An Essential Drop of the Ocean: Rites of Purifying Powerful Latencies* (25 pages)

NGE

> ***nad bdag stobs 'joms kyi man ngag zla Od 'bum 'dzad la/***
>
> *A Shower of Innumerable Moon Rays: A Quintessential Instruction on Destroying the Powerful Lord of Sickness* (50 pages)

CE

> ***nad bdag stobs 'joms kyi man ngag don 'dus la/***
>
> *An Abbreviated Version of a Quintessential Instruction on Destroying the Lord of Sickness* (5 pages)

CHE

> ***nad yams bsrung bsad kyi man ngag rig 'dzin lugs bzang /***
>
> *A Noble Tradition of Tantric Practitioners': A Quintessential Instruction on Protection from and Elimination of Epidemics* (14 pages)

JE

> ***phyugs nad sel thabs rdo rje sbyin byed la/***
>
> *Granting a Vajra Blessing: A Method to Get Rid of Sickness in Animals* (4 pages)

NYE

> ***bka' nan rab brjid bya tshul rdo rje'i gnya' shing la/***
>
> *A Vajra Yoke: How to Perform Consecrations* (24 pages)

TE

> ***bka' nan rab brjid bya tshul rdo rje'i rwa gdengs la/***
>
> *A Vajra Threat: How to Perform Consecrations* (10 pages)

THE

'gong po ar gtad kyi chog sgrigs rngams pa'i lcags khang la/

A Frightening Iron House: A Compilation of Rituals to Subjugate the Evil Spirit from the East Gongpo Arted

DE

brgyad brngan bsangs dang bcas pa'i cho ga spos sprin rgya mtshor/

An Ocean of Incense Clouds: Rites of Food Offering (35 pages)

VOLUME NYA

NE

bsam pa lhun grub ma'i las tshogs thugs rje'i bum bzang la/

A Noble Vase of Kindness: A Host of Activities of Sampa Lhundrup (22 pages)

PE

gegs sel snying po'i mthar thug la/

The Ultimate Essence: Getting Rid of Obstacles (21 pages)

PHE

rten 'brel gyi bcos thabs 'ja' klong 'khyil pa la/

A Swirl of Rainbows: Treatment through Dependent Arising (21 pages)

BE

mnga' dbang rin chen 'bar ba bskur tshul gyi cho ga dbang phyug 'phrul mdzod la/

A Miraculous Treasure of a Powerful One: Rites of Conferring the Blazing Jewel Empowering Empowerment (23 pages)

ME

> *grib sel gyi man ngag phan bde'i rol mtsho la/*

> *An Ocean of Benefit and Happiness: A Quintessential Instruction on Purifying Obscurations* (13 pages)

TSE

> *'byung lnga'i sats+tsha 'debs chog 'phrul gsang lde mig la/*

> *A Key to Secret Miracles: How to Make Sa-Tsa of the Five Elements* (5 pages)

TSHE

> *ser bdag bcu gsum mchod thabs bdud rtsi gar bu la/*

> *Excellent Nectar: How to Make Offerings to the Thirteen Lords of Gold* (8 pages)

DZE

> *gsal 'debs dang 'pho ba'i man ngag gsal byed gtan gyi lam grogs/*

> *A Permanent Companion: An Elucidation of a Quintessential Instruction on Supplication and Transference of Consciousness* (123 pages)

WE

> *'pho ba'i man ngag bklags chog ma la/*

> *A Straightforward Practice: A Quintessential Instruction on Transference of Consciousness* (5 pages)

ZHE

> *sgrol ma phyag 'tshal nyer gcig gi man ngag 'gro phan don bsdus/*

> *A Compendium of Meanings and Benefits for Sentient Beings: A Quintessential Instruction on the Twenty-One Taras* (20 pages)

ZE

sgrol ma maN+Dal bzhi pa'i cho ga g.yu mtsho'i snying po la/

An Essence af a Torquoise Ocean: Rites of Offering to Tara with Four Mandalas (8 pages)

'E

'jigs pa brgyad skyob tu bsgrub pa'i cho ga rdo rje'i go cha la/

Vajra Armor: Rites to Accomplish Protection from the Eight Fears (3 pages)

YE

mdangs bskangs kyi cho ga Od lnga'i rgya mtsho la/

An Ocean of Five Lights: Rites of Fulfilling Confession and Propitiation (46 pages)

RE

skong bshags kyi cho ga grub gnyis 'dod 'jo la/

Granting the Two Accomplishments: Confession and Propitiation (32 pages)

LE

brgya bzhi'i cho ga rin chen khang bzang la/

A Jewel House: The Rituals of the Four Hundred Offerings (25 pages)

VOLUME TA

SHE

'gong nad sel thabs gzhan phan bdud rtsi la/

Nectar Benefiting Others: A Method to Eliminate Sickness Caused by Evil Spirits (10 pages)

SE

sems bskyed cho gas 'dzin tshul kun mkhyen lam bzang la/

The Noble Path of the Omniscient One: How to Hold Bodhicitta by Means of Rituals (6 pages)

HE

sems bskyed mchod pa bya tshul rlabs chen rgya mtsho la/

An Ocean of Benefit: How to Make Offerings for Bodhicitta (90 pages)

E

rgyal mo chu bzlog gi lag len gsal byed gnam lcags nyi ma'i 'phrul mdzod la/

A Miraculous Treasure of Sun and Metoric Iron: An Elucidation of the Flood-Preventing Practice Known as Gyalmo Chudhog (21 pages)

KO

kha 'bar ma dkar nag khra gsum la brten nas 'chi blu byad bzlog mi kha sel ba'i man ngag rdo rje'i 'gro phan la/

A Vajra Benefiting Beings: A Quintessential Instruction on Saving Life and Getting Rid of Evil Spirits and Curses while Depending on White, Black, and Multi-Color Khabar Ma (the Flaming Mouth Deity)

KHO

las tshogs ci 'dod rgyan shar la/

An Ornament of a Wish-Fulfilling Host of Activities (36 pages)

GO

dbang sdud kyi las mtha' 'phrul zhags btab tshad myur 'gugs/

A Miraculous Lassoo: A Host of Speedy and Effective Subjugation Activities (26 pages)

NGO

'phrul zhags btab tshad myur 'gugs kyi lcags kyu wam mig

An Iron Hook with an Eye Like the Letter Wom: Speedy and Effective Subjugation Activities (9 pages)

CO

nyi ma mdung gang ma'i man ngag dug sel gsal sgron la/

A Clear Lamp for Eliminating Poison: A Quintessential Instruction of Nyima Dung Gangma (Rahula)

CHO

'dar phyar lugs kyi gza'i byad 'grol rdo rje'i sor mo la/

A Vajra Nail: A Release from the Harm of Sorcery according to the Master Darcher (8 pages)

JO

gza'i byad 'grol dug sel gAng+ga la/

The Poison-Cleansing Ganges: Release from the Harm of Sorcery (32 pages)

NYO

gza' bcos kyi mde'u rdo rje'i rkyen sel la/

A Vajra Elimination of Adverse Conditions: A Bullet to Counteract the Actions of Rahulas (5 pages)

TO

gdab las kyi rim pa gnam lcags 'khrul 'khor la/

A Miraculous Wheel of Meteoric Iron: Stages of Subjugation Activities (32 pages)

THO

de'i gsal byed gnam lcags lde mig la/

A Meteoric Iron Key: An Elucidation of a Miraculous Wheel of Meteoric Iron (19 pages)

DO

gnam lcags lde mig gi zur rgyan ur mo'i lcags gser la/

An Iron Nail of Aurmo: Appendices to a Meteoric Iron Key (6 pages)

NO

phrin las kyi le lag spu gri reg bcod la/

A Cutting Sword: Appendices to a Host of Beneficial Activities (12 pages)

PO

hrih dmar gshin rje'i man ngag gi gsal byed yid bzhin nor bu/

A Wish-Fulfilling Gem: An Elucidation of a Quintessential Instruction on Red Hri Yamantaka (13 pages)

PHO

dam can bran du bkol ba'i man ngag zil gnon snying por/

An Essence of Overcoming: A Quintessential Instruction on Summoning Damchan into Action (7 pages)

VOLUME THA

BO

maN+Dal gyi gsal byed mchod sbyin lam bzang la/

A Noble Path of Supreme Giving: An Elucidation of a Mandala Offering (23 pages)

MO

maN+Dal gyi zur rgyan tshon brgya'i ri mor la/

A Drawing of One Hundred Colors: Appendices to a Mandala Offering (32 pages)

TSO

las 'bras kyi rnam gzhag la yid ches pa'i gtam thugs rje'i rol mtsho la/

An Ocean of Compassion: A Trust-Inspiring Discourse Analyzing Karma and Its Results (280 pages)

VOLUME DA

TSHO

las 'bras kyi rnam gzhag phan bde'i srog gcig la/

A Single Life Pillar Bringing Benefit and Happiness: An Analysis of Karma and its Results (218 pages)

DZO

tshogs 'khor gyi rnam bshad nyi ma'i dkyil 'khor la/

A Sun Disc: A Commentary on Tsok Practice (50 pages)

VOLUME NA

WO

mi rtag pa'i rnam gzhag gnyen po'i lcags chen/par du ma 'khod/

An Iron-Heavy Antidote: A Presentation on Impermanence (text lost before woodblocks could be made)

ZHO

nges 'byung gi rnam bshad thar pa'i srog 'dzin la/

Cherishing a Life of Liberation: A Commentary on Renunciation (153 pages)

ZO

gser skyems gtong ba'i man ngag 'gro phan nyin byed la/

A Sunshine-Like Benefit to Beings: A Quintessential Instruction on a Golden Libation Offering (13 pages)

O

gtor ma'i rnam bshad grub pa'i bcud len la/

An Extracted Essence of Practice: An Explanation concerning Ritual Cakes (19 pages)

YO

bza' btung mchod pa'i zab gnad gsal bar byed pa 'phrul gyi man ngag la/

A Miraculous Quintessential Instruction: An Elucidation of the Vital Points of Offering Food and Drink (17 pages)

RO

rtsa sngags kyi rnam bshad mkha' 'gro'i snying khrag la/

The Heart Blood of the Dakinis: A Commentary on the Root Mantra (30 pages)

LO

'pho ba'i man ngag mchog lam yang rtser/

The Supreme and Highest Path: A Quintessential Instruction on the Transference of Consciousness (17 pages)

SHO

'pho ba'i mang ngag grub dbang zhal lung la/

An Oral Transmission of a Great Master: A Quintessential Instruction on the Transference of Consciousness (7 pages)

SO

sri can sbubs gshig gis man ngag rdo rje'i tho ba la/

A Vajra Hammer: A Quintessential Instruction for Killing a Harmful Spirit Within (6 pages)

HO

tshe sgrub kyi cho ga a haM rgyas 'debs la/

Enhancing the Letters Ah and Ham: Longevity Rituals (23 pages)

O

thod pa mchod pa'i man ngag bde skyong tshim byed la/

Sustaining Pleasure and Satisfaction: A Quintessential Instruction on the Skull Cup Offering (4 pages)

KA

mnan pa'i las mtha' ri rab lhun por/

Mount Meru, the King of Mountains: Activities of Subduing Evil Spirits (33 pages)

KHAM

de'i ngag 'don rgyas pa'i cha lag zur du bkol ba la/

Separate Supplementary Appendices to the Extensive Recitation of Mount Meru, the King of Mountains (17 pages)

GAM

rigs lnga'i mkha' 'gro'i 'gyu dus dang dbang ba'i gnas skabs kyi man ngag rnam gzhag drang por/

A Straightforward Presentation: A Quintessential Instruction on the Movements and Power of the Dakinis of the Five Families (4 pages)

NGAM

dam tshig gi glegs bam bri tshul gyi yi ge gsang mdzod kun gsal la/

A Clear Illumination of Secret Treasure: How to Write Scriptures about Samaya Deities (10 pages)

CAM

smon lam khyung chen rtsal rdzogs la/

Garuda with Fully Developed Strengths and Skills: Aspirational Prayers (3 pages)

CHAM

smon lam rdo rje'i 'phrul mig la/

A Vajra Miracle Eye: Aspirational Prayers (3 pages)

JAM

lus ngag gi brda khyad par can la 'jug tshul brda don kun gsal la/

An Elucidation of All Holy Codes: How to Engage in Special Physical and Verbal Codes (19 pages)

sle lung rje drung pad+ma bzhad pa'i rdo rje'i gsung bcom ldan 'das dpal 'khor lo sdom pa'i rtsa rgyud kyi dgongs 'grel glegs bam gyi dkar chag bzhugs so/

Appendix IV. A Catalogue of Lelung Pema Zhepai Dorje's Commentaries on the Root Tantra of Bhagavan Shri Chakrasamvara

Appendix IV. A Catalogue of Lelung Pema Zhepai Dorje's Commentaries on the Root Tantra of Bhagavan Shri Chakrasamvara

KA

dpal 'khor lo sdom pa'i rtsa rgyud rgya gar gyi mkhan po pad+ma kA ra war ma dang /zhu chen gyi lo tsA ba dge slong rin chen bzang pos zhus te gtan la phab pa/

The Root Tantra of Glorious Chakrasamvara Received and Edited by Indian Abbot Padmakara Varma and Great Lotsawa Bhikshu Rinchen Zangpo (117 pages)

KHA

bcom ldan 'das 'khor lo sdom pa'i rtsa rgyud kyi phan yon bklag thabs dang bcas pa stong srog gcig 'dus la/

An Embodiment of One Thousand Lives: The Benefits and Methods of Reading the Root Tantra of Glorious Chakrasamvara (20 pages)

GA

dpal 'khor lo sdom pa'i rtsa rgyud mchan 'grel dang bcas pa bstan 'gro'i spyi nor la/

A Universal Jewel for Dharma and Sentient Beings: An Annotated Commentary on the Root Tantra of Glorious Chakrasamvara (323 pages)

NGA

bcom ldan 'das 'khor lo sdom pa dril bu phyi nang gi bsnyen pa bya tshul gyi yi ge mkha' 'gro'i gsang mdzod la/

A Secret Treasure of Dakinis: A Retreat Manual of the Outer and Inner Dimensions of Enlightened Chakrasamvara according to the Gandapada Tradition (283 pages)

CA

dpal 'khor lo bde mchog gi thun mtshams kyi man ngag gsal bar byed pa snying nor kun gsal la/

An Elucidation of the most Cherished Heart Jewel: A Commentary on a Quintessential Instruction on Glorious Chakrasamvara during Post-Meditational Periods (19 pages)

CHA

dpal 'khor lo bde mchog gi rgyud nas gsungs pa'i lag mchod bya tshul kun mkhyen myur lam la/

A Speedy Path of Omniscient Ones: How to Perform Hand Gestures as Taught in the Glorious Chakrasamvara Tantras (14 pages)

JA

dpal 'khor lo sdom pa'i man ngag nas gsungs pa'i chos 'byung gi mchod pa bya tshul zab don snying bcud la/

An Innermost Essence of Profound Meaning: How to Make Offerings to the Double Triangle Mandala as Taught in the Quintessential Instruction on Glorious Chakrasamavara (9 pages)

NYA

dpal 'khor lo sdom pa'i rgyud nas gsungs pa'i g.yon pa'i kun spyod bya tshul kun spyod rab gsal la/

An Elucidation of All Activities: How to Perform Activities with the Left Hand as Taught in Glorious Chakrasamvara Tantras (4 pages)

TA

lag mchod dang 'brel ba'i smon lam e waM 'phrul mdzod/

The Miraculous Treasure of Aewam: Prayers Related to Hand Gesture Offerings (4 pages)

THA

dpal 'khor lo bde mchog gi sgo nas chu dang rlung gi lam khyer rlabs chen don 'grub la/

A Fulfilment of Great Purpose: Taking Water and Wind into the Path through Glorious Chakrasamvara (6 pages)

DA

dpal 'khor lo sdom pa'i dbang sdud kyi man ngag mdzes rgyan yid 'phrog la/

A Beautiful Heart-Captivating Ornament: A Quintessential Instruction on Subjugation through Glorious Chakrasamvara (4 pages)

NA

bcom ldan 'das 'khor lo sdom pa'i rnal 'byor ma'i dbang phyug sum cu rtsa drug gi 'gyu dus kyi man ngag gser gyi thur ma la/

A Golden Spoon: A Quintessential Instruction on the Time and Movements of the Thirty-Six Powerful Dakinis of Enlightened Chakrasamvara (12 pages)

PA

bde mchog gi sgo nas klu gtor gtong ba'i man ngag gdung sel dga' ston la/

A Joyous and Misery-Relieving Activity: A Quintessential Instruction on Offering Ritual Cakes according to Chakrasamvara (4 pages)

PHA

dpal 'khor lo bde mchog gi sgo nas 'chi ba blu ba'i man ngag tshe bcud kun 'dus la/

A Gathering of All Life Energies: A Quintessential Instruction on Deceiving Death according to Glorious Chakrasamvara (14 pages)

BA

bcom ldan 'das 'khor lo sdom pa'i rtsa sngags kyi rnam bshad mthar thug don gsal la/

An Elucidation of the Ultimate Meaning: An Explanation of the Root Mantras of Enlightened Chakrasamvara (11 pages)

MA

dpal 'khor lo sdom pa'i rtsa sngags kyi nang tshan yig 'bru drug gi rnam bshad gsang tshig brjen pa la/

Naked Disclosure of Secret Words: An Explanation of the Six Syllables from the Root Mantras of Glorious Chakrasamvara (8 pages)

TSA

dpal 'khor lo sdom pa'i yab kyi rkang brgyad kyi bstod pa'i gsal byed sbas don dgongs rgyan la/

An Ornament of Hidden Thought: An Elucidation of the Eight-Line Praises to the Father Deity Chakrasamvara (14 pages)

TSHA

tshogs kyi 'khor lo'i rnam bshad mkha' 'gro dgyes pa'i sgra dbyangs la/

Sound that Delights Dakinis: An Explanation of the Feast-Offering (67 pages)

DZA

dpal 'khor lo sdom pa'i man ngag zab bcud bdud rtsi la/

Nectar of Profound Taste: A Quintessential Instruction on Glorious Chakrasamvara (9 pages)

WA

zab don gyi legs bshad yungs 'bru nam mkha' la/

A Mustard Seed with Infinite Meanings: An Excellent Explanation of Profound Reality (5 pages)

Innermost essence: Pith Instructions of Necessary Elements for Sexual Union (5 pages)

An Explanation of the Definitive Meaning of the Varahi Mantra (1 page)

A Drop of Heart's Blood: Top Secret Pith Instructions on the Sadhana of Lama Vajrasattva (11 pages)

NB: It is not clear how many volumes there are in regard to Jedrung Rinpoche's commentaries on glorious Chakrasamvara. I am grateful to have recently found several, notably Chapter Ka: *The Root Tantra of Glorious Chakrasamvara as Received and edited by Indian Abbot Padmakara Varma and Great Lotsawa Bhikshu Rinchen Zangpo.*

Lelung Tulku, 3 June 1999

Appendix V. A Catalogue of Damchan Be'u Bum from the Collected Works of Lelung Pema Zhepai Dorje

KA

> ***dam can mgar ba nag po'i sgrub skor las stag sbyang rol pa'i rgyud lefu dgu pa la/***
>
> *Chapter Nine of the Tagjang Rolpa Tantras from the Sadhana Cycle of Black Damchan Garwa* (9 pages)

KHA

> ***gnod sbyin ha la 'bar ba'i rgyud la/***
>
> *The Yaksha Hala Barwa Tantra* (7 pages)

GA

> ***gnod sbyin rdo rje'i stag mda'i rgyud la/***
>
> *The Yaksha Dorje Tagda Tantra* (11 pages)

NGA

> ***bdud rgyal thod pa'i phreng ba can gyi rgyud la/***
>
> *The Tantra of the King of the Demons with a Garland of Skulls* (6 pages)

CA

> ***srog gzer nag po'i rgyud la/***
>
> *The Black Sogzer Tantra* (6 pages)

CHA

> ***srog zan dmar po'i rgyud la/***
>
> *The Red Sogzen Tantra* (21 pages)

JA

dge bsnyen dgra gsang nag po'i rgyud la/

The Dark Upasaka Drasang Tantra (13 pages)

NYA

'phung byed nor srung ba'i rgyud la/

The Phungjed Norsung Tantra (5 pages)

TA

dam can rdo rje legs pa mgar ba nag po'i sgrub skor las mgar ba nag po rdo rje legs pa'i rgyud le'u bcu la/

Ten Chapters of Black Garwa Dorje Legpa from the Sadhana Cycle of Black Damchan Garwa Dorje Legpa (9 pages)

THA

yang 'khol mgar nag rdor legs kyi sgrub thabs la/

A Sadhana of Yangkhol Garnag Dorleg (2 pages)

DA

rdzogs chen gu ru'i thugs sgrub las rgyal ba'i bka' bsrungs dam can rdo rje legs pa gter bdag gi sgrub pa'i 'phrin la/

A Sadhana of Damchan Dorje Legpa, Lord of Treasure, Guardian of Buddha's Words, from the Heart Practice of Dzogchen Guru (3 pages)

NA

srog sgrub yang snying 'dus pa stag zhon bdun 'gros kyi bsgrub pa bzhugs so//sprul sku gu ru jo rtses kong po gre la tse rnon nas gter bston pa la/

An Innermost Essence of Life Accomplishment: A Practice of the Seven Tiger Riders, a Treasure Discovered by Tulku Guru Jotse from Drela Tsenon in Kongpo (14 pages)

PA

dam can ldang lha'i gsol mchod la/

A Supplication and Offering to Damchan Danglha (3 pages)

PHA

rdor legs lha btsan ging gi cho 'phrul la/

Miracles of Ging Dorleg Lhatsan (1 page)

BA

rdor legs gsol kha la/

A Propitiation of Dorleg (5 pages)

MA

dam can sgrub thabs kyi thems yig la/

Inscribed Words: A Sadhana to Accomplish Damchan (1 page)

TSA

dam can gyi gsang sgrub srog gi spu gri la/

A Life-Threatening Sword: A Secret Practice of Damchan (6 pages)

TSHA

dpe ma rnyed/

[text missing]

DZA

rat+na'i thugs gter shis bstan pa dam can sgrub thabs la/

Revealing Shiten, Ratna's Heart Treasure: A Sadhana of Damchan (2 pages)

WA

dam can chen po rdo rje legs pa'i bskang gso chen mo la/

An Extensive Propitiation of Great Damchan Dorje Legpa (12 pages)

ZHA

dam can rdo rje legs pa'i las tshogs rin chen spungs pa zhes bya ba rat+na'i gter ma la/

A Heap of Jewels: A Host of Activities of Damchan Dorje Legpa, Ratna's Treasure (6 pages)

ZA

skyes bu chen po'i jag chings la/

The Great Being Damchan's Binding of Robbers (2 pages)

'A

dam can rdo rje'i legs pa'i nor sgrub dbang sdud kyi gdams pa zab mo la/

A Profound Instruction on the Influential Power and Wealth Accomplishment of Damchan Dorje Legpa (3 pages)

YA

nor sgrub dbang sdud kyi gdams pa snying gi dum bu'i gnas yig go/nor sgrub gnad yig bzhugs pa'i dbu la/

A Piece of Heart: A Guide to "A Profound Instruction on the Influential Power and Wealth Accomplishment," the beginning of the Guide to Wealth Accomplishment (3 pages)

RA

dgra la cho 'phrul ltas ngan gtong thabs la/

How to Direct Miracles and Bad Omens to Enemies (3 pages)

LA

mon pa nag po'i ltas ngan cog brdungs la/

Beating Bad Omens from Black Monpa (1 page)

SHA

skyes bu chen po rdo rje legs pa'i gsol kha la/

A Propitiation of the Great Being Dorje Legpa (3 pages)

SA

rdo rje bsam 'grub rtsal gyi nor sgrub la/

A Wealth Accomplishment of Dorje Samdrup Tsal (2 pages)

HA

dam can gyi gsang sgrub srog gi spu gri la/

A Life-Threatening Sword: A Secret Practice of Damchan (4 pages)

A

dgra lha'i cho 'phrul dam can lnga bsdus yang zab cog brdungs/

Beating Dharma Enemies by Practicing Dralha's Manifestation: The Innermost Profound Five-Fold Damchan, (4 pages)

KI

(dpe ma rnyed)

[text missing]

KHI

dam can skyes bu'i mdos rat+na gling pa'i gter ma la/

A Crossed-Thread Ritual of Damchan: Ratna Lingpa's Treasure (8 pages)

GI

dam can skyes bu chen po'i rjes gnang la/

A Permission Blessing of the Great Being Damchan (2 pages)

NGI

dam can bla rdo'i man ngag u pa de sha la/

Upa Desha: An Instruction on Damchan's Life Stone (1 page)

CI

> *dam can nor scgrub rin chen gter mchod la/*

> A Jewel Treasure Offering: A Wealth Accomplishment of Damchan (4 pages)

CHI

> *(dpe ma rnyed)*

> [text missing]

JI

> *dam can sgrub skor la/ (dpe ma rnyed)*

> Regarding a Damchan Sadhana Cycle (1 page [text missing])

NYI

> *(dpe ma rnyed)*

> [text missing]

TI

> *dam can rno mthong gi sgrub thabs la/*

> A Liturgy of Damchan Nothong (2 pages)

THI

> *dam can dmar nag gi sgrub pa rno myur dregs pa tshar gcod la/*

> Defeat of a Haughty Spirit: A Liturgy of Dark Red Damchan (6 pages)

DI

> *thugs rje chen po don gsal sgron me las bka' bsrung dam can rdo rje legs pa gsang ba srog gi 'khor lo'i sgrub skor phyi sgrub/*

> An Outer Sadhana of Great Damchan from the Practice Set of the Secret Wheel of Life of Damchan Dorje Legpa, Guardian of the Avalokiteshvara Lamp Illuminating Clear Meaning (3 pages)

NI

thugs rje chen po don gsal sgron me'i bka' bsrung dam can rdo rje legs pa gsang ba srog gi 'khor lo'i sgrub skor las nang sgrub/

An Inner Sadhana of Great Damchan from the Practice Set of the Secret Wheel of Life of Damchan Dorje Legpa, Guardian of the Avalokiteshvara Lamp Illuminating Clear Meaning (3 pages)

PI

thugs rje chen po don gsal sgron me'i bka' bsrung dam can rdo rje legs pa gsang ba srog gi 'khor lo'i sgrub skor las gsang sgrub/

A Secret Sadhana of Great Damchan from the Practice Set of the Secret Wheel of Life of Damchan Dorje Legpa, Guardian of the Avalokiteshvara Lamp Illuminating Clear Meaning (5 pages)

PHI

thugs rje chen po don gsal sgron me'i bka' bsrung dam can rdo rje legs pa gsang ba srog gi 'khor lo'i sgrub skor las nor sgrub/

A Wealth Sadhana of Great Damchan from the Practice Set of the Secret Wheel of Life of Damchan Dorje Legpa, Guardian of the Avalokiteshvara Lamp Illuminating Clear Meaning (4 pages)

BI

de'i gnas yig la/

A Guide to the Pilgrimage Sites of Eight Classes of Violent Deities of Great Damchan from the Practice Set of the Secret Wheel of Life of Damchan Dorje Legpa, Guardian of the Avalokiteshvara Lamp Illuminating Clear Meaning (3 pages)

MI

gsang ba gnad kyi dril sgrub la/

A Combined Sadhana of Secret Vital Points of Great Damchan from the Practice Set of the Secret Wheel of Life of Damchan Dorje Legpa, Guardian of the Avalokiteshvara Lamp Illuminating Clear Meaning (3 pages)

TSI

> *thugs rje chen po don gsal sgron me'i bka' bsrung dam can rdo*
> *rje legs pa'i gsang ba srog gi 'khor lo'i sgrub skor las dam can*
> *chen po'i rten mdos la/*

> A Crossed-Thread Rite of Great Damchan from the Sadhana Cycle
> of the Secret Wheel of Life of Damchan Dorje Legpa, Guardian
> of the Avalokiteshvara Lamp Illuminating Clear Meaning (3
> pages)

TSHI

> *thugs rje chen po don gsal sgron me'i bka' bsrung dam can rdo*
> *rje legs pa'i gsang ba srog gi 'khor lo'i sgrub skor las gser*
> *skyems phrin las kun 'grub la/*

> A Golden Libation Offering Fulfilling All the Activities from the
> Sadhana Cycle of the Secret Wheel of Life of Damchan Dorje
> Legpa, Guardian of the Avalokiteshvara Lamp Illuminating Clear
> Meaning (6 pages)

DZI

> *dam can rdo rje legs pa'i las byang gnas lcags 'bar ba spu gri*
> *dmar len la/*

> A Slaying Sword of Meteoric Iron: A Sadhana Instruction of
> Damchan Dorje Legpa (6 pages)

WI

> *thugs rje chen po don gsal sgron me lasaHbka' bsrung dam can*
> *rdo rje legs pa yiHgsang ba srog gi 'khor lo'i sgrub skor*
> *lasaHsde brgyad las la bskul ba'i gnad yig/*

> A Guide to Motivating the Eight Protectors from the Sadhana Cycle
> of the Secret Wheel of Life of Damchan Dorje Legpa, Guardian of
> the Avalokiteshvara Lamp Illuminating Clear Meaning (2 pages)

ZHI

thugs rje chen po don gsal sgron me'i bka' bsrung dam can rdo rje legs pa gsang ba srog gi 'khor lo'i sgrub skor las rjes gnang la/

A Permission Blessing from the Sadhana Cycle of the Secret Wheel of Life of Damchan Dorje Legpa, Guardian of the Avalokiteshvara Lamp Illuminating Clear Meaning (3 pages)

ZI

dam can rdo rje legs pa'i sgrub thabs la/

A Sadhana of Damchan Dorje Legpa (4 pages)

'I

dam can mgar ba nag po la/

Black Damchan Garwa (4 pages)

YI

dam can mgar ba'i sgrub thabs la/

A Sadhana of Damchan Garwa (5 pages)

RI

dge bsnyen rdo rje legs pa'i nor sgrub la

A Wealth Accomplishment of Upasaka Dorje Legpa (2 pages)

LI

bla ma yang tig gi nang tshan las dam can pa'i chos skor la/

A Cycle of Teachings on Damchan from the Collection of Lama Yang Tig (6 pages)

SHI

dam can mgar nag gi sgrub thabs mgar gyi me dpung 'bar ba la/

A Blazing Heap of Fire: A Sadhana of Black Damchan Garwa (10 pages)

SI

dam can chos skor la/(dpe tshan nyer bzhi'i mtshan byang /)

A Cycle of Teachings on Damchan (A List of Twenty-Four Chapter Names

HI

skyes bu chen po'i sgab 'dre mnan pa la/

Subduing Evil Spirits by the Great Being Dorje Legpa (3 pages)

I

sgrub thabs mdod 'jo'i bum bzang las skyes mchog rdo rje legs pa'i sgrub thabs la/

A Sadhana of the Great Being Dorje Legpa from a Wish-Fulfilling Vase of Sadhanas (5 pages)

KU

the rang ber ka can gyi nye 'byed zab mo lugs gcig la/

A Single Profound Method: A Ritual to Produce Contention by Means of Iron Stick Holding Therangs (1 page)

KHU

dam can skyes bu rdo rje legs pa'i sgo nas rigs brgyud 'phel bar byed pa la ltas ngan g.yang du 'gugs pa'i man ngag la/

An Instruction to Summon Bad Omens as Good Fortune for the Procreation of the Lineage by Practicing Damchan Dorje Legpa (1 page)

GU

stong bdud tshe bdud rgyal po'i sgrub thabs bon lugs lag len ma la/

A Sadhana of Tongdue Tshedue Gyalpo according to Bon Tradition (3 pages)

NGU

> *dpe ma rnyed/*

> [text missing]

CU

> *dam can gyi gsang sgrub cho 'phrul gyi gdams pa la/*

> *A Miraculous Instruction on a Secret Practice of Damchan* (2 pages)

CHU

> *rdor legs pa'i gsol kha yig rnying las byung ba la/*

> *A Propitiation of Damchan from Archives* (2 pages)

JU

> *dpe ma rnyed/*

> [text missing]

NYU

> *thugs rje chen po 'khor ba las sgrol las bka' srung bye brag pa bshan pa ra mgo'i sgrub thabs la/*

> *A Sadhana of the Goat-Headed Butcher, a Special Guardian, from Avalokiteshvara, Liberator from Samsara* (4 pages)

TU

> *dam can sgrub skor la/dpe ma rnyed/*

> *Regarding a Sadhana Cycle of Damchan* (1 page [text missing])

THU

> *dam can rdo rje legs pa'i las byang 'phrin las kyi rim pa nor bu'i bang mdzod bzhugs pa'i dbu phyogs dam can lcam dral chos tshan gcig pa la/*

> *A Single-Chaptered Practice of Damchan Chamdrel from "A Treasury of Jewels": A Series of Activities of Damchan Dorje Legpal* (6 pages)

DU

*dam can lcam dral gyi rbad bskul dregs pa'i dmag tshogs gnam
lcags 'jigs pa'i dpal zhes pa dmag bskul dang bcas pa shin tu
gnyan pa la/*

*A Top Secret Command of Damchan Chamdrel's Wrathful Armed
Force Known as the Power to Destroy Meteoric Iron* (10 pages)

NU

*dam can skyes bu chen po rdo rje legs pa'i 'phrin las bsdus pa
nor bu'i phreng ba la/*

*A Rosary of Jewels: A Short Version of the Blessings of the Great
Being Damchan Dorje Legpa* (2 pages)

PU

*dam can rdo rje legs pa thig le rtsal gyi gsol kha 'phrin las myur
'grub la/*

*Quick Accomplishing Activities: A Propitiation of Damchan Dorje
Legpa Thigle Tsel* (3 pages)

PHU

*dam can rdo rje legs pa'i bskang ba bsam pa'i don 'grub ces bya
ba bzhugs/dam can lcam dral gyi chos sde la/*

*A Wish-Fulfilling Propitiation of Damchan Dorje Legpa from a
Set of Teachings of Damchan Chamdrel* (7 pages)

BU

*dam can rdo rje legs pa'i srog sgrub drag po lha lnga'i dril sgrub
srog sel cho 'phrul chen po la/*

*A Great Trouble-Shooting Miracle: A Five Wrathful Deity Sadhana
of Damchan Dorje Legpa's Life Accomplishment* (4 pages)

MU

dam can rdo rje legs pa'i rten bca' dam sre gnyer gtad bcol dam rim pa la/

Creating the Environment, Mending Samaya, Entrusting Oneself, Invoking, and Making Promises to Damchan Dorje Legpa (5 pages)

TSU

dam can lcam dral yab yum dril sgrub nor lha ltar sgrub thabs dgos 'dod kun 'byung bzhugs/phyi sgrub dgos 'don kun 'byung la/

Fulfilling the Outer Dimension: A Wish-Fulfilling Sadhana of Damchan Chamdrel Father and Mother in Union as Wealth Deities (7 pages)

TSHU

dam can rdo legs pa'i srog sgrub drag po mthu yi las bsad pa hom sgrub spu gri'i dug 'khor la/

Poisons Spinning on a Sharp Sword: A Hung Practice to Slay Enemies from the Wrathful Power Activities of Damchan Dorje Legpa's Power Activities (3 pages)

DZU

dam can lcam dral gyi rtags yig gsal ba'i lde mig dang sgrub pa'i zhal bkod gnad dbab shis bstan pa'i man ngag

A Key to Clarifying the Symbols of Damchan Chamdrel and a Sadhana: A Quintessential Instruction on the Vital Points of Practice (4 pages)

WU

dam can lcam dral las mngon shes 'phrul gyis gsal ba'i sgron me/yab yum gnyis med rten 'bri mo'i las/

A Miraculous Lamp of Illumination: Achieving Clairvoyance by Practicing Damchan Chamdrel (9 pages)

ZHU

> *dam can lcam dral gyi srog 'khor nor sgrub dbang sdud kyi tsakra bri ba'i yig chung la/*

> *A Short Note on Drawing the Wheel of Wealth Accomplishment and Subjugation: A Life Accomplishment Sadhana of Damchan Chamdrel* (4 pages)

ZU

> *dam can lcam dral nor sgrub gter gyi lde mig yab yum dril ba'i gsang sgrub glog zhags ma la/*

> *A Key to the Treasure House: An Electric Lassoo-Like Sadhana of Wealth-Accomplishing Damchan Chamdrel in Secret Union* (4 pages)

'U

> *dam can lcam dral yab yum gyi 'gyu dus bstan pa'i man ngag sogs gces gnad zab mo la/*

> *Precious Vital Points: Quintessential Instructions Revealing the Time and Movements of Damchan Chamdrel in Secret Union* (4 pages)

YU

> *ma mo brtan ma rdo rje g.yu sgron ma rtsa ba'i sgrub pa 'phrul gyi me long phyi sgrub pad+ma'i ljon shing la/*

> *A Lotus Plant-Like Accomplishment of the Outer Dimension: A Miraculous Mirror for Accomplishing Mamo Dorje Yudon Ma as Principal Deity* (4 pages)

RU

brtan ma chen mo rdo rje g.yu sgron ma'i nang bsgrub gnod sbyin mo phag gdong can la brten pa'i dbul sel nor gyi sgrub pa dngos grub rgya mtsho la/

An Ocean of Wealth Accomplishment to Alleviate Poverty Relying upon Boar-Faced Yaksha: A Sadhana of the Inner Dimension of Great Protectress Dorje Yudon Ma (3 pages)

LU

ma mo brtan ma chen mo rdo rje g.yu sgron ma'i gsang sgrub lha mo 'bar gdong ma tsaN+Di ka'i sgrub thabs spu gri la/

A Sharp Sword-Like Sadhana of the Blazing-Faced Goddess Chandrika from an Accomplishment of the Secret Dimension of Great Mamo Protectress Dorje Yudon Ma (4 pages)

SHU

ma mo brtan ma rdo rje g.yu sgron ma shin tu khros ma spyang zhon nag mo'i sgrub thabs yang gsang mchog sgrub dug mtsho 'khyil ma/

A Swirling Lake of Poison: A Top Secret Sadhana of the Extra Wrathful Mamo Dorje Yudon Ma Riding on a Black Jackal (5 pages)

SU

brtan ma rdo rje g.yu sgron ma'i 'phrul sgrub mngon shes gsal sgron/

A Clear Lamp Illuminating Clairvoyance: An Accomplishment of the Miracles of Mamo Dorje Yudon Ma (3 pages)

HU

brtan ma chen mo g.yu sgron ma'i bskang gso dngos grub 'khyil ba/

A Swirling Lake of Attainments: A Propitiation of the Great Protectress Yudon Ma (4 pages)

U

rdo rje g.yu sgron ma'i rten 'dzugs ri rab lhun po dang rten 'dzugs bstod pa la/

Mount Meru: Erecting a Residence for Dorje Yudon Ma and Offering Praises to It (5 pages)

KE

rdo rje legs pa'i gsol kha nyung bsdus la/

A Short Version of a Propitiation of Dorje Legpa (1 page)

KHE

gter srung gi sgrub thabs gter byung sor bzhag la/

A Sadhana of Treasure Guardians According to the Treasure Text (1 page)

GE

dam can skyes bu myur mgyogs can la/

Swift-Footed Damchan (4 pages)

NGE

dam can rdo rje legs pa thig le rtsal gyi rtsa ba'i sgrub thabs kyi sgrub pa chen mo gnad yig gsol kha dang bcas la/

The Vital Points of Engaging in the Greater Sadhana, from the Root Sadhana, including a Propitiation of Damchan Dorje Legpa Thigletsal (6 pages)

CE

dam can rdo rje legs pa'i nang sgrub la/

A Sadhana of the Inner Dimension of Damchan Dorje Legpa (3 pages)

CHE

> *dam can badz+ra swa d+hu'i gsang sgrub zhal shes dang bcas pa la/*
>
> *A Sadhana of the Secret Dimension of Damchan Dorje Legpa* (4 pages)

JE

> *dam can rdo rje legs pa'i bskang ba mchod bstod kyi rim pa stobs ldan yid 'gul la/*
>
> *Powerful Inspiration: Rites of Invocation, Offering and Praises to Damchan Dorje Legpa* (8 pages)

NYE

> *dam can rdo rje legs pa'i bskang gso chen mo dngos grub nam mkha' la/*
>
> *An Infinite Space of Attainments: A Great Propitiation of Damchan Dorje Legpa* (55 pages)

TE

> *dam can rdo rje legs pa'i stag zhon bdun 'gros kyi 'bod rbad bsad gsum gyi man ngag thog gi gan mdzod la/*
>
> *A Store of Thunderbolt-Like Pith Instructions: Calling, Encouraging, and Slaying by Practicing Seven-Fold Tiger-Riding Damchan Dorje Legpa* (24 pages)

THE

> *dam can rdo rje legs pa'i nor sgrub srid zhi'i g.yang bum la/*
>
> *A Fortune Vase of Samsara and Nirvana: A Wealth Accomplishment of Damchan Dorje Legpa* (8 pages)

DE

> *dam can rdo rje legs pa'i nor sgrub gter dung g.yas 'khyil/*
>
> *A Right-Coiling Treasure Conch: A Wealth Accomplishment of Damchan Dorje Legpa* (7 pages)

NE

rig 'dzin nus ldan rdo rje'i gter byon dam can gyi nor sgrub bya tshul gter dung g.yang 'khyil gyi zur rgyan no/

An Appendix to the Right-Coiling Treasure Conch: A Wealth Accomplishment of Damchan by the Treasure Discoverer and Knowledge Holder Nunden Dorje (3 pages)

PE

dam can rdo rje legs pa'i sgo nas mngon shes sgrub thabs cer mthong mdzub tshugs la/

Naked Perception and Pointing Out the Unknown: A Liturgy to Accomplish Clairvoyance through Damchan Dorje Legpa (5 pages)

PHE

dam can rdo rje legs pa'i bla rdo srog 'khor bca' tshul gyi man ngag rgya mtsho'i bcud dril la/

An Essence of the Ocean: A Quintessential Instruction on How to Make a Life Stone and Wheel of Life of Damchan from the Practice Set of the Secret Wheel of Life of Damchan Dorje Legpa, Guardian of the Avalokiteshvara Lamp Illuminating Clear Meaning (15 pages)

BE

dam can rdo rje legs pa'i las sbyor gyi gnad yig mngon spyod 'phrul gyi lde mig la/

A Miraculous Key of Wrathfulness: Notes on the Vital Points of Wrathful Activity Rites of Damchan Dorje Legpa (7 pages)

ME

dam can rdo rje legs pa'i 'gyu dus kyi man ngag rnam gzhag kun gsal la/

A Complete Elucidation of the Stages of a Quintessential Instruction on the Time and Movements of Damchan Dorje Legpa (12 pages)

TSE

dam can skyes bu chen po'i gdab las kyi dar 'dogs rdo rje'i brdar rdo la/

A Grindstone for Vajra Tied with a Magic Cord: Cultivating Activities by Practicing Great Damchan (6 pages)

TSHE

dam can rdo rje legs pa'i 'khon sbyong gi man ngag snying khrag hub len la/

Sucking in Heart Blood: A Quintessential Instruction on Purifying the Wrath of Damchan Dorje Legpa (2 pages)

DZE

dam can rdo rje legs pa'i bsnyen sgrub las gsum gyi man ngag stong gsum khyon yangs la/

The Infinite Space of the Three Thousand Worlds: A Quintessential Instruction on the Three Activities of Practice, Retreat, and Actions of Damchan Dorje Legpa (6 pages)

WE

dam can rdo rje legs pa'i las sbyor gyi yang yig dug gi rgya mtsho la/

An Ocean of Poison: A Core Note on Wrathful Activity Rites of Damchan Dorje Legpa (8 pages)

1

dam can bstan srung rgya mtsho'i rnam par thar pa cha shas tsam brjod pa sngon med legs bshad stod cha deb gzugs ldi li dpar ma la/

Unprecedented Holy Lineage Histories: A Partial Presentation from the Liberating Chronicles of Damchan, an Ocean of Protectors, Part I, Book Format, Delhi Edition (311 pages)

2

dam can bstan srung rgya mtsho'i rnam par thar pa cha shas tsam brjod pa sngon med legs bshad smad cha deb gzugs ldi li dpar ma la/

Unprecedented Holy Lineage Histories: A Partial Presentation from the Liberating Chronicles of Damchan, An Ocean of Protectors, Part II, Book Format, Delhi Edition (346 pages)

It appears that the last two volumes constitute one of the most authoritative and latest sources of *An Ocean of Dharma Protectors*. Kyabje Dilgo Khyentse Rinpoche had the oral transmission of this text and kindly accepted my request to give it to me. Unfortunately, however, I was unable to receive it due to my single-pointed pursuit of my monastic education and metaphysical debate, my lack of financial resources, and also obstacles created by some of his attendants who were unduly caught up with the eight worldly concerns. I very much regret not having received it.

Appendix VI. A Bibliography of the Handwritten Works of Lelung Pema Zhepai Dorje

1

mkha' spyod du byin dbab pa'i lo rgyus ngo mtshar mod tshal zhes bya ba/

A Garden of Wonderful Aspiration: An Account of Summoning Holy Deities into Oneself at Khachod in Lelung (13 pages)

2

gnas yig dang lo rgyus gsar du 'khod pa rnams kyi dkar chags sgo brgya 'byed pa'i lde mig ces bya ba/

A Key to Open Hundreds of Doors: A Catalogue of Guides to Pilgrimage Sites and Some New Accounts (3 pages)

3

don mthun 'dus pa'i tshom bu du mar ngo mtshar ba'i ltad mo mthong ba'i lo rgyus rig rtsal sgyu 'phrul dra ba zhes bya ba/

An Illusory Emanation Net of Creative Intelligence: An Account of a Spectacle of Miracles at a Gathering of Karmically Linked Practitioners (24 pages)

4

me mo sbrul lo'i zab 'khrid chen mo'i stong thun rdzu 'phrul rang shar zhes bya ba'i rtsa tshig don bsdus/

Self-Arisen Thousand-Fold Miracles: The Root Text and Summary of the Great and Profound Commentary Given in the Fire Snake Year (6 pages)

5

'khrungs rabs gsol 'debs/

A Supplication to the Line of Reincarnations (4 pages)

6

sa ga zla ba'i tshes nyer drug gi nub rje bla ma yab yum 'dus par bcas pa la mchog sprul rdo rje ngo mtshar gyis bdud rtsi'i mchod pa bstab pa'i tshe rje bla ma'i ngo mtshar gyi mdzad pa ji ltar rtogs pa'i tshul gsal bar brjod pa/

A Clear Report of the Most Venerable Lama's Wonderful Deeds at the Event where Supreme Emanation Dorje Ngotsar Made a Nectar Offering to the Most Venerable Lama and His Consort on the Evening of the Twenty-Sixth Day of the Fourth Lunar Month (11 pages)

7

dpa' bo chen po khrag 'thung rnam par rol bas mdzad pa'i bdud rtsi mchod pa las 'phros pa'i lo rgyus gnas lugs kun gsal zhes bya ba/

A Complete Illumination of All the Vital Points: An Account from a Nectar Offering Authored by the Great Being Tragthung Nampar Rolpa (175 pages)

8

rig 'dzin bzhad pa'i rdo rje'i bskang gso gtad med nyams dga' zhes bya ba/

Flawless Joy: A Propitiation of Rigzin Zhepai Dorje (6 pages)

9

dam rdzas yig drug ril bu'i dkar chag snyigs dus mdzes rgyan zhes bya ba/

A Beautiful Ornament of the Degenerate Time: A Catalogue of the Blessed Mani Pills (8 pages)

10

gar dbang dang po'i sangs rgyas ng+harma'i mtshan can zhing brjes dus kyi dgongs rdzogs zin bris/

Notes on the Passing Away of Dharma, the Primordial Buddha of Garwang (31 pages)

11

bshes gnyen bstan pa dar rgyas kyi 'khrungs rabs gsol 'debs zhabs brtan smon lam dang bcas pa/

A Lineage Supplication for Spiritual Teacher Tenpa Dhargye's Reincarnation and His Long-Life Prayer (3 pages)

12

bcom ldan 'das mgon po byams pa'i bstod pa'i tshigs su bcad pa gtsug rgyan nor bu 'dud pa'i sbyor ba zhes bya ba/

An Action to Procure a Crown Jewel: Verses of Praise to Buddha Maitreya (4 pages)

13

sangs rgyas byang sems rnams la phyag 'tshal ba'i cho ga sdig sgrib sbyongs thabs zla zhun 'khyil ba zhes bya ba/

A Swirl of the Moon: A Method to Purify Negativities through the Rite of Prostrating to Buddhas and Bodhisattvas (4 pages)

14

sangs rgyas phal po che las gsungs pa'i rgyal ba sras bcas la gsol ba gdab pa'i rim pa kun bzang nam mkha'i mdzod sprin zhes bya ba/

Clouds of Samantabhadra's Space Treasure: Rites of Supplication to Buddhas and Bodhisattvas from the Avatamsaka Sutra (6 pages)

15

rnam grol gling gi skor tshad kyi rim pa gsal bar byed pa'i yi ge gang 'dod lam ston zhes bya ba/

A Wish-Fulfilling Guide: Clear Measurements of the Circumambulatory Benefits of the Path Around Namdrol Ling (3 pages)

16

blta na sdug gi gtsug lag khang gi ldebs bris kyi gsham du 'khod pa'i bden tshig

Words of Truth Inscribed Beneath the Murals in Tanaduk Temple (10 pages)

17

rnam dgar rdzogs byang du bsngo ba'i ngag 'don nges legs rgya mtshor 'jug pa'i gru rdzings/

A Ship to Enter the Ocean of Ultimate Excellence: A Dedication Prayer of Virtuous Actions for Complete Enlightenment (4 pages)

18

gsang ba ye shes kyi mkha' 'gro'i sgo nas bsngo ba bya tshul/

How To Practice Dedication by Way of Sangwa Yeshe (4 pages)

19

bsngo ba rgyas pa phan bde'i Od dkar/

Beneficial White Light: A Long Dedication (3 pages)

20

dag snang pad+ma mkha' 'gro'i mngon rtogs/

Clear Understanding of Pema Dakini from Pure Vision (2 pages)

21

hum sgrub dang 'brel ba'i bla ma'i rnal 'byor gyi rim pa/

Rites of Guru Yoga Related to the Actualization of Hung (2 pages)

22

thun drug gi rnal 'byor gyi rgyun khyer gnad 'gag kun 'dus kyi gsal byed rgyas can drang po zhes bya ba/

Honest Words Arising from Experience: A Commentary on All the Vital Points of the Daily Practice of Six Session Yoga (3 pages)

23

rta mgrin phug gi gnas bshad dad pa'i nyin byed ces bya ba/

Radiance of Faith: An Explanation of the Pilgrimage Cave of Haya-griva (6 pages)

24

mkha' spyod kyi 'khor phigs sdeb bris kyi dkar chag rje nyid kyis gnang ba/

A Catalogue of the Murals in Kha Choed written by the Master Himself (2 pages)

25

yig drug gi 'khor lo 'gro 'dren rnams rol gyi dkar chag smon lam dang bcas pa/

A Dedication Prayer Together with a Catalogue of the Wheel of the Six Syllables Liberating Sentient Beings (5 pages)

26

dag snang i yig gi sgrub pa mdor bsdus/

A Short Practice of the Syllable "AI" from Pure Vision (2 pages)

27

chos srung spyi'i 'phrin bcol bsam don lhun grub ma/

A Spontaneous Fulfilment of Wishes: A General Invocation of All Dharma Protectors (2 pages)

28

gzhung pa rin po che nas rta lo khra 'brug gi zhig bso gnang ba'i dkar chag gi 'dra 'bag

A Copy of the Catalogue of the Restoration of Tradruk in the Horse Year by Zhungpa Rinpoche (8 pages)

29

rdo rje chos srung spyi sgos la 'phrin las bcol ba mi bslu'i bden 'grub ces bya ba/

The Unfailing Power of Truth: An Invocation to the Vajra Dharma Protectors in General and Some Individual Protectors (3 pages)

30

chu glang lo'i nyams snang zin bris/

A Journal of Pure Visions in the Water Ox Year (161 pages)

31

shing stag lo nang du phebs pa'i nyams snang zin bris su bkod pa/

A Journal of Pure Visions which Appeared in the Wood Tiger Year (76 pages)

32

snyan dar zhal byang gi rim pa sna tshogs/

A Miscellaneous Collection of Wishing Verses for Silk Offering Scarves (45 pages)

33

shing 'brug lo'i nyams snang zin bris kyi le'u/

A Chapter of Notes of Pure Visions in the Wood Dragon Year (79 pages)

34

sman sgrub kyi man ngag khams gsum bde byed gzhan phan nyi ma'i dkyil 'khor zhes bya ba/

A Solar Disc-Like Benefit to Others: A Quintessential Instruction on Preparing and Accomplishing Medicinal Pills for the Well-Being of the Three Realms (95 pages)

35

shing sbrul lo'i nyams snang zin bris kyi le'u/

A Journal of Pure Visions in the Wood Snake Year (110 pages)

36

me rta lo'i nyams snang zin bris kyi le'u tshan/

A Chapter of Notes of Pure Visions in the Fire Horse Year (261 pages)

37

rig 'dzin chen po pad+ma bzhad pa'i rdo rje'i bslab bya zhal gdams thor bu sna tshogs phyogs gcig tu bsdus pa skal ldan yid kyi re skong zhes bya ba/

Fulfilling the Hopes of the Fortunate Ones: A Collection of Miscellaneous Advice and Testaments of the Great Vajra Master Pema Zhepai Dorje (36 pages)

38

rig 'dzin chen po pad+ma bzhad pa'i rdo rje'i gsung 'bum las chab shog gi rim pa sna tshogs phyogs gcig tu bkod pa ngo mtshar rdo rje'i rol mo zhes bya ba/

Wonderful Vajra Music: A Collection of Miscellaneous Letters from the Collected Works of the Great Vajra Master Pema Zhepai Dorje (72 pages)

39

lha sras da las ba dur gyis bsam yas zhig gso sgrub pa'i legs gso'i 'bul tho ga'u le/

A Chart of Gift Records: A Congratulatory Gift to Prince Dale Badur for the Completion of the Renovation of Samye (3 pages)

40

> *sa rta mdo sde mchod pa'i dus lha sras da las sku zhabs su legs 'bul phul ba'i 'bul tho zin bris/*

> *A Record of the Gifts Presented to His Excellency Prince Dale on the Occasion of the Offering to Sutras' in the Earth Horse Year* (4 pages)

41

> *zhu yig 'bul ba'i dper brjod/*

> *Examples of Petitions* (5 pages)

42

> *bzhad pa'i rdo rje'i bu rgyud rnams la gdams pa'i bslab bya snying gi dwangs ma zhes bya ba/*

> *Clear Heart Essence Advice Given to the Inheritors of Zhepai Dorje's Lineage* (12 pages)

43

> *g.yung drung sprul pa'i sku gtso bor gyur pa'i bzhad pa'i rdo rje'i rjes su zhugs pa rnams la gdams pa'i bslab bya nye kho kun gsal zhes bya ba/*

> *A Clear Illumination of All Needs: Advice Given to the Followers of Zhepai Dorje Headed by Yungdrun Tulku* (12 pages)

44

> *mtsho rgyal bdun pa Og min sprul pa'i skur 'phrin yig tu spel ba bdud rtsi'i thigs pa zhes bya ba/*

> *A Drop of Nectar: A Letter Sent to Tsogyal Dunpa Ogmin Tulku* (3 pages)

45

dpal mkha' 'gro yang tig gi khrid kyi brgyud 'debs byin rlabs char 'bebs/

A Cascade of Blessings: A Supplication to the Lineage of the Commentary on Glorious Dakini Yangtig (4 pages)

46

'chi ba'i gnad gcod sel ba'i gdams pa rdo rje'i zhun thigs zhes bya ba/

A Drop of Vajra Essence: An Instruction on Eliminating the Major Causes of Death (3 pages)

47

rang la gces pa'i gros 'debs nyung ngur smras pa/

Brief Advice to Myself on My Personal Necessities (3 pages)

48

blo gsal rnams la gros 'debs tam bu ra'i sgra dbyangs zhes bya ba/

The Sound of a Lute: A Discussion Addressed to Intelligent Ones (3 pages)

49

fchi ba bskul ba'i gros 'debs rkang drug gi glu dbyangs/

The Song of Bees: A Discussion on Remembering Death (4 pages)

50

blang dor gyi bslab bya srid zhi'i 'dod 'jo zhes bya ba/

Fulfilling the Wishes of Samsara and Nirvana: Advice on Abandonment and Cultivation (3 pages)

51

sde pa nor 'dzin dbang po bdud las rnam par rgyal ba la stsal ba'i bslab bya spang blang kun gsal zhes bya ba/

A Clear Illumination of All Abandonment and Cultivation Actions: Advice Addressed to Chief Norzin Wangpo Dudle Namgyal (4 pages)

52

chos mdzad bstan 'dzin rgya mtshor gsung lan yid kyi gdung sel/

Eliminating Mental Agony: A Reply to a Letter from Choeze Tenzin Gyatso (4 pages)

53

ri sgo gnyer pa 'chi med bde ldan la gdams pa'i man ngag zab gnad gcig 'dus/

A Summary of the Vital Points: A Quintessential Instruction Given to Chime Dedan, Manager of Rigo (3 pages)

54

phyag mdzod rdo rje gsang bdag gi nyams len gsal byed/

A Clear Illumination of Practice for Treasurer Dorje Sangdag (4 pages)

55

'bel gtam gyi sngon 'gro mchod brjod sogs bkra shis dga' ston/

A Festivity of Auspiciousness and Joy: A Salutation before a Discourse (4 pages)

56

rgyab byang sna tshogs gras/

A Collection of Miscellaneous Addresses (84 pages)

57

nag zla'i dus ston chen mo'i deb ther rin chen snang gsal zhes bya ba/

A Precious Bright Lamp: A Book Recording the Great Festive Event in the Third Month (14 pages)

58

shing mo yos kyi lo'i nyams snang zin bris su bkod pa'i le'u/

A Chapter of Pure Visions in the Wood Hare Year (19 pages)

59

me pho 'brug gi lo'i nyams snang zin bris su bkod pa'i le'u/

A Chapter of Pure Visions in the Fire Dragon Year (20 pages)

60

me mo sbrul gyi lo'i nyams snang zin bris su bkod pa'i le'u/

A Chapter of Pure Visions in the Fire Snake Year (9 pages)

61

sa pho rta lo'i nyams snang zin bris su bkod pa'i le'u/

A Chapter of Pure Visions in the Earth Horse Year (43 pages)

62

sa mo lug gi lo'i nyams snang zin bris su bkod pa'i le'u/

A Chapter of Pure Visions in the Earth Sheep Year (15 pages)

63

gsang 'dzin las kyi rdo rje'i 'khrungs rabs gsol 'debs/

A Supplication to the Line of Reincarnations of Drupchen Namkha Gyaltsen (5 pages)

64

lha gcig nyi ma gzhon nu'i mdzad pa'i lo rgyus ngo mtshar ba thor bu'i le'u tshan/

A Chapter on Certain Wonderful Deeds of Lhacig Nyima Zhonnu (55 pages)

65

nyi gzhon dga' tshal du bzhugs pa'i lha gcig gi rdo rje'i rnam thar gsol 'debs byin rlabs nor bu'i dkar chag

A Catalogue of Jewel Blessings: A Supplication to the Vajra Biography of Lhacig, Who Resided in the Garden of the Young Sun (7 pages)

66

rig pa 'dzin pa chen po bzhad pa'i rdo rje'i rnam thar gsol 'debs byin rlabs char 'bebs zhes bya ba/

A Cascade of Blessings: A Supplication including the Deeds of the Great Vajra Master Zhepai Dorje (5 pages)

67

sa mo bya yi lo sbas yul pad+ma bkod du bskyod pa'i lo rgyus mdo tsam bshad pa ngo mtshar do shal zhes bya ba/

A Magnificent Garland: A Short Account of a Visit to the Hidden Land of Pema Koe in the Female Earth Bird Year (29 pages)

68

dwags kyi rgyud las dpal kun tu bzang po'i phreng gi gnas zhal gsar du phye ba'i lo rgyus tshangs dbyangs snyan mgur/

A Melodic Song of Brahma: An Account of the Inauguration of a New Pilgrimage Site of the Samantabhadra Deities in the Dagpo Region (27 pages)

69

dwags po kun bzang pho brang gi gnas bshad nyi zla'i tshom bu/

A Heap of Suns and Moons: An Explanation of Kunzang Palace in Dagpo (11 pages)

70

shing yos zla ba lnga pa'i tshes bco lnga'i nyin Og min du rje bla ma yab yum sku 'khor dang bcas pa spyan drangs pa'i lo rgyus srin bu'i Od snang/

A Radiance of Fireflies: An Account of the Invitation to the Most Venerable Lama, his Consort, and their Retinue to Mondroling, the Akanishta Pure Land, on the Fifteenth Day of the Fifth Month of the Wood Hare Year (5 pages)

71

byar phu tshogs bdag nor bu'i phreng gi gnas zhal gsar du phye ba'i lo rgyus bstan pa thog babs zhes bya ba/

A Timely Appearance: An Account of the Newly Discovered Spiritual Site of Jar Phu Tshog Dag Nor Bu'i Treng (5 pages)

72

mtsho sna brgyud dkar po zangs su bskyod pa'i lo rgyus kun gsal shel khang ngo mtshar bden pa'i zungs ldan zhes bya ba/

The Power of Truth: A Magnificent All-Seeing Crystal House-Like Account of Going to Karpozang in the Tsonna Region (32 pages)

73

chos 'khor rgyal mi 'gyur lhun gyis grub pa'i gtsug lag khang dang 'brel ba'i dben gnas ljongs lnga lung bstan tshul gyi lo rgyus brda' gsal don 'byed ces bya ba/

A Revelation of Symbols and Meaning: An Account of the Prediction about the Five Solitary Valleys Site Related to Migyur Lhungyi Drupai Temple in Choekhor Gyal (7 pages)

74

rgyal yum nyi ma gzhon nu'i rdzu 'phrul gyi bkod pa las cha shas tsam brjod pa rgya mtsho chu thigs zhes bya ba/

A Drop from the Ocean: A Partial Presentation from the Miracles of Gyalyum Nyima Zhonnu (22 pages)

75

ru mtshams rgyal byed tshal gyi gnas zhal gsar du phye ba'i lo rgyus dad pafi lde mig ces bya ba/

A Key of Faith: An Account of the Inauguration of a New Pilgrimage Site in Rutsam Gyalje Tsal (9 pages)

76

lha gcig yid bzhin nor bu'i rdzu 'phrul gyi byung ba brjod pa skar phran tshom bu zhes bya ba/

A Cluster of Stars: Annals of the Miracles of Lhacig Yidzhin Norbu (6 pages)

77

dbu mdzad dgra 'dul las 'phros pa'i lha gcig gi rdzu 'phral brjod pa yang dag pa'i gtam bya ba/

Pure Talk: A Presentation of Lhacig's Miracles Relating to Chant Leader Dradul (5 pages)

78

shing yos lo phu thang spyan g.yas chos grwar klu rten btsugs pa'i lo rgyus dga' bskyed snang ba zhes bya ba/

A Radiance of Joy: An Account of the Construction of a Naga's Residence at Phuthang Chanye Monastery in the Wood Hare Year (6 pages)

79

rnam sras kyi bskang ba mdor bsdus re skong zhes bya ba /

Fulfilling Hopes: A Short Version of a Propitiation of Vaishramana (3 pages)

80

me 'brug lo lcang skya rin po che rtsed thang du mjal bar bskyod pa'i lo rgyus stabs bde/

A Convenient Account of Visiting Changkya Rinpoche in Tsethang in the Fire Dragon Year (5 pages)

81

gsang ye'i lo dgra'i 'jigs bsrung las 'bu bsrung 'khol bur phyungs pa/

A Method to Protect Crops from Pests from Sangwa Yeshe's "Protecting Crops from Harm" (2 pages)

82

me 'brug rgyal zlar me mchod bgyid pa'i lo rgyus dri za'i ltad mo zhes bya ba/

A Spectacle of Fire Gods: An Account of a Fire Offering in the Twelfth Month in the Fire Dragon Year (4 pages)

83

bde ldan ma'i rgyun 'khyer/

A Daily Practice of Dedan Ma (2 pages)

84

me 'brug spyan g.yas su bskyod pa'i lo rgyus snang la 'byams klas zhes bya ba/

An Excellent Appearance: An Account of Visiting Chanye in the Fire Dragon Year (19 pages)

85

sa ga zla ba'i dus chen dang bstun pa'i zab khrid chen po'i 'dus par 'du Os rnams kyi dran tho drang po'i lam ston zhes bya ba/

Showing the True Path: A Record of the Worthy Gathering at the Great Profound Commentary during the Wonderful Event of the Fourth Month (1 page)

86

hum chen sgang gi dur khrod du phung po skyel mi rnams la stsal ba'i bka' lung/

Advice Given to the Pall Bearers of Hungchen Gang Cemetery (2 pages)

87

hUM chen sgang gi dur khrod du bgyi Os kyi bslab bya/

Advice on Proper Conduct at Hungchen Gang Cemetery (2 pages)

88

yar lo cho 'aprul zla ba'i tshes gcig nas bco lnga bar mched lcam rnams kyi dge sbyor bsgrub rgyu'i zhal bkod/

An Instruction on Virtuous Practices for Dharma Brothers and Sisters from the First to the Fifteenth Day of the Sixth Month of the Yar Year (2 pages)

89

mkha' spyod kyi yar mar tshes bcu'i thebs su bsod snyoms rgyag pa'i bka' shog 'dod dgu'i char 'bebs/

Wish-Fulfilling Rain: Decrees on Alms-Begging on Dakini Days— the Tenth Day of the Waxing and Waning Moon (2 pages)

90

smyon pa bzhad pa'i rdo rje'i dge sbyor gyi dran tho/

A Record of the Virtuous Practices of Crazy Zhepai Dorje (10 pages)

91

rdo rje skyob byed kyi nyin ltar dge sbyor khrid chags su byed dgos kyi dran tho/

A Reminder of Dorje Kyobjed's Daily Virtuous Practices (2 pages)

92

chu glang lo sbas yul pad+ma bkod du chibs bskyod gnang skabs kyi tho sgrigs zhal bkod/

A Record of Visiting the Hidden Land of Pema Koe in the Water Ox Year (6 pages)

93

zab khrid chen mo'i skabs ja thug gtong dgos sogs kyi thob bsgrigs/

A Record of Tea and Soup Servings during the Great Profound Commentary (3 pages)

94

spyan g.yas su dam can pa'i rten 'dzugs gnang ba'i zhal bkod thol byung rgyan shar/

An Ornament: A Spontaneous Instruction for the Construction of Damchan's Residence at Chanye (4 pages)

95

mkha' 'gro rgya mtshos byin gyis brlabs pa'i ming gi rab byed 'phrul gyi dra mig ces bya ba/

A Miraculous Plot: A Set of Names Blessed by Oceans of Dakinis (14 pages)

96

ming gi rab byed kyi sde tshan gsum pa rma bya'i zlos gar/

A Peacock's Dance: Chapter Three of a Set of Names (10 pages)

97

rje bla ma mchog nas stsal ba'i ming gi rab byed khag cig

Some of the Set of Names Given by the Excellent Guru (10 pages)

98

sa skyong rgya ri ba'i 'phrul blon chen po se ra gong bsod nams bstan 'dzin la gdams pa'i bslab bya rtsa gsum snying dril/

Three-Fold Core Advice Given to Sera Gong Sonam Tenzin, Great Minister of King Gyari (11 pages)

99

sa rta zla ba dgu pa nas sa lug gi mgo sgang bar 'di kha'i mched lcam rnams kyi spang blangs sgrub dgos kyi ljags bsgrigs/

A Text about What should be Adopted and Abandoned by Dharma Brothers and Sisters Residing Here, Compiled between the Ninth Month of the Earth Horse Year and the Beginning of the Earth Sheep Year (2 pages)

100

bzhad pa'i rdo rje me 'brug lo dge ba'i bshes gnyen 'ba' rong pa chen pos dag snang du stsal ba'i bla ma ro snyoms chos ldan gyi man ngag sku gsum ngo sprod ces bya ba/

An Introduction to the Three Enlightened Bodies, a Quintessential Instruction of Lama Ronyom Choeden, Given to Zhepai Dorje in Pure Vision in the Fire Dragon Year, by the Great Guru Barong Pa (2 pages)

101

gzims mal sku 'dra rin po che'i dkar chag rin chen 'phreng ba/

A Precious Garland: A Catalogue of the Statues of Zimmal (9 pages)

102

na len+d+ra'i dpon slob dag snang rol pa las 'phros pa'i lo rgyus snang ba rgya mtsho zhes bya ba/

An Ocean of Appearances: An Account Relating to Nalanda's Pandita Dagnang Rolpa (3 pages)

103

shing yos khrums zla'i nang du dbang drag rol pa'i gur khang gsar skrun gyi zhal spro'i lo rgyus nyung gsal don bsdus zhes bya ba/

A Short, Clear Summary: A Joyful Account of the New Construction of the Temple of Wangdak Rolpa in the Eighth Month of the Wood Hare Year of 1735 (5 pages)

104

shing yos lo khrums zla'i tshes bcur dpon slob dag snang rol pas mkhar spyod du tshogs 'khor gyi yon sbyor mdzad dus las 'phros pa'i lha gcig gi che brjod dam dpag bsam yongs 'du zhes bya ba/

A Gathering of All Wish-Fulfilling Trees: Praises to Lhacig from an Account of Master Dagnang Rolpa, Who Sponsored a Tsok in Khachod on the Tenth Day of the Eighth Month of the Wood Hare Year of 1735 (5 pages)

105

dpa' bo khyu mchog khrag 'thung rnam rol dang rje'i zhal snga nas mkha' btsun rgya mtsho las 'phros pa'i zhing skyong ma'i che ba brjod pa rmad byung gtam rgyud zhes bya ba/

An Excellent Narrative: A Presentation of the Qualities of Dakini Zhingkhong Ma Relating to the Masters Khatsun Gyatso and Hero Khyuchog Tragthung Namrol (9 pages)

106

*lha gcig yid bzhin nor bu sprul gzhi sprul gzugs dang bcas pa'i
rnam par thar pa las brtsams pa'i lo rgyus mdza' mo'i gdung
dbyangs zhes bya ba snying la lhag par 'babs pa/*

A Lover's Heart-Enchanting Lamentation: Stories from the Life of
Lhacig Yidzhin Norbu, Where She Emanated from and Her Own
Emanations (28 pages)

107

*yongs grags shing yos hor zla bcu gnyis pa'i tshes kyi lo gsar las
'phros pa'i 'phags ma gzhan gyis mi thub pa chen po nyi ma
gzhon nu'i rdzu 'phrul gyi byung ba mdo tsam brjod pa byi ru'i
lding khang bya ba/*

A House of Coral: A Short Presentation of the Miracles of Nyima
Zhonnu, the Female Bodhissatva Undefeated by Others, Relating
to the Well-Known New Year of the Twelfth Month of the Wood
Hare Year of 1735 (14 pages)

108

*shing yos hor zla bcu gnyis pa'i tshes bcu rang lugs me 'brug
gsar du tshes pa'i lo gsar gyi rjes thogs kyi bya ba las 'phros
pa'i rgyal yum rdo rje skyabs byed dang nyi ma gzhon nu zung
du 'jug pa'i rdzu 'phrul gyi byung ba brjod pa'i gtam a la la'i
gad mo zhes bya ba/*

Delighted Laughter: Accounts of the Miracles of Gyalyum Dorje
Kyabjed in Conjunction with Nyima Zhonnu, relating to the Sub-
sequent Activities of the New Year of the Fire Dragon Year in the
Tibetan Calendar and the Tenth Day of the Twelfth Month of the
Wood Hare Year according to the Mongolian System (5 pages)

109

gsang ye dang 'brel bar tshe sgrub byed lugs/

How to Practice a Longevity Ritual Connected to Sangwa Yeshe (2
pages)

110

> *me 'brug lo cho 'phrul zla bar rgyal yum ye shes mtsho rgyal gyi sgrub par zhugs pa'i tshe lha gcig nyi ma gzhon nu'i rdzu 'phrul gyi skal bzang ji ltar stsal zhing mngon sum pa'i yul du gyur tshul gyi lo rgyus gtam snyan phul byung bya ba/*

> *Most Excellent and Melodious Words: An Account of the Fortune of Lhacig Nyima Zhonnu's Miracles Appearing Directly to the Senses during the Retreat of Gyalyum Yeshe Tsogyal in the First Month of the Fire Dragon Year of 1736* (34 pages)

111

> *nyi gzhon dga' tshal du klu dren btsugs pa dang rjes su 'brel bar lha gcig yid bzhin nor bu'i rdzu 'phrul gyi rnam par bkod pa brjod pa'i gtam nyi ma'i shel mig zhes bya ba/*

> *A Magnifying Glass: An Account of the Miracle Activities of Lhacig Yidzhin Norbu Related to the Event of Erecting a Naga Memorial in Nyima Zhonnu's Garden* (7 pages)

112

> *me 'brug lha gcig dang gnod sbyin chen po'i mdos skongs dag snang du shar ba'i skor las 'phros pa'i lo rgyus kyi yi ge snying sdug bu mo'i snang glu zhes bya ba/*

> *A Song for Attracting Sweethearts: A Record of Accounts of Crossed-Thread and Propitiation Rituals of Lhacig and Great Yaksha which Appeared in Pure Vision in the Fire Dragon Year of 1736* (8 pages)

113

> *me 'brug nag zla'i dus ston chen mo dang 'brel ba'i lo rgyus tshangs dbyangs sprin sgra zhes bya ba/*

> *A Thundering Sound of Brahma: An Account related to the Great Festivity of the Third Month of the Fire Dragon Year of 1736* (24 pages)

114

> *me 'brug zab khrid chen mo'i lo rgyus las brtsams pa'i byung ba brjod pa ngo mtshar thol byung zhes bya ba/*

> A Wonder of Spontaneity: An Account relating to the Great Profound Commentary of the Fire Dragon Year (49 pages)

115

> *dge bsnyen chen mo snyon kha'i pho brang gi skyed mos tshal las 'phros pa'i lha gcig zhing skyong chen mo'i rdzu 'phrul gyi byung ba brjod pa dad pa'i shing rta zhes bya ba/*

> A Chariot of Faith: A Recollection of the Miracles of Great Lhacig Zhingkyong relating to the Garden of the Palace of Great Upasika Nyon Kha (8 pages)

116

> *lha gcig rdzu 'phrul gyi bdag mo'i bka' drin rjes su dran pa'i gtam in+d+ra'i bum bzang zhes bya ba/*

> A Magnificent Diamond Vase: A Recollection of the Kindnesses of Lhacig, Holder of Miracles (27 pages)

117

> *shing mo yos kyi lo lha mi'i rnam 'dren dam pa rgyal dbang phyag na pad+mo bdun pa kun mkhyen bskal bzang rgya mtsho mi nyag 'gar thar gyi sa'i cha nas slar yang chibs kyi kha lo bskyod dus phebs bsur bgrod tshul ngo mtshar mtha' yas zhes bya ba/*

> Infinite Wonder: An Account of the Welcoming Back Reception for Omniscient Kalzang Gyatso, the Seventh Dalai Lama, Lotus Holder and Ultimate Lord of Humans and Divine Beings, on His Return from Minyak Garthar (62 pages)

118

dmag dpon chen po jo bo rgyal mtshan dang klu mo dung skyong ma 'dzin pa lag mangs zung 'brel gyi gsol mchod dwangs shel 'dod bum zhes bya ba/

A Wish-Fulfilling Crystal Vase: A Supplication and Offering to Great Commander Jowo Gyaltsen in Conjunction with the Many-Armed Naga Holding Dungkyong Ma (1 page)

119

legs ldan tshogs rje chen po'i mchod sprin las bzhi'i bang mdzod ces bya ba/

A Treasure of the Four Activities: Clouds of Offerings to Great Legden Tsogje (5 pages)

120

dpal mgon ma ning gi drag bskul dbang med las byed ces bya ba/

Rendering Powerless to Resist: An Invocation to the Wrath of Palgon Maning (2 pages)

121

myur mdzad phyag bzhi pa'i rgyun khyer snying por dril ba/

Gathered Essences: A Daily Practice of Four-Armed Mahakala (3 pages)

122

me sbrul zla ba drug pa'i tshes nyer drug gi nyin Og min du skyabs mgon yab yum spyan 'dren zhus pa'i lo rgyus ngo mtshar mi zad pa'i zlos gar zhes bya ba/

An Endless Wonder of Dance: An Account of the Invitation Given to the Master and His Consort, Refuge and Protector, to Visit Mindrolling on the Twenty-Sixth Day of the Sixth Month of the Fire Snake Year (11 pages)

123

nyang gter ye shes mgon po'i sgrub 'phrin snying po'i gsal byed/

A Commentary on the Essence of the Practice and Blessing of Mahakala from Nyangter (4 pages)

124

chu mo glang gi lo dre'u lhas su bskyod pa'i lo rgyus ngo mtshar mtha' yas zhes bya ba/

Endless Wonder: An Account of Visiting Driwulhe in the Water Ox Year (29 pages)

125

bdud mgon trag bshad nag po'i drag bskul bskal me'i thog mda' zhes bya ba/

A Lightning Strike from the World-Ending Conflagration: An Invocation to the Wrath of Black Dudgon Tragshad (2 pages)

126

mgon po phyag drug pa'i thugs dam bskang ba'i rim pa yid kyi re skong zhes bya ba/

Fulfilling Hopes: Rites to Fulfill the Commitments of Six-Armed Lord Mahakala (6 pages)

127

mgon po snying zhugs kyi nyams len pho ba'i man ngag dang dbang bcas rgyud sde'i yang bcud ces bya ba/

An Innermost Essence of Tantra: An Empowerment and Quintessential Instruction on the Transfer of Consciousness Practice of Inviting Mahakala into the Heart (7 pages)

128

sa pho rta'i lo zab khrid stong thun smra ba'i sgo 'byed ces bya ba/

Opening the Door to Awareness: A Profound Thousand-Fold Commentary Given in the Earth Horse Year (2 pages)

129

shing mo yos kyi lo sa ga zla ba'i nang du 'dus pa phyed lnga brgya brdal tsam la gsang ye'i zab khrid phebs dus kyi ngo mtshar ba'i lo rgyus yid ches gdengs khel zhes bya ba/

Confident Trust: A Wonderful Account of a Profound Commentary on Sangwa Yeshe Given to a Gathering of over 500 Devotees in the Fourth Month of the Wood Hare Year (83 pages)

130

shing mo yos lo'i char 'bebs las 'phros pa'i lo rgyus ltad mo'i bang mdzod/

A House of Entertainment: An account regarding the Production of Rain in the Wood Hare Year (6 pages)

131

lha gcig gi rdzu 'phrul byung tshul dad pa'i bsos spel la/

An Enhancement of Faith: The Origin of the Miracles of Lhacig (5 pages)

132

dpa' bo rdo rje 'dod dgu las 'phros pa'i gtam brgyud ya mtshan ltad mo zhes bya ba/

A Wondrous Spectacle: An Account relating to Hero Dorje Dodgu (8 pages)

133

rtsa gsum dam can rgya mtsho'i mchod 'phrin bde chen mchog rtsol zhes bya ba/

A Bestowal of Great Bliss: Clouds of Offerings to Oceans of Damchans, Manifestations of the Three Roots (3 pages)

134

me 'brug bcad rgyar zhugs pa'i skabs las 'phros pa'i gtam mchog gsang khyab brdal zhes bya ba/

An Open Secret: Great Words about the Fire Dragon Retreat (21 pages)

135

sbas yul pad+ma bkod du bgrod pa'i smon lam/

A Prayer to be in the Hidden Land of Pema Koe (3 pages)

136

zangs mdog dpal ri'i gtsug lag khang gi ldebs bris gsham gyi bden tshig tshangs pa'i rnga chen/

Brahma's Great Drum: Words of Truth Inscribed Beneath the Murals in the Temple of Zangdog Pelri (8 pages)

137

lha mo dpal lha beg tse rgyal mtshan pa rnams kyis gtor 'bul rgyun khyer bsdus pa/

A Short Daily Practice of Offering Ritual Cakes to the Protectress Palden Lhamo, Pelha, Begtse, and Gyaltsen Pa (4 pages)

138

dam can kun 'dus kyi ngo bo snyon kha nag po'i bskang ba rgya mtsho khyab gdal zhes bya ba/

A Surge of the Ocean: A Propitiation of Black Nyonkha, Embodiment of All Damchans (11 pages)

139

*zhang blon chen po rdo rje bdud 'dul gyi thugs dam bskul ba'i
bstod pa legs tshogs sgo 'byed ces bya ba/*

*Opening the Door to All Goodness: Praises to Remind Great
Zhanglong Dorje Duddul of His Promises* (3 pages)

140

dam can rgya mtsho'i mchod 'phrin 'dod yon rgya mtsho/

*An Ocean of Sensual Objects: Clouds of Offerings to the Oceans of
Damchans* (3 pages)

141

*dge bsnyen ra mgo can pa'i mdos kyi cho ga nag 'gros su bkod
pa bshan pa dgyes bskongs zhes bya ba/*

*Delighting Butchers: An Orderly Guide to a Crossed-Thread Ritual
of Goat-Headed Upasaka* (7 pages)

142

*dam can rgya mtsho'i gtso bo rgyal po gnod sbyin chen po bse
khrag pa'i bskang ba'i cho ga bla med don sbyor zhes bya ba/*

*A Collection of Ultimate Meanings: Propitiation Rites to the Great
Royal Yaksha Setrab, Head of Damchan Gyatso* (7 pages)

143

*rgyal po gnod sbyin chen po bse khrab pa'i bskang ba bla med
don sbyor gyi le lag*

*Activity Appendices to "A Collection of Ultimate Meanings": Pro-
pitiation Rites to the Great Royal Yaksha Setrab* (2 pages)

144

*gnod sbyin mig dmar chen po dang klu rgyal mal dro gzi can gyi
drag bskul/*

*An Invocation to the Wrath of Both Great Red-Eyed Yaksha and
Naga King Maldro Zichan* (2 pages)

145

rtsa gsum dam can rgya mtsho'i bskang ba 'dod dgu'i bang mdzod ces bya ba/

A Wish-Fulfilling Treasure: A Propitiation to the Oceans of Dam-chans, Protectors of the Three Roots (5 pages)

146

sku lha ne rang gi gsol mchod nor bu'i rgya mtsho zhes bya ba/

An Ocean of Jewels: A Supplication and Offering to Kulha Ne (6 pages)

147

'phrin bcol snying gi thig le zhes bya ba/

A Drop of Heart Essence: An Invocation to Dharma Protectors (3 pages)

148

'phrin bcol 'dod 'jo'i dpal ster zhes bya ba/

A Wish-Granting Invocation to Dharma Protectors (2 pages)

149

lha gcig zhing skyong ma rdzong btsan chen po rdo rje legs pa gnod sbyin chen po bcas kyi gsol mchod 'di phyi'i don grub/

Fulfilling the Purposes of Current and Future Lives: A Supplication and Offering to Great Lhacig Zhingkyong Ma, Great Zongtsan, Dorje Legpa, and Great Yaksha (3 pages)

150

dge bsnyen nyer gcig bod kyi mthu chen dgu srid pa'i lha chen dgu rje'i mgur lha bcu gsum rnams kyi gsol mchod/

A Supplication and Offering to the Twenty-One Genyen, the Nine Thuchen of Tibet, the Nine Great Sidpai Lha, and the Thirteen Protectors according to Lama Tsong Khapa (4 pages)

151

gnod sbyin chen po ra mgo can pa'i mchod 'phrin las bzhi myur 'grub ces bya ba/

Speedy Accomplishment of the Four Activities: An Offering and Invocation to Great Goat-Headed Yaksha (5 pages)

152

ging chen bshan pa dmar po'i dam bsgrags rdo rje'i mna' tshig ces bya ba/

A Vajra Pledge: Proclaiming the Commitments relating to the Red Butcher of Gingchen (8 pages)

153

zo lha'i gsol kha rnams sras longs spyod bya ba/

The Enjoyment of Vaishramana's Wealth: A Propitiation to Zolha (2 pages)

154

gzi can gyi gsol kha khyer bde/

A Convenient Rite of Propitiation to Zichan (2 pages)

155

ging lnga'i gsol mchod re skong don 'dus zhes bya ba/

Concise Meanings and Hope Fulfilment: A Supplication and Offering to the Five Gings (3 pages)

156

lha chen Od de gung rgyal gyi gsol mchod dgyes skong bde ster zhes bya ba/

Giving Bliss and Joy: A Supplication and Offering to the Great Protector Od De Gung Gyal (3 pages)

157

zab pa skor bdun gyi nang tshan bdag 'dzin 'joms byed rkyen ngan lam khyer gyi khrid rtsa ba'i dmigs rkang snying por dril ba/

A Condensation of the Root Points of Visualization: A Commentary on Taking Adverse Conditions into the Path and Destroying all Aspects of Self-Grasping from the Seven Discourses on Profundities (3 pages)

158

myur mdzad mahA kA la phyag bzhi pa'i bskang ba thog med las mdzad ces bya ba/

Beginningless Actions: An Invocation to the Four-Armed Mahakala (3 pages)

159

tshangs pa dung thod can dpon blon gyi rten mdos kyi cho ga snang srid zil gnon zhes bya ba/

Overpowering Appearances: Rites of Crossed-Thread Bases for Conch-Crowned Brahma and His Ministers (4 pages)

160

zhing skyong chen mo'i rdzu 'phrul gyi bkod pa gsal bar brjod pa'i gtam sna tshogs rgyan snang zhes bya ba/

A Variegated Ornament: A Clear Account of the Miracles of the Great Zhingkyong Ma (56 pages)

161

gar dbang khyab brdal las 'phros pa'i lha gcig gi che brjod gnad 'gag lhug 'akrol zhes bya ba/

Demystifying the Vital Points: Recounting the Greatness of Lhacig Connected to Garwang Khyabdel (17 pages)

162

btags grol gyi rdzing bu'i gnas bshad bya tshul/

How to Illustrate the Water Spring of Tagdrol (8 pages)

163

mkha' 'gro rgya mtsho'i pho brang zung 'jug rnam rol gyi ka ba las 'phros pa'i lha gcig gi rdzu 'phrul brjod pa yid kyi dga' ston zhes bya ba/

A Festivity of Heartfelt Joy: An Account of the Miracles of Lhacig Relating to the Pillar of Zungyuk Namrol Palace of a Myriad of Dakinis (10 pages)

164

rgyal yum ye shes mkha' 'gro'i bka' drin rjes su dran pa'i gtam phyogs bcu'i sgo 'byed ces bya ba/

Opening the Doors to the Ten Directions: A Recollection of the Kindnesses of Gyalyum Yeshe Khandro (9 pages)

165

dre'u lhas sprul pa'i sku chibs bsgyur dus kyi byed sgo brjod pa'i rjed byang/

A Journal of Activities regarding the Visit of the Dre'u Lha Incarnation (3 pages)

166

zhing skyong chen mo'i rdzu 'phrul gyi byung ba brjod pa rab snyan ya to kha zhes bya ba/

Incomparable Music: An Account of the Miracles of Great Zhingkyong Ma (17 pages)

167

bde ldan ma'i 'phrin las kha skong 'jug bde/

Convenient Ease: A Supplement to the Propitiation of Deden Ma (3 pages)

168

rdo rje tshig gi zab don 'grel par byed pa rdo rje'i sgron me la/

A Vajra Lamp: A Commentary on the Profound Meaning of Vajra Words (58 pages)

169

rig 'dzin chen po pad+ma bzhad pa'i rdo rje'i gsung 'bum las gsol 'debs smon lam thor bu sna tshogs skor phyogs bsgrigs su bgyis pa ci 'dod re skong zhes bya ba/

Fulfilling Hopes: A Collection of Miscellaneous Supplications and Prayers from the Collected Works of the Great Vajra Master Pema Zhepai Dorje (115 pages)

170

rig 'dzin chen po pad+ma bzhad pa'i rdo rje'i bka' 'bum las zhabs brtan gsol 'debs bden tshig smon lam gyi skor sna tshogs 'khrigs bsdebs su bgyis pa g.yung drung rdo rje'i rang bzhin zhes bya ba/

A Swastika of Vajra Strength: A Collection of Miscellaneous Prayers of Truthful Words and Long Life from the Collected Works of the Great Vajra Master Pema Zhepai Dorje (65 pages)

171

rig 'dzin chen po pad+ma bzhad pa'i rdo rje'i gsung 'bum las bshes gnyen dam pa rnams kyis yang srid myur byon gyis rim pa sna tshogs gcig bsdus re 'bras lhun grub zhes bya ba/

A Spontaneous Fulfilment of Hopes: A Collection of Prayers for the Speedy Return of the Reincarnations of Great Masters from the Collected Works of the Great Vajra Master Pema Zhepai Dorje (8 pages)

172

rig 'dzin chen po pad+ma bzhad pa'i rdo rje'i bka' 'bum las gsung mgur gyi rim pa sna tshogs skal ldan 'dus pa'i re skongs zhes bya ba/

Fulfilling the Hopes of the Fortunate Gathering: A Collection of Miscellaneous Spiritual Songs from the Collected Works of the Great Vajra Master Pema Zhepai Dorje (19 pages)

173

rig 'dzin chen po pad+ma bzhad pa'i rdo rje'i gsung 'bum las gsung mgur rim pa thol byung rdo rje'i glu dbyangs zhes bya ba/

A Spontaneous Vajra Song: A Collection of Spiritual Songs from the Collected Works of the Great Vajra Master Pema Zhepai Dorje (8 pages)

174

gsung mgur gsungs rbad sna tshogs/

A Collection of Miscellaneous Reflections and Spiritual Songs (8 pages)

175

don grub nag pa zla ba'i yar tshes brgyad kyi nyin rje bla mas thol byung du gsung pa'i bka' lung /

The Master's Excellent Spontaneous Words on the Eighth Day of the Waxing Moon of the Third Month (4 pages)

176

ja mchod kun bzang mchod sprin 'gyed pa'i khang bzang zhes bya ba/

A House of Delight: A Tea Offering Prayer as a Samantabhadra Offering Cloud (1 page)

177

rig 'dzin chen po pad+ma bzhad pa'i rdo rje'i gsung 'bum las par byang sna tshogs gras/

A Collection of Miscellaneous Dedications for Printed Works from the Collected Works of the Great Vajra Master Pema Zhepai Dorje (4 pages)

178

rig 'dzin chen po pad+ma bzhad pa'i rdo rje'i gsung 'bum las 'dod gsol sna tshogs gras/

A Collection of Miscellaneous Request Prayers from the Collected Works of the Great Vajra Master Pema Zhepai Dorje (10 pages)

179

dregs pa rnams la bsngags pa'i spring yig thor bu/

A Collection of Praises to Wrathful Ones (3 pages)

180

gsang bdag ha s+ya badz+ra mkha' 'gro dga' ba'i lang tshos mdzad pa'i thabs lam zhal gdams/

An Instruction on the Skilful Path by the Secret Lord Youthful Pema Zhepai Dorje, Lover of Dakinis (12 pages)

Appendix VII. Anniversaries of the Lelung Jedrung Reincarnations

	European dates	Age	Tibetan date of birth		Tibetan date of death	
			Year	Rab-jung	Year	Rab-jung
Lhodrak Namkha Gyaltsen	1326–1401	75	Fire Tiger	5	Iron Snake	7
Jedrung Ngagrampa Gendun Tashi	1486–1559	73	Fire Horse	8	Earth Sheep	9
Jedrung Gendun Tenpa Gyatso	1560–1625	65	Iron Monkey	9	Wood Ox	10
Jedrung Gendun Choegyal Wangchuk	1646–1696	50	Fire Dog	11	Fire Mouse	12
Jedrung Losang Trinley	1697–1740	43	Fire Ox	12	Iron Monkey	12
Losang Lhundrup Trinley Gyaltsen	1741–1811	70	Iron Bird	12	Iron Sheep	14
Jedrung Ngawang Tenzin Gyatso	1812–?		Water Monkey	14		
Jedrung Kalzang Tenzin	?					
Jedrung Tenzin Choekyi Wangchuk	1905–1908	3	Wood Snake	15	Earth Monkey	15
Thupten Lungtok Choekyi Wangchuk	1909–1962	53	Earth Bird	15	Water Tiger	16

Appendix VIII. Map of the Lelung Region

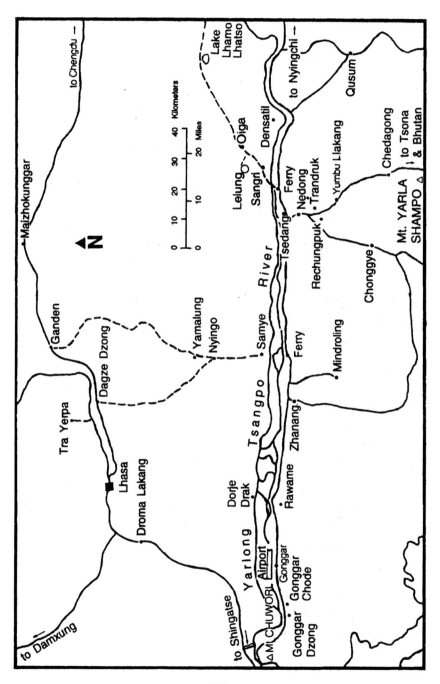

Dedication Verses

A drop has been recorded in this book,
From the ocean of marvellous Lelung histories,
Whose line of reincarnations rendered unrepayable
      kindness,
Appearing as teachers of the people of the Land of Snows

May the merit accumulated through good deeds,
Performed with virtuous motivation from beginning to
      end,
Become a cause for all beings including this benefactor
To enter the city of enlightenment.

I, Tenzin Phuntsok Loden, holder of the honorable and heavy title of Lelung Rinpoche, lately become a black sheep, maintaining immutable faith in all the old and new Buddhist traditions of the Land of Snows, composed the above dedication verses on May 26 2002 on behalf of Tessa Heron. With pure thoughts and prayers she very kindly sponsored the publication of this book.

Wishing Prayer

With much delight, I send my prayers to a number of Dharma friends who have helped with this book. May your far-reaching beneficial wishes be duly fulfilled. My friend Beri Jigme Wangyal took upon himself the responsibility of proof-reading the Tibetan version. He might have been motivated by a strong wish to follow the disciplined conduct of the fifth Jedrung, or an appreciation free from expectations and doubts of my crazy-seeming conduct. Alternatively his motivation might have been his attachment to our native land and traditions. Whatever it was, I want to thank him particularly.

CPSIA information can be obtained at www.ICGtesting.com
Printed in the USA
BVOW070012030413

317119BV00002B/5/P